Global Transformations

Global Transformations

Anthropology and the Modern World

Michel-Rolph Trouillot

GLOBAL TRANSFORMATIONS
© Michel-Rolph Trouillot, 2003

First published 2003 by
PALGRAVE MACMILLAN™
175 Fifth Avenue, New York, N.Y. 10010 and
Houndmills, Basingstoke, Hampshire, England RG21 6XS
Companies and representatives throughout the world

PALGRAVE MACMILLAN is the global academic imprint of the Palgrave Macmillan division of St. Martin's Press, LLC and of Palgrave Macmillan Ltd. Macmillan® is a registered trademark in the United States, United Kingdom and other countries. Palgrave is a registered trademark in the European Union and other countries.

ISBN 0–312–29520–0 hardback
ISBN 0–312–29521–9 paperback

Library of Congress Cataloging-in-Publication Data
Trouillot, Michel-Rolph
    Global transformations: anthropology and the modern world/by
    Michel-Rolph Trouillot.
        p.cm.
    includes bibliographical references and index.
    ISBN 0–312–29520–0
    ISBN 0–312–29521–9 (pbk.)
        1. Anthropology—Philosophy. 2. Globalization. I. Title.

GN33.T76 2003
301'.01—dc22   2003058078

A catalogue record for this book is available from the British Library.

Design by Letra Libre.

First edition: November, 2003
10 9 8 7 6 5 4 3

Printed in the United States of America.

A Canel,
Citoyenne d'un monde à construire

Contents

Acknowledgments

This book has been an ongoing project since 1991 and many parts of it have appeared elsewhere as individual publications. However, the framework offered here allowed me the opportunity to draw this work and research together in ways that I could not have envisioned when I first began working on what would later become this book. My acknowledgments must therefore of necessity be incomplete, since I could not hope to mention all the colleagues, graduate students, and others with whom conversations and debates have shaped my thinking.

Most of chapter 1 was originally published in 1991 as "Anthropology and the Savage Slot: The Poetics and Politics of Otherness," in Richard G. Fox's edited volume, *Recapturing Anthropology: Working in the Present*. Drafts of that article were commented on by participants at the Santa Fe Seminar, graduate students and faculty at Johns Hopkins University and at the New School for Social Research, and readers for the School of American Research. Kamran Ali, Talal Asad, Lanfranco Blanchetti, Ashraf Ghani, Ananta Giri, Richard Fox, Richard Kagan, and Eric Wolf all offered comments and suggestions on that piece at the time. I have updated this piece here, especially the introductory section on postmodernism that now, a decade after its original publication, seems somewhat dated.

The bulk of chapters 2 and 3 of this volume began in 1999 as an introduction to an edited volume that I intended to produce as a reader on the anthropology of globalization, but which never went to publication. In retrospect, working on that piece provided the inspiration to pull together thematically related research into the current volume once the project for the reader was shelved. Parts of chapter 2 originally appeared in 2002 as "The Otherwise Modern: Caribbean Lessons from the Savage Slot," in the volume *Critically Modern: Alternatives, Alterities, Anthropologies*, edited by Bruce M. Knauft, and as "North Atlantic Universals: Analytic Fictions, 1492–1945," in a special issue of *South Atlantic Quarterly* edited by Saurabh Dube. Parts of chapter 3 were written in 1998, when versions of it were presented at Stanford University, the University of Chicago, the University of Virginia at Morgantown, Duke University, and at the workshop on Theory and Politics after Postcoloniality (Institute for Global Studies, Johns Hopkins University). This paper was later published in a 2002 volume edited by Elisabeth Mudimbe-Boyi, *Beyond Dichotomies: Histories, Identities, Cultures, and the Challenge of Globalization*. My thanks also to Michael Dorsey, Jeffrey Mantz, Nabiha Megateli, and Clare Sammells, whose research tips inform this text, and to Vivek Dhareshwar, for the ongoing conversation that provoked some of these lines.

Chapter 4 was prepared for the "Close Encounters" Conference held at the Department of Cultural Anthropology of Stanford University on April 9–10, 1999, and a revised version was later presented at the colloquium, "Resilience or Erosion? The State under Attack from Above and Below," of the Centre d'Etudes de Relations Internationales (CERI), Paris, June 15–16, 2000. At both of these meetings participants offered helpful suggestions. After many revisions, it was then published in 2001 as "The Anthropology of the State in the Age of Globalization: Close Encounters of the Deceptive Kind" in *Current Anthropology* with the encouragement of the journal's editor, Benjamin Orlove, and with further comments from Gavin Smith, Kay Warren, and the anonymous referees for that journal. Sections of that article were then presented at the Conference "Identity, Difference and Globalization" at Candido Mendes University, Rio de Janeiro, on May 24, 2001, and at the Conference "'Globalisation studies': Epistemological and Methodological Considerations from Anthropology" at the University of Oslo on June 7, 2001. Comments I received at both of these presentations helped me shape that article into its current form. Gwen Faulkner and Clare Sammells both provided useful research assistance on this project.

The "adieu" of chapter 5 took a long time to say. My uneasiness with the race-culture complex in North American anthropology dates back to graduate school. I first put it into words at the presidential session on race at the 1991 American Anthropology Association meetings in San Francisco. My arguments were revived for the paper "Exploring The Limits of Liberal Discourse: American Anthropology and U.S. Racism," presented at the symposium "Anthropologists of Color Speak Out: Perspectives on Race and Public Anthropology" at American University on October 25, 1997. This essay in its current form was first proposed at the Ben-Gurion University in the Negev (Israel) in April 2000 with the encouragement of Sam Kaplan. It was later discussed at the Wenner-Gren Conference that led to its appearance in the 2002 volume *Anthropology Beyond Culture*, edited by Richard G. Fox and Barbara J. King. I thank participants to all these venues and also Xavier Andrade, Lee D. Baker, Bruce Knauft, Sam Kaplan, Richard A. Schweder, George W. Stocking, Jr., and especially Richard G. Fox for their substantial comments.

Special thanks to Brackette F. Williams, from whom I continue to learn both in print and conversation. I also owe my thanks to the many graduate students at Duke University, Johns Hopkins University, and the University of Chicago who took my "Concepts and Categories" seminar during the last 16 years. I extend my thanks also to Clare Sammells, who has been my graduate research assistant at the University of Chicago for over three years. She worked on this project (among many others) from its inception, finding and suggesting research materials, tracking down citations, reading drafts, offering comments, and proofreading the final manuscript. Thanks also to Greg Beckett and Michelle Knip-Beckett, both of whom provided additional research assistance and proofreading during the final stages of preparation. I am indebted to Kristi Long, Amanda Fernández, and all those at Palgrave Macmillan who patiently supported me throughout the preparation of this book.

My wife Anne-Carine and my daughter Canel have supported and encouraged me throughout this project and many others, and they have my love as well as my thanks. Despite all the talented individuals that have challenged and encouraged me to express the ideas I present here, ultimately I must claim full and sole responsibility for what some will see as the outrageous conclusions of this book.

Introduction

Anthropology is what anthropologists do.[1] That is to say, the boundaries as well as the distinctive features of the discipline vary with time. Changes in the world at large and in academe, anthropologists' responses to these changes, and their individual and collective initiatives all contribute to the dynamism of the discipline.

Since the 1980s one major change in sociocultural anthropology has been an increased focus on global flows of populations, ideas, goods, and resources and on the transformations that such massive movements provoke among the populations involved. As the word "globalization" becomes part of our vocabulary, sociocultural anthropologists struggle to understand the ongoing transformations that its use evokes and the implications for our theories and methodologies.

This book is an attempt to face those challenges, yet its point of departure precedes most studies of globalization by five centuries. One of the many reasons for that greater time-depth must be stated at the onset: This book aims to critically reassess the challenges that typify our times in light of history—both the history of anthropology and the history of the West. Its central premise is that these two histories have been intertwined from the very beginning, that the geography of imagination inherent in the creation of the West five centuries ago is a condition of possibility of anthropology. One of its goals is to unravel some of the major knots of this interconnectedness.

This, in turn, means taking some distance from dominant histories of both the West and anthropology. Historical narratives necessarily produce silences that are themselves meaningful (Trouillot 1995). What are the major silences in the history the West tells about itself? What are some of the related silences that anthropology as a discipline produces about its own history?

North Atlantic Geographies

In creating "the West," the European Renaissance shaped a global geography of imagination. That geography required a "Savage slot," a space for the inherently Other. Martinican author Edouard Glissant (1989:2) writes: "The West is not in the West. It is a project, not a place." Indeed, the place we most often call the West is best called the North Atlantic—not only for the sake of geographical precision but also because such usage frees us to emphasize that "the West" is always a fiction, an exercise in global legitimation. That exercise sometimes takes the form of an explicit project in the hands of intellectual, economic, or political leaders.

Yet most humans who see themselves as Westerners, aspire to become so, or criticize that aspiration experience the West in the form of a projection: the projection of the North Atlantic as the sole legitimate site for the universal, the default category, the unmarked—so to speak—of all human possibilities.

Thus, the West has never had a fixed content, nor is it an unchanging site: Its center moves from Rome to Lisbon, from Vienna to London, from Washington to Geneva, and from Venice to Grenada depending on the claims being made. It can absorb parts of Eastern Europe or Latin America, and more recently, Japan—not because of any feature common to these areas, but rather depending on who else is being excluded. As all default categories, the West as the universal unmarked operates only in opposition to the populations that it marks.

Anthropology emerged in the nineteenth century as a separate discipline specializing in the occupants of the Savage slot. However noble their political values or accurate their theories, anthropologists have inherited the structural limitations of the slot that they share with the Savage. To put it differently, anthropology as a practice is part of the very geography of imagination that it seeks to understand. Anthropology as a discipline emerges from the projection of the West, from the gap between the Here and the Elsewhere, in ways that no other discipline does. No wonder it has been accused of being an inherent tool of North Atlantic power in ways that no other discipline has been charged, as being a child of both colonialism and imperialism. These charges are deserved only to the extent that many anthropologists have ignored the duality of the West and thus the global inequalities that make their work possible. Indeed, anthropologists sometimes forget that the projection of the West entails not one but two intertwined geographies.

From the beginning, the geography of imagination went hand in hand with a geography of management that made possible—and was in turn refueled by—the development of world capitalism and the growing power of North Atlantic states. Just as the West was global from the start, capitalism, as an economic system premised on continuous spatial expansion, was also global from the start (see chapters 2 and 3). So was the modern state system, since the existence of any single state rested on the recognition of that system as a whole. Thus management and imagination have always been connected globally and locally, as distinguishable yet intertwined phenomena connecting space and time, politics and economics, production and consumption. Insofar as Renaissance imagination entailed a universal hierarchy, control and order were also premised on this enterprise (chapter 1). So was colonization. So were profits from trade. So was the extraction of forced labor in the colonies for the improvement of free trade in North Atlantic states. In short, the geography of imagination was always sustained on the ground, both at home and abroad, by the elaboration and implementation of procedures and institutions of control, and by a global geography of management that this imagination helped to consolidate and reproduce. That the two maps generated by these two geographies do not fully overlap should not surprise us. Indeed, it is in the interplay of these geographies that we are likely to identify processes most relevant to the joint production of sameness and difference that characterizes the dual expansion of the North Atlantic and of world capitalism.

Anthropology's sharpest critics—internal and external—argue that the discipline has privileged one of these geographies at the expense of the other.

Yet if the West is a claim to universal legitimacy, it is fair to say at anthropology's partial discharge that no other discipline has sustained such an explicit questioning of that claim. Thanks in part to anthropology, many humans inside and outside of the North Atlantic now accept the proposition that there may not always be one way for collectivities to do the right thing, that goals and values, truths and practices deemed to be self-evident and therefore universal in one place are not necessarily accepted as such elsewhere. In documenting this human record, anthropology has necessarily relativized the North Atlantic and revealed some of the gaps and connections between its two geographies. Because of their discipline's location at the borders of the institutionalized divide between the humanities and the social sciences, anthropologists have had the leisure to look both ways—and often enough took advantage of this duality.

What we need to do today is to systematize the benefits of that doubly ambiguous location at the border between the humanities and the social sciences and between the Here and the Elsewhere. If the modern world entails two geographies rather than one, it makes no sense to artificially isolate one as a privileged object of study. If, as critics of anthropology argue, it takes the entanglement of these two geographies to make our practice both necessary and possible, then it is both possible and necessary to turn these geographies themselves into heuristic devices. We can spell out better than most how the geography of imagination and the geography of management constantly intertwine to construct the management of imagination.

This means that we cannot completely abandon history to the historians, sociology to the sociologists, and economics to the economists. Not only do these disciplines have their own institutional biases—as does ours—but the materials with which they deal have immediate impacts on the geography of imagination of which we claim to be the experts. The analysis of the rhetoric, clichés, changes in sensibilities, and self-perceptions of individuals and communities that accompany our current global era require a preliminary assessment of the extraordinary changes that the domination of finance capital has imposed upon the majority of humanity since the 1980s. In no way can a symbolic analysis of globalization today avoid addressing the rise of the financiers. We need not approach symbols as a mere outcome of material life to acknowledge these links. On the contrary, we need to approach the geography of imagination and the geography of management as distinct yet necessary domains of our intellectual enterprise.

Anthropology for a Changing World

The history of the changing relations between these two geographies and what that history teaches us about our own times is a leitmotif of this book. Planetary flows of populations, of crops and animals, of goods, ideas, motifs, resources, techniques, religions, languages, and ideologies date back to the sixteenth century's first wave of colonization and the conquest of the Americas. Only by calling attention to these five centuries of global transformations can we distinguish between them and the trends that characterize our times. The more we insist on the relevance of previous global flows, the more likely we are to identify changes in the nature, magnitude, speed, and directions of these flows today without presuming a moral teleology. *purpose/design that all th. are moving twds. in the world.*

Critical distance from a moral teleology is not easy to establish, especially since globalization today sustains two major but opposite ideological illusions: euphoria and nostalgia. Observers who know little—or prefer to forget—about the history of the world before the nineteenth century tend to be most euphoric about the promises of globalization. Observers who tend to reduce the possibilities of a better world to the promises first evoked in that same nineteenth century tend to be most nostalgic about a past they did not live. Others vacillate between these two poles.

The effort to distinguish our times from previous eras thus requires that we account for the very difficulty of establishing a viewpoint that incorporates our own temporality. It also requires that we take more critical distance from the terms under which the nineteenth century taught us to both approach world history and to frame our present (see chapters 3, 4, 5). Reliance on the terms of the nineteenth century only increases the difficulty of securing a reliable viewpoint from which to look at global transformations today.

That difficulty is not only temporal. It is also spatial, since it has to do with the porousness and malleability of borders. The two geographies that ushered in the creation of the West proposed a world of fixed units and identifiable entities, later reinforced by the intellectual and political practices of the Enlightenment and the nineteenth century. Once circumnavigation sketched the material limits of the earth, it became easier to claim unchanging boundaries for entities that were as much social and ideological as geographical. The limits of the Orient were supposed to be known. So were those of the Seven Seas, or indeed, of the West Indies. The fact that the limits of France or Navarre, of Prussia or Italy were themselves contested and constantly redefined by blood did little to change the fundamental proposition that Europeans knew how to divide the rest of the world.

The nineteenth century further solidified the borders of units—both the units that supposedly referred to entities existing out there (such as races or nation-states) and the units supposedly resting halfway between observation and analysis (such as societies, economies, cultures, or politics). Indeed, the intense and joint solidification of political and intellectual borders in Europe during the nineteenth century should remind us that the sciences of humankind as we now know them are products of the very world that they try to explain. The social sciences in particular solidified as disciplines in degree-granting departments during a nineteenth century marked by both nationalist fervor in the North Atlantic and colonial domination almost everywhere else.

Were we to look for a single collective sentiment to identify our times, it might be the feeling that the many kinds of borders first proposed by the Renaissance, reinforced by the Enlightenment, and institutionalized in the nineteenth century have become increasingly difficult to reconcile with the reality we perceive. To be sure, these units never fully matched the daily experiences of millions of humans. Yet as tropes they were both convenient and powerful enough to sustain an illusion of fixed boundaries that was not shared by social scientists alone. The visibility, speed, and magnitude of global flows in our times makes this illusion of fixity increasingly hard to maintain. Anthropology must adapt to a world where none of us can take refuge in the illusion that we have found the uncontaminated Savage, the bearer of that pristine culture supposedly untouched by its Western alter-ego.

This book is a contribution to this much-needed adaptation and revitalization of anthropology. I hope that it will help sharpen our critical distance from the geography of imagination that we seek to understand. Buried in the critique of anthropology as the child of colonialism are positive proposals for a better evaluation of the narratives of the West and their global reach. Anthropologists have been quite productive at showing how these narratives could be falsified in specific places and times. As masters of the particular we have exposed thousands of small silences and discrepancies in the projection of the North Atlantic. This book is an attempt to pursue this anthropological critique of North Atlantic fictions. Yet it is deliberately self-reflective: that critique cannot spare anthropology itself.

Conceptually, the critique of anthropology proposed here sets up two preferential targets: empiricism and essentialism, which have been closely tied into our practice so far. In *The Poverty of Philosophy*, Karl Marx makes fun of philosophers looking for the fruitness of fruit, anticipating Ludwig Wittgenstein's critique of the futile search for the common essence that makes all games tokens of a type. In many ways, the social sciences have to different degrees pursued the search for content, when not directly searching for essences. A recurring theme of this book is the futility of that search: There is no stateness to states, no essence to culture, not even a fixed content to specific cultures, let alone a fixed content to the West. We gain greater knowledge of the nation, the state, the tribe, modernity, or globalization itself when we approach them as sets of relations and processes rather than as ahistorical essences.

Read one way, this book is an examination of such key words and their silences as they relate to anthropological history, theory, and practice: the West (chapter 1); modernity (chapter 2); globalization (chapter 3); the state (chapter 4); culture (chapter 5); the field, ethnography, and anthropology itself (chapter 6). Yet this examination does not exhaust the project. First, it requires a serious engagement with the history of the North Atlantic, without which the close reading of its fictions is impossible. Second and more importantly, this exercise in disciplinary reflexivity matters because of the long-term questions it raises about the insertion of the discipline into a larger world. Ultimately, anthropology will only matter to the populations that we study and to most of our readers if it evokes a purpose outside of itself. This purpose need not be found in the immediate applications of our research, but does not imply that it should not be a central object of debate within the discipline. To whom does—and should—anthropology make sense? This book is an invitation to such a debate.

Chapter 1

Anthropology and the Savage Slot: The Poetics and Politics of Otherness

Anthropology discovered globalization before the term became fashionable. By the late 1970s changes in the dynamism, mass, speed, and direction of global flows had seriously affected anthropological practice through their impact on the feasibility and relevance of ethnographic fieldwork. What did it mean to do fieldwork in India when there were so many Indians in New Jersey? Could one still pretend that non-Western peoples were so untouched by North Atlantic power that they truly constituted cultural isolates? Then, in the mid-1980s, as postmodernism announced ever louder the death of the grand narratives associated with Western modernity, a number of anthropologists tried to reassess ethnography— both fieldwork and writing—in relation to the increasingly suspect claims inherent in these narratives. They not only pursued the critique of progress launched by earlier anthropologists, but also engaged in a critique of representation that directly addressed fundamental assumptions of anthropological practice. The new wave of challenges brought forward by changes within and outside of academe required an archaeology of the discipline and a careful examination of its implicit premises.

From 1982 to the early 1990s, one of the most powerful attempts at that reexamination in the United States was what I call, in short, the postmodernist critique of anthropology. The label is a convenient shortcut: It includes scholars who never saw themselves as part of a single movement. Indeed, postmodernism never became a school in anthropology. Furthermore, the postmodernist melancholy of the 1980s has been outflanked in anthropology, as elsewhere, by the euphoria, outrage, or confusion spurred by the rise of the narratives of globalization— a shift that, temporary though it may be, we need to incorporate in our appraisal of globalization (chapter 3). Yet the reassessment of representation, the calls for a cultural critique of the discipline and for a greater individual reflexivity that proliferated in the 1980s offered both a diagnostic package of anthropological problems and a related set of solutions. Decades later both packages are still instructive in spite of, or even because of, their limitations. Their critique is also instructive because many of the sensibilities and assumptions of postmodernism—minus the gloomy mood—have since passed into anthropological approaches to globalization. Yet the diagnostic package of the postmodernist critique falls short of building the archaeology that it rightly sees as necessary because it tends to treat the discipline as a closed discourse. Similarly, the set of solutions proposed, from the reevaluation of ethnography as text to the greater reflexivity of individual anthropologists as writers and fieldworkers, does not address anthropology's relationship to the geography of imagination of the West. Nor does it question the Savage slot.

This chapter expands on a critique of that dual package to present an argument central to this book. I contend that anthropology belongs to a discursive field that is an inherent part of the West's geography of imagination. The internal tropes of anthropology matter much less than this larger discursive field within which it operates and upon whose existence it is premised. Any critique of anthropology requires a historicization of that larger discursive field—and thus an exploration of the relations between anthropology and the geography of imagination indispensable to the West. New directions will come only from the new vantage points discovered through such a critique.

Challenges and Opportunities

Academic disciplines do not create their fields of significance, they only legitimize particular organizations of meaning. They filter and rank—and in that sense, they truly *discipline*—contested arguments and themes that often precede them. In doing so, they continuously expand, restrict, or modify in diverse ways their distinctive arsenal of tropes, the types of statements they deem acceptable. But the poetics and politics of the "slots" within which disciplines operate do not dictate the enunciative relevance of these slots. There is no direct correlation between the "electoral politics" of a discipline and its political relevance. By "electoral politics," I mean the set of institutionalized practices and relations of power that influence the production of knowledge from within academe: academic filiations, the mechanisms of institutionalization, the organization of power within and across departments, the market value of publish-or-perish prestige, and other worldly issues that include, but expand way beyond, the maneuvering we usually refer to as "academic politics." Coalitions of variable durations coalesce intellectual, institutional, and individual affinities and contribute to propelling certain scholars to the forefront of their discipline in ways that make their voices more authoritative within the guild and more representative of that guild to the outside world.

Changes in the types of statements produced as "acceptable" within a discipline, regulated as they are—if only in part—by these "electoral politics," do not necessarily modify the larger field of operation, and especially the enunciative context of that discipline. Changes in the explicit criteria of acceptability do not automatically relieve the historical weight of the field of significance that the discipline inherited at birth. More likely, the burden of the past is alleviated when the sociohistorical conditions that obtained at the time of emergence have changed so much that practitioners face a choice between complete oblivion and fundamental redirection. At one point in time, alchemists become chemists or cease to be—but the transformation is one that few alchemists can predict and that even fewer would wish.

Anthropology is no exception to this scenario. Like all academic disciplines, it inherited a field of significance that preceded its formalization. Like many of the human sciences, it now faces dramatically new historical conditions of performance. Like any discourse, it can find new directions only if it modifies the boundaries within which it operates. These boundaries not only predated the emergence of anthropology as a discipline, but they also prescribed anthropology's roles (and ethnography's ultimate relevance) to an extent not yet unveiled. Anthropology fills a pre-established compartment within a wider symbolic field, the "Savage" slot[1] of a thematic trilogy that helped to constitute the West as we know it. A critical and reflexive anthropology requires, beyond the self-indulgent condemnation of traditional techniques and tropes, a reappraisal of this symbolic organization upon which anthropological discourse is premised.

Anthropology's future depends largely on its ability to contest the Savage slot and the *thématique* that constructs this slot. The times are ripe for this questioning. More important, solutions that fall short of this challenge can only push the discipline toward irrelevance, however much they reflect serious concerns. In that light, calls for reflexivity in the United States are not products of chance, the casual convergence of individual projects. Nor are they a passing fad, the accidental effect of debates that stormed philosophy and literary theory.[2] Rather, they are timid, yet spontaneous—and in that sense genuinely American—responses to major changes in the relations between anthropology and the wider world, provincial expressions of wider concerns, allusions to opportunities yet to be seized. What are those changes? What are these concerns? What are the opportunities?

On sheer empirical grounds, the differences between Western and non-Western societies are blurrier than ever before. Anthropology's answer to this ongoing transformation has been typically ad hoc and haphazard. The criteria according to which certain populations are deemed legitimate objects of research continue to vary with departments, with granting agencies, with practitioners, and even with the mood shifts of individual researchers. Amid the confusion, more anthropologists reenter the West cautiously, through the back door, after paying their dues elsewhere. By and large this reentry is no better theorized than were previous departures for faraway lands.[3]

While some anthropologists are rediscovering the West without ever naming it, what "the West" stands for is itself an object of debate within and outside the gates of academe. The reactionary search for a fundamental Western corpus of "great texts" by many intellectuals and bureaucrats in the English-speaking world is both the reflection of a wider conflict and a particular response to the uncertainties stirred by this conflict. Interestingly, few anthropologists have intervened in that debate. Fewer even among those thought to be at the forefront of the discipline have deigned to address directly the issue of Western monumentalism, with one or two exceptions (e.g., Rosaldo 1989). Even more interestingly, anthropological *theory* remains irrelevant to—and unused by—either side of the "great texts" debate, rhetorical references notwithstanding. Today, the statement that any canon necessarily eliminates an unspecified set of experiences need not come only from anthropology—thanks, of course, to the past diffusion of anthropology itself, but thanks especially to changes in the world and to the experiences that express and motivate these changes. Minorities of all kinds can and do voice their cultural claims, not on the basis of explicit theories of culture but in the name of historical authenticity. They enter the debate not as academics—or not only as academics—but as situated individuals with rights to historicity. They speak in the first person, signing their argument with an "I" or a "we," rather than invoking the ahistorical voice of reason, justice, and civilization.

Anthropology is caught off guard by this reformulation. Traditionally, it approached the issue of cultural differences with a monopoly over "native discourse," hypocritically aware that this discourse would remain a quote. It is too liberal to accept either the radical authenticity of the first person or the conservative reversion to canonical truths—hence, its theoretical silence.

Silence seems to me a hasty abdication. At the very least, anthropology should be able to illuminate the myth of an unquestioned Western canon upon which the debate is premised.[4] In so doing it would certainly undermine some of its own premises; but that risk is an inherent aspect of the current wave of challenges: its numerous opportunities are inseparable from its multiple threats. Nowhere is this combination of threats and opportunities as blatant as in the postmodern admission that the metanarratives of the West are crumbling.

The Fall of the House of Reason

Whatever else postmodernism means, it remains inseparable from the acknowledgment of an ongoing collapse of metanarratives in a world where Reason and Reality have become fundamentally destabilized (Lyotard 1979, 1986).[5] To be sure, the related claim (Tyler 1986:123) that "the world that made science, and that science made, has disappeared" is still premature. The growing awareness among literati that rationality has not fulfilled its promises to uncover the absolute becoming of the spirit does not alter the increasing institutionalization of rationality itself (Godzich 1986:xvii–xix). Indeed, one could argue that the spectacular failure of science and reason, judged on the universal grounds that scholars love to emphasize, serves to mask success on more practical and localized terrains into which academics rarely venture.

But if the world that science made is very much alive, the world that made science is now shaky. The crisis of the nation-state, the crisis of the individual, the crisis of the parties of order (liberal, authoritarian, or communist), terrorism, the crisis of "late capitalism"—all contribute to a Western malaise and, in turn, feed upon it (Aronowitz 1988; Jameson 1984). Philosophers reportedly asked: Can one *think* after Auschwitz? But it took some time for Auschwitz to sink in, for communism to reveal its own nightmares, for structuralism to demonstrate its magisterial impasse, for North and South to admit the impossibility of dialogue, for fundamentalists of all denominations to desacralize religion, and for reenlightened intellectuals to question all foundational thought. As the walls crumbled—North and South and East and West—intellectuals developed languages of postdestruction. It is this mixture of negative intellectual surprise, this postmortem of the metanarratives, that situates the postmodernist mood as primarily Western and primarily petit bourgeois.

These words are not inherently pejorative, but they are meant to historicize the phenomenon—an important exercise if we intend to have relevance outside the North Atlantic. First, it is not self-evident that all past and present worldviews required metanarratives up until their current entry into postmodernity. Second, if the collapse of metanarratives alone characterized the postmodern condition, then some of those populations outside of the North Atlantic that have been busily deconstructing theirs for centuries, or that have gone through mega-collapses of their own, have long been "postmodern," and there is nothing new under the sun. Things fell apart quite early on the southern shores of the Atlantic, and later in the hinterlands of Africa, Asia, and the Americas. Third, even if we concede, for the sake of argument, that metanarratives once were a prerequisite of humankind and are now collapsing everywhere at equal rates (two major assumptions, indeed), we cannot infer identical reactive strategies to this collapse.

Thus, we must distinguish between postmodernism as a mood, and the recognition of a situation of postmodernity, especially now that the melancholy is fading. The acknowledgment that there is indeed a crisis of representation, that there is indeed an ongoing set of qualitative changes in the international organization of symbols (Appadurai 1991, 1996), in the rhythms of symbolic construction (Harvey 1989), and in the ways symbols relate to localized, subjective experience, does not in itself require a postmortem. In that light, the key to dominant versions of postmodernism is an ongoing destruction lived as shock and revelation. Postmodernism builds on this revelation of the sudden disappearance of established rules, foundational judgments, and known categories (Lyotard 1986:33). But the very fact of revelation implies a previous attitude toward such rules, judgments, and categories—for instance, that they have been taken for granted or as immutable. The postmortem inherent in the postmodernist mood implies a previous "world of universals" (Ross 1988a:xii–xiii). It implies a specific view of culture change. It implies, at least in part, the Enlightenment and nineteenth-century Europe.

In cross-cultural perspective the dominant mood of postmodernism thus appears as a historically specific phenomenon, a reaction provoked by the revelation that the Enlightenment and its conflicting tributaries may have run their course. This mood is not inherent in the world situation, but neither is it a passing ambience as many of the postmodernists' detractors would have—even though it ushers in fads of its own. It is a mood in the strong sense in which Geertz (1973:90) defines religious moods: powerful, persuasive, and promisingly enduring. But contrary to religions, it rejects both the pretense of factuality and the aspiration to realistic motivations. It seeks a "psychoanalytic therapeutic" from the "modern neurosis," the "Western schizophrenia, paranoia, etc. all the sources of misery *we* have known for two centuries" (Lyotard 1986:125–6).

"We," here, *is* the West, though not in a genealogical or territorial sense. The postmodern world has little space left for genealogies, and notions of territoriality are being redefined right before our eyes (Appadurai 1991, 1996). It is a world where black American Michael Jackson starts an international tour from Japan and imprints cassettes that mark the rhythm of Haitian peasant families in the Cuban Sierra Maestra; a world where Florida speaks Spanish (once more); where a Socialist prime minister came to Greece by way of New England and the fundamentalist imam came from Paris to turn Iran into an Islamic state. It is a world where a political leader in reggae-prone Jamaica traces his roots to Arabia, where U.S. credit cards are processed in Barbados, and Italian designer shoes are made in Hong Kong or Shangai. It is a world where the Pope can be Polish and where most orthodox Marxists live on the Western side of a fallen iron curtain. It is a world where the most enlightened are only part-time citizens of part-time communities of imagination.

But these very phenomena—and their inherent connection with the expansion of what we conveniently call the West—are part of the text that reveals the post-modernist mood as eventuating from a Western *problématique*. The perception of a collapse as revelation cannot be envisioned outside of the trajectory of thought that has marked the West and spread unevenly outside its expanding boundaries. Its conditions of existence coalesce within the West. The stance it spawns is unthinkable outside of the West, and has significance only within the boundaries set by the Western reading of world history.

Millennial Historicity

Human beings participate in history both as actors and as narrators, yet the boundaries between these two sides of historicity, necessary as they are as heuris-tic devices, are themselves historical, and thus fluid and changing. The interface between what happened and that which is said to have happened is thus always a matter of struggle, a contested field within which uneven power is deployed (Trouillot 1995). I have insisted so far that the West is a historical projection, a projection *in* history. But it is also a projection *of* history, the imposition of a par-ticular interface between what happened and that which is said to have happened.

As anchor of a claim to universal legitimacy, the geography of imagination inherent in the West since the sixteenth century imposes a frame within which to read world history. Thematic variations and political choices aside, from Las Casas to Condorcet, to Kant, Hegel, Marx, Weber, and beyond, this framework has always assumed the centrality of the North Atlantic not only as the site from which world history is made but also as the site whence that story can be told. Eric Wolf (1982) has argued that the human disciplines have treated the world outside of Europe as people without history. One can more precisely claim that they were also treated as people without historicity. Their capacity to narrate anecdotal parts of the world story was always subsumed under a North Atlantic historicity that was deemed universal.

The linear continuity that Western universalism projects—the sense of a telos, if not all the teleological variations that punctuate the literature from Condorcet to Engels—reflected and reinforced implicit and explicit persuasions of a growing general public within and outside the North Atlantic. During the last two cen-turies, it became obvious to increasing segments of otherwise diverse populations that history was going somewhere. With the certitude of a telos—or at the very least, of a universal "meaning" to history—came a particular twist on periodization: Chunks of chronology could be read backwards or in their contemporaneity as temporary moments of regress or, more often, as indications of progress. Not only was world history going somewhere, but one could tell how far it had gone and guess how much further it had to go.

Within this continuity and the global temporality that it entailed, the nineteenth century emerges as an era of certitudes, of truths worth dying for—and killing for—in the name of a species suddenly united in spite of its inequalities, and indeed often because of them. Yet the twentieth century was, from that same perspective, a century of paradoxes (Todorov 2001). It was an age of extremes (Hobsbawm 1962) during which the incompatibilities of Western universalism—evident in the Renaissance yet quickly masked by the rhetoric of the Enlightenment and the enormous deployment of North Atlantic power in the nineteenth century—revealed themselves in full force. The last hundred years of this now defunct millennium were those during which the global domination of North Atlantic institutional forms became so pervasive that subjugated peoples everywhere found it impossible to formulate the terms of their liberation and to envision their futures outside of these forms. It was the century of hope, yet it was also the century of violent deaths—almost eighteen million in World War I alone, twice as many in World War II, and twice as many again since then in ethnic, civil, and national wars, border conflicts, and separatist struggles. It was the century during which international institutions gained legitimacy, yet it was also the century that fully institutionalized international disparities. It was the century of medicine and technological miracles, yet it was also the century during which humanity measured the full horror of technology and its capacity for mass destruction.

As that century drew to a close, its contradictory path—long covered up by the partisans of communism and capitalism alike—could not be hidden anymore, especially once the fall of the Soviet Union had removed one of the necessary components of the teleological discourses that nurtured the cover-up. Maybe world history was going nowhere. With that creeping sense of loss, moods and affects began to replace the analytical schemes that once promised a universal future that now appeared increasingly dubious. Postmodernist melancholy mourned the death of utopias: There was never a future. Globalitarist euphoria claimed the end of history: Our present is the future. Both reflect the millennial historicity of a North Atlantic incapable of inserting the history of the last one hundred years in a single universal narrative. Utopia and progress both became concrete in the twentieth century, but neither survived intact.

If the postmodern mood is fundamentally Western in the sense delineated above, what does this mean for an anthropology of the present? It means that the present that anthropologists must confront is the product of a particular past that encompasses the history and the pre-history of anthropology itself. Consequently, it also means that the postmodernist critique within North American anthropology remains within the very thematic field that it claims to challenge. Finally, it means that a truly critical and reflexive anthropology needs to contextualize Western metanarratives and read critically the place of the discipline in the field so discovered. In short, anthropology needs to turn the apparatus elaborated in the observation of non-Western societies on itself, and more specifically, on the history from which it sprang. That history does not begin with the formalization of the discipline, but with the emergence of the symbolic field that made this formalization possible.

The Savage and the Innocent

In 1492, Christopher Columbus stumbled upon the Caribbean. The admiral's mistake would later be heralded as "The Discovery of America," a label challenged only in the last century during its quincentennial celebration. To be sure, it took Nuñez de Balboa's sighting of the Pacific in 1513 to verify the existence of a continental mass, and Amerigo Vespucci's insistence on a *mundus novus* for Christendom to acknowledge this "discovery." Then it took another fifty years to realize its symbolic significance. Yet 1492 was, to some extent, a discovery even then, the first material step in a continuously renewed process of invention (Ainsa 1988). Abandoning one lake for another, Europe confirmed the sociopolitical fissure that was slowly pushing the Mediterranean toward northern and southern shores. In so doing, it created itself, but it also discovered America, its still unpolished alter ego, its elsewhere, its Other. The Conquest of America stands as Europe's model for the constitution of the Other (Todorov 1982; see also Ainsa 1988).

Yet from the beginning, the model was Janus-faced. The year 1516 saw the publication of two anthropological precursors: the Alcalá edition of the *Decades* of Pietro Martire d'Anghiera (a paraethnographic account of the Antilles, and in many ways one of Europe's earliest introductions to a "state of nature" elsewhere) and one more popular edition of Amerigo Vespucci's epistolary travel accounts. In that same year too, Thomas More published his fictional account of an "ideal state" on the island of *Utopia*, the prototypical nowhere of European imagination.

The chronological coincidence of these publications, fortuitous as it may be, symbolizes a thematic correspondence now blurred by intellectual specialization and the abuse of categories. We now claim to distinguish clearly between travelers' accounts, colonial surveys, ethnographic reports, and fictional utopias. Such cataloging is useful, but only to some extent. In the early sixteenth century, European descriptions of an alleged state of nature in the realist mode filled the writings of colonial officers concerned with the immediate management of the Other. The realist mode also pervaded travelers' accounts of the sixteenth and seventeenth centuries, before settling in the privileged space of learned discourse with eighteenth-century philosophers and the nineteenth-century rise of armchair anthropology. Even then, the line between these genres was not always clear-cut (Thornton 1983; Weil 1984). The realist mode also pervaded fiction—so much so that some twentieth-century critics distinguish between utopias and "extraordinary voyages," or trips to the lands of nowhere with the most "realistic" geographical settings. On the other hand, fantasies about an ideal state increased in fiction, but they also found their way into theater, songs, and philosophical treatises.

Classifications notwithstanding, the connection between a state of nature and an ideal state is, to a large extent, in the symbolic construction of the materials themselves. The symbolic transformation through which Christendom became the West structures a set of relations that necessitate both utopia and the Savage. What happens within the slots so created—and within the genres that condition their historical existence—is not inconsequential. But the analysis of these genres cannot explain the slots nor even the internal tropes of such slots. To wit, "utopia" has been the most studied form of this ensemble, yet there is no final agreement on which works to include in the category (Andrews 1937 [1935]; Atkinson 1920, 1922; Eliav-Feldon 1982; Kamenka 1987; Manuel and Manuel 1979; Trousson 1975). Further, when reached, agreement is often ephemeral. Even if one could posit a continuum from realist ethnography to fictional utopias, works move in and out of these categories and categories often overlap on textual and non-textual grounds. Finally, textuality is rarely the final criterion of inclusion or exclusion. From the 200-year-long controversy about the *Voyage et aventures de François Leguat* (a 1708 best-seller believed by some to be a true account and by others, a work of fiction), to the Castañeda embarrassment[6] to professional anthropology, to debates on *Shabono*[7] or the existence of the Tasaday,[8] a myriad of cases indicate the ultimate relevance of issues outside of "the text" proper (Atkinson 1922; Pratt 1986; Weil 1984).

That the actual corpus fitting any of these genres at any given period has never been unproblematic underscores a thematic correspondence that has survived the increasingly refined categorizations. In the 1500s, readers could not fail to notice the similarities between works such as Jacques Cartier's *Brief Récit*, which features paraethnographic descriptions of Indians, and some of Rabelais's scenes in *Gargantua*. Montaigne, an observant traveler himself within the confines of Europe, used descriptions of America to set for his readers issues in philosophical anthropology—and in the famous essay "Des cannibales," he is quick to point out the major difference between his enterprise and that of his Greek predecessors, including Plato: The Greeks had no realistic database (Montaigne 1952). Early in the seventeenth century, Tommaso Campanella produced his *La Città del Sole* (1602) informed by descriptions that Portuguese missionaries and Dutch mercenaries were bringing back from Ceylon and by Jesuit reports of socialism within the Inca kingdom.

Utopias were both rare and inferior—by earlier and later standards—during the seventeenth century. Few are now remembered other than those of Campanella, Sir Francis Bacon, and François Fénelon. But the search for an exotic ideal had not died, as some authors (Trousson 1975) seem to suggest. Fénelon's *Aventures de Télémaque* went into 20 printings. The *History of the Sevarites* of Denis Vairasse d'Alais (1677–79) was published originally in English, then in a French version that spurred German, Dutch, and Italian translations (Atkinson 1920). Utopias did not quench the thirst for fantasy lands but only because relative demand had increased unexpectedly.

Travel accounts, of which the numbers kept multiplying, filled the demand for the Elsewhere. Some did so with reports of unicorns and floating isles, then accepted as reality by their public, including some of the most respected scholars of the time. But most did so with what were "realist" pictures of the savage, pictures that would pass twentieth-century tests of accuracy and are still being used by historians and anthropologists. Jean-Baptiste Du Tertre (1973 [1667]), Jean

Baptiste Labat (1972 [1722]), or Thomas Gage (1958 [1648])—to take only a few recognizable authors writing on one hemisphere—familiarized readers with the wonders of the Antilles and the American mainland.

Outside of a restricted group of overzealous scholars and administrators, it mattered little to the larger European audience whether such works were fictitious or not. That they presented an elsewhere was enough. That the Elsewhere was actually somewhere was a matter for a few specialists. The dream remained alive well into the next century. Baron de Montesquieu was so much aware of this implicit correspondence that he gambled on reversing all the traditions at the same time, with considerable aesthetic and didactic effect, in his *Lettres Persanes* (1721). The Elsewhere became Paris; the Other became French; the utopia became a well-known state of affairs. It worked, because everyone recognized the models and understood the parody.

The thematic correspondence between utopias and travel accounts or paraethnographic descriptions was not well camouflaged until the end of the eighteenth century. The forms continued to diverge, while the number of publications within each category kept increasing. Utopias filled the century that gave us the Enlightenment, from Jonathon Swift's parodic *Gulliver's Travels* (1702) to Bernadin de Saint Pierre's unfinished *L'amazone* (1795). But so did realistic descriptions of far away peoples, and so did, moreover, crossnational debates in Europe on what exactly those descriptions meant for the rational knowledge of humankind. In the single decade of the 1760s, England alone sent expeditions like those of Commodore Byron, Captains Cartwright, Bruce, Furneaux, and Wallis, and Lieutenant Cook to savage lands all over the world. Bruce, Wallis, and Cook brought home reports from Abyssinia, Tahiti, and Hawaii. Byron and his companions carried back accounts "of a race of splendid giants" from Patagonia. Cartwright returned with five living Eskimos who caused a commotion in the streets of London (Tinker 1922:5–25).

Scholars devoured such "realistic" data on the Savage with a still unsurpassed interest while writing didactic utopias and exploring in their philosophical treatises the rational revelation behind the discoveries of the travelers. Voltaire, who read voraciously the travel descriptions of his time, gave us *Candide* and *Zadig*. But he also used paraethnographic descriptions to participate in anthropological debates of his time, siding for instance with the Göttingen school on polygenesis (Duchet 1971). Denis Diderot, who may have read more travel accounts than anyone then alive, and who turned many of them into paraethnographic descriptions for the *Encyclopédie*, wrote two utopias true to form.[9] Jean Jacques Rousseau, whom Claude Lévi-Strauss called "the father of ethnology," sought the most orderly link between "the state of nature" first described by Martire d'Anghiera and the "ideal commonwealth" envisioned by More and his followers. He thus unwittingly formalized the myth of the "noble savage," renewing a theme that went back not only to Alexander Pope and Daniel Defoe, but to now forgotten travelers of the sixteenth and seventeenth centuries. Long before Rousseau's *Social Contract*, Pietro Martire already thought that the Arawak of the Antilles were sweet and simple. Ferdinand Magellan's companion, Antonio Pigafetta, claimed in 1522 that the Indians of Brazil were "*creduli e boni*" by instinct. And Pierre

Boucher, writing of the Iroquois in 1664, had confirmed that "*tous les Sauuages ont l'esprit bon*" (Atkinson 1920:65–70; Gonnard 1946:36).

The myth of the noble Savage is not a creation of the Enlightenment. Ever since the West became the West, Robinson has been looking for Friday. The eighteenth century was not even the first to see arguments on or around that myth (Gonnard 1946). The verbal duel between Bartolomé de Las Casas and Juan Gines de Sepúlveda on the "nature" of the Indians and the justice of their enslavement, fought at Valladolid in the early 1550s in front of Spain's intellectual nobility, was as spectacular as anything the Enlightenment could imagine (Las Casas 1992 [1552]; André-Vincent 1980; Pagden 1982). Rather, the specificity of eighteenth-century anthropological philosophers was to dismiss some of the past limitations of this grandiose controversy and to claim to resolve it not on the basis of the Scriptures, but on the open grounds of rationality and experience. But the debate was always implicit in the thematic concordance that had tied the observation of the savage and the hopes of utopia since at least 1516. Swiss writer Isaac Iselin, a leading voice of the Göttigen school of anthropology, criticized Rousseau's ideals and the state of savagery as "disorderly fantasy" (Rupp-Eisenreich 1984:99). The fact that the Göttingen school did not bother to verify its own "ethnographic" bases, or that it used travelers' accounts for purposes other than Rousseau's (Rupp-Eisenreich 1985), matters less than the fact that Rousseau, Iselin, Christoph Meiners, and Joseph-Marie De Gérando shared the same premises on the relevance of savagery. For Rousseau, as for More and Defoe, the Savage is an argument for a particular kind of utopia. For Iselin and Meiners, as for Swift and Thomas Hobbes in other times and contexts, it is an argument against it. Given the tradition of the genre being used, the formal terrain of battle, and the personal taste of the author, the argument was either tacit or explicit and the Savage's face either sketched or magnified. But argument there was.

The nineteenth century blurred the most visible signs of this thematic correspondence by artificially separating utopia and the Savage. To schematize a protracted and contested process, it is as if that century of specialization subdivided the Other that the Renaissance had set forth in creating the West. From then on, utopia and the Savage evolved as two distinguishable slots. Immanuel Kant had set the philosophical grounds for this separation by laying out his own teleology without humor or fiction while moving away from the *Naturinstink*. Nineteenth-century French positivists, in turn, derided utopias as chimeric utopianisms (Manuel and Manuel 1979).

The growing fictional literature in the United States also modified the forms of utopia (Pfaelzer 1984). To start with, America had been the imagined site of traditional utopias, Alexis de Tocqueville's *feuille blanche*, the land of all (im)possibilities. Defining an elsewhere from this site was a dilemma. Ideally, its Eden was within itself (Walkover 1974). Not surprisingly, William Dean Howells brings *A Traveler from Altruria* (1894) to the United States before sending his readers back to utopia. Edward Bellamy chose to look "backward." More important, America's Savages and its colonized were also within itself—as American Indians and black Americans, only one of whom white anthropologists dared to study before the latter part of this century (Mintz 1971a, 1990). With two groups of savages to pick from, specialization set in, and Indians (especially "good" Indians) became the preserve of anthropologists.[10]

At the same time, a black utopia was unthinkable, given the character of North American racism and the fabric of black/white imagery in American literature (Levin 1958). Thus the black pastoral (the unmatched apex of which is *Uncle Tom's Cabin* [1851]—but note that the flavor is also in Faulkner) played the role that Saint Pierre's *Paul et Virginie* (1787) had played earlier in European imagination.[11] But true-to-form utopia writers in North America moved away from the specter of savagery.

Other factors were at play. The nineteenth century was America's century of concreteness, when its utopias became reachable. Of the reported 52 million migrants who left Europe between 1824 and 1924, more than ninety percent went to the Americas, mostly to the United States. In the United States, and in Europe as well, decreasing exchange among writers—who were involved in different forms of discourse and seeking legitimacy on different grounds—contributed even more to giving each group of practitioners the sentiment that they were carrying on a different enterprise. As they believed their practice and practiced their beliefs, the enterprises indeed became separated, but only to a certain extent. By the end of the nineteenth century, utopian novelists accentuated formal interests while utopianisms were acknowledged primarily as doctrines couched in nonfictional terms: Saint-Simonism, Fabian Socialism, Marxism (Gonnard 1946). Travel accounts came to pass as a totally separate genre, however Robinson-like some remained. The "scientific" study of the Savage *qua* Savage became the privileged field of academic anthropology, soon to be anchored in distinguished chairs, but already severed from its imaginary counterpart.

A Discipline for the Savage

The rest of the story is well known, perhaps too well known, inasmuch as the insistence on the methods and tropes of anthropology as a discipline may obscure the larger discursive order that made sense of its institutionalization. Histories that fail to problematize this institutionalization—and critiques premised on that naïve history—necessarily fall short of illuminating the enunciative context of anthropological discourse. To be sure, anthropologists to this day keep telling both undergraduates and lay readers that their practice is useful to better understand "ourselves," but without ever spelling out exactly the specifics of this understanding, the utopias behind this curiosity turned profession.

It has often been said that the Savage or the primitive was the alter ego the West constructed for itself. What has not been emphasized enough is that this Other was a Janus, of whom the Savage was only the second face.[12] The first face was the West itself, but the West fancifully constructed as a utopian projection, and meant to be, in that imaginary correspondence, the condition of existence of the Savage. This thematic correspondence preceded the institutionalization of anthropology as a specialized field of inquiry. Better said, the constitutive moment of ethnography as metaphor antedates the constitution of anthropology as discipline, and even precedes its solidification as specialized discourse.

Anthropology's disciplinary emergence was part of the institutionalization of the social sciences from the mid-nineteenth century to the start of World War II. That institutionalization closely followed the rise of nationalism and the consolidation of state power in North Atlantic countries where the social science disciplines first solidified. It paralleled the partition of the world mainly by the same countries (Wallerstein et al. 1996). Eurocentric ideas first developed and nurtured successively by the Renaissance, the first wave of colonialism, the Enlightenment, and the practice of plantation slavery in the Americas, had gathered new momentum with colonialism's second wave. By the time the social sciences were standardized in degree-granting departments, non-Western areas and peoples were thought to be fundamentally different both in essence and in practice. They could not be known through the same scientific procedures or subjected to the same rules of management. At the same time, the desire to know and manage them had increased.

It is in that context that cultural anthropology became, almost by default, a discipline aimed at exposing the people of the North Atlantic to the lives and mores of the Other. Anthropology came to fill "the Savage slot" of a larger thematic field, performing a role played, in different ways, by literature and travel accounts—and at times, by unexpected media.[13] The contingent factors of that institutionalization now seem irrelevant. Yet had Classics maintained a more sustained dialogue with Orientalism, had Oriental Studies remained vibrant in France and especially in Britain, had sociology become an institutional arm of the state abroad as it was at home, cultural anthropology's niche and formalization would have been different. There would have been a division of academic labor on the Savage slot. As there was not such a division, anthropology inherited a disciplinary monopoly over an object that it never bothered to theorize.

Yet that theorization is necessary. For the dominant metamorphosis, the transformation of savagery into sameness by way of Utopia as positive or negative reference is not the outcome of a textual exercise within anthropological practice, but part of anthropology's original conditions of existence. That the discipline was positivist in a positivist age, and structuralist in a context dominated by structuralism, is not very intriguing; as Tyler (1986:128) acutely notes, the more recent "textualization of pseudo-discourse" can accomplish "a terrorist alienation more complete than that of the positivists." Thus attempts at disciplinary reflexivity cannot stop at the moment of institutionalization, or emphasize the internal tropes of late modern ethnographies, even though some rightly allude to the correspondence between savagery and utopia, or the use of the pastoral mode in anthropology (e.g., Clifford 1986b; Rosaldo 1986; Tyler 1986). Such attempts are not *wrong*. But the primary focus on the textual construction of the Other *in* anthropology may turn our attention away from the construction of Otherness upon which anthropology is premised, and further mask a correspondence already well concealed by increasing specialization since the nineteenth century.

Indeed, the savage-utopia correspondence tends to generate false candor. It rarely reveals its deepest foundations or its inherent inequality, even though it triggers claims of reciprocity. From Pietro Martire to North American anthropology's forays into postmodernist reflexivity, the Savage has been an occasion to profess innocence. We may guess at some of the reasons behind this recurrent tendency to exhibit the nude as nakedness. Let me just say this much: In spite of such old claims, the utopian West dominated the thematic correspondence. It did so from behind the scenes, at least most of the time. It showed itself in least-equivocal terms in just a few occasions, most notably the philosophical jousts over American colonization in sixteenth-century Spain (Pagden 1982) and in the anthropological debates of the eighteenth century (Duchet 1971).

But visible or not, naïve or cynical, the West was always first, as utopia or as challenge to it—that is, as a universalist project, the boundaries of which are no-where, u-topous, non-spatial. And that, one needs to repeat, is not a product of the Enlightenment, but part and parcel of the horizons set by the Renaissance and its simultaneous creation of Europe and Otherness, without which the West is inconceivable. Thomas More did not have to wait for ethnographic reports on the Americas to compose his *Utopia*. Similarly, eighteenth-century readers of travel accounts did not wait for verification. Even today, there is a necessary gap between the initial acceptance of the most fanciful "ethnographies" and the "restudies" or "reassessments" that follow. The chronological precedence reflects a deeper inequality in the two faces of Janus: the utopian West is first in the construction of this complementarity. It is the first observed face of the figure, the initial projection against which the Savage becomes a reality. The Savage *makes sense* in terms of utopia.

The Mediation of Order

Utopia itself made sense only in terms of the absolute order against which it was projected, negatively or not.[14] Utopias do not necessarily advance foundational propositions, but they feed upon foundational thought. Fictional "ideal states," presented as novels or treatises, suggest a project, or a counter-project. It is this very projection, rather than their alleged or proven fanciful characteristics, that makes them utopias. Here again, we need to go back to the Renaissance, that fictional rebirth through which Christendom became the West, where two more snapshots may clarify the issue.

From the point of view of contemporaries, the most important event of the year 1492 was not Columbus's landing in the Antilles, but the conquest of the Muslim kingdom of Granada and its incorporation into Castile (Trouillot 1995:108–40). The gap between the three religions of Abraham had paralleled the sociopolitical fissure that split the Mediterranean, but because of that fissure religious intolerance increasingly expressed itself in ways that intertwined religion, ethnicity, territory, and matters of state control. To put it simply, as Christendom became Europe, Europe itself became Christian. It is no accident that the fall of Muslim Granada was immediately followed by the expulsion of the Jews from the now Christian territory. It is no accident either that the very same individual who signed the public order against the Jews also signed Ferdinand and Isabella's secret instructions to Columbus. Indeed, nascent Europe could turn its eyes to the Atlantic only because the consolidation of political borders and the concentration of political power in the name of the Christian God presaged the advent of internal order.

Order—political and ideological—was high on the agenda, both in theory and in practice; and the increased use of the printing press stimulated the interchange between theory and practice. Thus, in 1513, three years before Thomas More's *Utopia*, Niccolò Machiavelli wrote *The Prince*. In retrospect, that work signified a threshold: Some leaders of the emerging Western world were ready to phrase the issue of control in terms of *realpolitik* long before the word was coined. The Machiavelli era encompassed Desiderius Erasmus's *Education of a Christian Prince*, Guillaume Budé's *Education of a Prince*, and other treatises that shared an "emphasis on the workable rather than the ideal," a belief that "men's destinies were to some extent within their own control and that this control depended upon self-knowledge" (Hale 1977 [1971]:305).[15]

The seminal writings that inscribed savagery, utopia, and order were conceived in the same era. This simultaneity is but one indication that these slots were created against the backdrop of one another. In the context of Europe, the works that set up these slots were part of an emerging debate that tied order to the quest for universal truths, a quest that gave savagery and utopia their relevance. Looming above the issue of the ideal state of affairs, and tying it to that of the state of nature, was the issue of order as both a goal and a means, and its relation with reason and justice. Campanella's *City*, the runner-up to *Utopia* in the critics' view, clearly engaged some of Machiavelli's proposals and those of contemporary Spanish philosophers (Manuel and Manuel 1979:261–88). Campanella, like More, also wrote in nonfictional modes. He commented on European political regimes in terms of their ultimate justification. He proposed to various European monarchs a nonfictional plan of rule based on his religious and philosophical views. Indeed, the opinions expressed in his treatises got him thrown into a Spanish jail where he wrote his fictionalized utopia (Manuel and Manuel 1979; Trousson 1975:39, 72–8). Sir Thomas More, in turn, was executed.

The relation between fictionalized utopias and matters of political power goes way back to the ancestral forms of the genre in ancient Greece (Trousson 1975:39). So do debates on the nature of otherness. But we need not take the naïve history of the West at face value: Greece did not beget Europe. Rather, Europe claimed Greece. The revisionist historiography through which the Renaissance turned Christendom into Europe and gave it its Greek heritage is itself a phenomenon that needs to be placed in history. The distinctiveness of the Renaissance was, in part, the invention of a past for the West.[16] It was also, in part, an emerging claim to universality and to an absolute order inconceivable without that claim. As Las Casas, Montesquieu, and Montaigne were quick to point out in different terms and times, a major difference between Europe and ancient Greece was the reality of the Savage as experienced by Europe after 1492. Unlike that of Greece and Rome, or that of the Islamic world, the West's vision of order implied from its inception two complementary spaces, the Here and the Elsewhere, which premised one another and were conceived as inseparable.[17]

In imaginary terms that Elsewhere could be Utopia; but in the concrete terms of conquest, it was a space of colonization peopled by others who would eventually become "us"—or at the very least who *should*—in a project of assimilation antithetic to the most liberal branches of Greek philosophy (Hartog 1988 [1980]).

In that sense, order had become universal, absolute—both in the shape of the rising absolutist state (quite opposed, indeed, to Greek democracy) and in the shape of a universal empire stretching the limits of Christendom out into nowhere. Colonization became a mission, and the Savage became absence and negation.[18] The symbolic process through which the West created itself thus involved the universal legitimacy of power—and order became, in that process, the answer to the question of legitimacy. To put it otherwise, the West is inconceivable without a metanarrative. Since their common emergence in the sixteenth century, world capitalism, the modern state, and colonization posed—and continue to pose—the issue of the philosophical base of order to the West. What language can legitimate universal control? Here again the geography of imagination and the geography of management appear to be distinct yet intertwined, both empirically and analytically.

Chronological convergences again illustrate the point. At about the time Machiavelli wrote *The Prince*, the Spanish Crown made known its supplementary laws on American colonization and the Medici clan in 1513 secured the papacy with the nomination of Leo X—the same Leo, Bishop of Rome, to whom Pietro Martire dedicated parts of his ethnography. Two years later, the accession of Francis I as king of France signaled the self-conscious invention of the traditions constitutive of the French nation-state—a self-consciousness manifested in the imposed use of the French dialect and the creation of the Collège de France.[19] One year after Francis's advent, Charles I (later Charles V) became king of Castille and of its New World possessions, and Martin Luther published the theses of Wittenberg. The second decade of the new century ended quite fortuitously with a semblance of victory on the side of order, that is, with Charles's "election" to the imperial crown in 1519. But the condemnation of Luther (1520), rural agitation within Castille itself, and the so-called Oriental menace (culminating with the 1529 siege of Vienna by the Turks) kept reminding a nascent Europe that its self-delivery was not to happen without pains. The notion of a universal empire that would destroy the borders of Christendom through its ineluctable expansion became both more attractive in thought and more unattainable in practice.[20]

The fictionalized utopias that immediately followed More's and overlapped with the practical reshaping of power in a newly defined Europe were by and large reformist rather than revolutionary, hardly breaking new imaginary grounds (Trousson 1975:62–72). This is not surprising, for just as the Savage is in an unequal relationship with utopia, so is utopia in an uneven relationship with order. Just as the Savage is a metaphorical argument for or against utopia, so is utopia (and the Savage it encompasses) a metaphorical argument for or against order, conceived of as an expression of legitimate universality. It is the mediation of universal order as the ultimate signified of the Savage-utopia relation that gives its full sense to the triad. In defense of a particular vision of order, the Savage became evidence for a particular type of utopia. That the same ethnographic source could be used to make the opposite point did not matter beyond a minimal requirement for verisimilitude. To be sure, Las Casas had been to the New World, Sepúlveda had not; and this helped the cause of the *Procurador*. To be sure, the Rousseauists were right and Göttingen was wrong about cranial sizes. To be sure, the empirical verdict is not yet in on the Tasaday. But now as before, the

	The West	The Rest	
The Observer			The Other
Culture			Nature
History			Stories
	ORDER	SAVAGE	
		Noble	
		Barbarian	
		Wise	
		Evil	
	State: Justice	UTOPIA	
		Paradisiac	
		Communist	
		Innocent	
		Illusory	
	Thought: Reason		
Here			Elsewhere

Figure 1   The symbolic organization of the Savage Slot, ca. 1515–1990

Savage is only evidence within a debate, the importance of which surpasses not only his understanding but his very existence.

Just as utopia itself can be offered as a promise or as a dangerous illusion, the Savage can be noble, wise, barbaric, victim or aggressor, depending on the debate and on the aims of the interlocutors. The space within the slot is not static, and its changing contents are not pre-determined by its structural position. Regional and temporal variants of the Savage figure abound, in spite of recurring tendencies that suggest geographical specialization.[21] Too often anthropological discourse modifies the projection of non-academic observers only to the extent that it "disciplines" them.[22] At other times, anthropologists help create and buttress images that can question previous permutations.[23] Thus what happens within the slot is neither doomed nor inconsequential (Fox 1991; Vincent 1991). The point is, rather, that a critique of anthropology cannot skirt around this slot. The direction of the discipline now depends upon an explicit attack on that slot itself and the symbolic order upon which it is premised (figure 1). As long as the slot remains, the Savage is at best a figure of speech, a metaphor in an argument about nature and the universe, about being and existence—in short, an argument about foundational thought.

Portrait of the Artist as a Bubble

This brings us back to the present. I have argued that to historicize the West is to historicize anthropology and vice versa. I have also suggested that ongoing changes in the world within and outside of academe make that two-pronged historicization both urgent and necessary. If these two arguments are correct, together they expose the seriousness of the challenges we face. Yet they also expose the limitations of some of the solutions proposed. The portrait of the postmodernist anthropologist that emerges from this dual exercise is not a happy one indeed. Camera and notebooks in hand, he is looking for the Savage, but the Savage has vanished. The problem starts with the fated inheritance of the moderns themselves. The world that the anthropologist inherits has wiped out the empirical trace of the Savage-object: Coke bottles and cartridges now obscure the familiar tracks. To be sure, one could reinvent the Savage, or create new Savages within the West itself. Solutions of this kind are increasingly appealing (see chapters 3 and 6). The very notion of savagery is increasingly redundant on empirical grounds, irrespective of the Savage-object. Lingering conditions of modernity make the notion a hard one to evoke in imagination, now that hordes of Savages have joined the slums of the Third World or touched the shores of the North Atlantic. We are far from the days when five Eskimos caused an uproar in London. The primitive has become terrorist, refugee, freedom fighter, opium or coca grower, or parasite. He can even play anthropologist, at times. Televised documentaries show his "real" conditions of existence; underground newspapers expose his dreams of modernity. Thanks to modernity and modernization, the savage has changed, the West has changed, and the West knows that both have changed empirically.

But modernity is only part of the anthropologist's difficulty. Modern obstacles have modern (technical) answers, or so we used to think. The more serious issue is that technical solutions do not suffice anymore. At best, they can solve the problem of the empirical object by removing the Cokes and cartridges. At worst, they can fabricate an entire new face for savagery. But they cannot remedy changes in the larger thematic field, especially since the Savage never dominated this field. He was only one of the requisite parts of a tripartite relation, the mask of a mask. The problem is not simply that the masks are torn, that true cannibals are now rare, nor even that now—as in Norman Mailer's *Cannibals and Christians* (1966)—both are equally good or equally evil (Walkover 1974), if evil itself can be defined (Lyotard 1986).

This is altogether a *post*modern quandary. It is part of the world of constructs and relations revealed by our juxtaposed snapshots, and it is an intrinsic dilemma of postmodern anthropology. For if indeed foundational thoughts are seen as collapsing, if indeed utopias are arguments about order and foundational thoughts, and if indeed the Savage exists primarily within an implicit correspondence with utopia, the specialist in savagery is in dire straits. He does not know what to aim at. His favorite model has disappeared or, when found, refuses to pose as expected. The fieldworker examines his tools and finds his camera inadequate. Most importantly, his very field of vision now seems blurred. Yet he needs to come back home with a picture. It's pouring rain out there, and the mosquitoes are starting to bite. In desperation, the baffled anthropologist burns his notes to create a moment of light, moves his face against the flame, closes his eyes and, hands grasping the camera, takes a picture of himself.

Tactics and Strategy

Lest this portrait be taken to characterize the postmodernist anthropologist as the epitome of self-indulgence (as many critics, indeed, imply), let me say that narcissist labels characterize postmodernist anthropologists as individuals no better than they typify their predecessors or adversaries. Intellectuals as a group claimed and gained socially sanctioned self-indulgence long before postmodernism. Individual intent is secondary here. At any rate, anthropology's situation warrants more sober reflection than petty accusations of egomania across theoretical camps.

I may end up being both more lenient and more severe—thus risking the condemnation of foes and proponents alike—by saying that the perceived self-indulgence of postmodernist anthropologists inheres in the situation itself. That is what makes it so obvious and such an easy target for opponents. If we take seriously the perception of an ongoing collapse of the Western metanarratives, the vacuum created by the fall of the house of Reason in the once fertile fields of utopian imagination, and the empirical destruction of the Savage-object, then the anthropologist aware of this situation has no target outside of himself (as witness) and his text (as pretext) within the thematic universe he inherits.

Once phrased in these terms, the dilemma becomes manageable. One obvious solution is to confront and change the thematic field itself and claim new grounds for anthropology—which is just what some anthropologists have been doing, though without explicit programs. But the dilemma as lived by the postmodernists is no less real, and the epiphany of textuality cannot be reduced to a mere aggregate of individual tactics of self-aggrandizement or preservation.[24] If electoral politics may explain either overstatements or the craving for new fads in North American anthropology and elsewhere, they say little of the mechanisms leading to specific choices among myriad possibilities.[25] Why the text? Why the sudden (for anthropologists, to some extent) rediscovery of literature, and of only some literature at that? However much the (re)discovery of textuality and authorial legitimation may be associated with midterm maneuvers, it also must be seen in another context. In that context—the thematic field delineated by order, utopia, and the Savage—this emphasis on textuality represents a strategic retreat triggered by the perception of ongoing destruction. In other words, electoral politics alone cannot explain postmodernist anthropology. To propose viable alternatives, one needs to take the ideological and theoretical context of postmodernism seriously, more seriously than the postmodernists do themselves. One needs also to take more seriously both literary criticism and philosophy.

Metaphors in Ethnography and Ethnography as Metaphor

The discovery of textuality by North American anthropologists in the 1980s was based on a quite limited notion of the text (see chapter 6). The emphasis on "the *independent* importance of ethnographic writing as a genre" (Marcus 1980:507), the dismissal of pre-text, con-text, and content, all contribute to reading the anthropological product as isolated from the larger field in which its conditions of existence are generated. Passing references aside, the course of inquiry on the relations among anthropology, colonialism, and political "neutrality" that opened in the late 1960s and early 1970s (e.g., Asad 1973) is considered closed because it allegedly revealed all its partial truths. Passing mentions of gender aside, feminism—as a discourse that claims the specificity of (some) historical subjects—is bypassed because it is said to deal only with "content."[26] Passing references to the Third World notwithstanding, the issues raised by Wolf's historicization of the Other (1982), an inquiry that inherently makes anthropology part of this changing world, are considered moot. Mentions of relations of textual production notwithstanding, the mechanisms and processes emphasized are those that singularize the voice of anthropology, as if anthropological discourse was either self-enclosed or self-sufficient.

Not surprisingly, the archaeological exploration that underpins the North American exercise in reflexivity tends to stop at the institutionalization of anthropology as a discipline in the Anglophone world, or at best to the delineation of a specialized anthropological discourse in the Europe of the Enlightenment. In spite of the professed renunciation of labels, boundaries are set in modern terms to produce a history of the discipline, albeit one with different emphases. The construction exposed is a discursive order *within* anthropology, not the discursive order within which anthropology operates and makes sense—even though, here again, this larger field seems to warrant passing mention. The representational aspect of ethnographic discourse is attacked with a vigor quite disproportionate to the referential value of ethnographies in the wider field within which anthropology finds its significance. To use a language that still has its validity, the object of inquiry is the "simple" rather than the "enlarged" reproduction of anthropological discourse. Terminology and citations notwithstanding, the larger thematic field on which anthropology is premised is barely scratched.

If we take seriously the proposition to look at anthropology as metaphor—as I think we can, given the thematic field outlined—we cannot just look at metaphors in anthropology. The study of "ethnographic allegory" (Clifford 1986b; Tyler 1986) cannot be taken to refer primarily to allegorical forms *in* ethnography without losing sight of the larger picture. Our starting point cannot be "a crisis in anthropology" (Clifford 1986a:3), but the histories of the world.[27] We need to go out of anthropology to see the construction of "ethnographic authority" not as a late requirement of anthropological discourse (Clifford 1983) but as an early component of this wider field that is itself constitutive of anthropology (see chapter 6). Would that the power of anthropology hinged upon the academic success of genial immigrants such as Franz Boas and Bronislaw Malinowski! It would allow us to find new scapegoats without ever looking back at the Renaissance. But the exercise in reflexivity must go all the way and examine fully the enlarged reproduction of anthropological discourse.[28]

Observers may wonder why the postmodernist experiment in U.S. anthropology has not encouraged a surge of substantive models. The difficulty of passing from criticism to substance is not simply due to a theoretical aversion to content or an instinctive suspicion toward exemplars. After all, the postmodernist wave revitalized substantive production in other academic fields. It stimulated architects and political theorists alike. At the very least, it has provoked debates on and of substance. Further, some political radicals advocate the possibility of militant practices rooted in postmodernism—although not without controversies

(Arac 1986b; Laclau and Mouffe 1985; Ross 1988b). More important, the implicit awareness of an expanding situation of postmodernity continues to motivate grass-roots movements all over the world with their partial truths and partial results. In fact, an anthropologist could well read postmodernism, or at the very least the postmodern situation, as a case for the specificity of otherness, for the destruction of the Savage slot.

To claim the specificity of otherness is to suggest a residual of historical experience that always escapes universalisms exactly because history itself always involves irreducible objects. It is to reserve a space for the subject—not the existential subject favored by the early Sartre and who keeps creeping back into the mea culpa anthropology, but the men and women who are the subjects of history.[29] It is to acknowledge that this space of the historical subject is out of reach of all metanarratives, not because all metanarratives are created equal and are equally wrong—which is the claim of nihilism and always ends up favoring *some* subjects and *some* narratives—but because those claims to universality necessarily imply the muting of first persons, singular or plural, that are deemed marginal. To say that otherness is always specific and historical is to reject this marginality. The Other cannot be encompassed by a residual category: there is no Savage slot. The "us and all of them" binary, implicit in the symbolic order that creates the West, is an ideological construct and the many forms of Third-World-ism that reverse its terms are its mirror images. There is no Other, but multitudes of others who are all others for different reasons, in spite of totalizing narratives, including that of capital.

Many propositions follow from this statement, not the least of which may be that a discipline whose object is the Other may in fact have no object—which may lead us to take a much needed look at the methodological specificity of anthropology. It also follows that the authenticity of the historical subject may not be fully captured from the outside even by way of direct quotes; there may be something irreducible in the first person singular. This, in turn, raises two related issues: that of the epistemological status of native discourse;[30] and that of the theoretical status of ethnography. I will turn to these issues in chapter 6, but some preliminary conclusions are worth posting now.

First, anthropology needs to evaluate its gains and losses with a fair tally of the knowledge anthropologists have produced in the past, sometimes in spite of themselves and almost always in spite of the Savage slot. We owe it to ourselves to ask what remains of anthropology and specific monographs when we remove this slot—not to revitalize disciplinary tradition through cosmetic surgery, but to build both an epistemology and a semiology of what anthropologists have done and can do. We cannot simply assume that modernism has exhausted all its potential projects. Nor can we assume that "realist ethnography" has produced nothing but empty figures of speech and shallow claims to authority.

Second, armed with this renewed arsenal, we can recapture domains of significance by creating strategic points of "reentry" into the discourse on otherness: areas within the discourse where the production of new voices or new combinations of meaning perturbate the entire field and open the way to its (partial) recapture.[31] This chapter is not the place to expand in the directions of these many queries, which are best addressed in chapters 4, 5, and 6. I can only tease the reader by pointing to a few tasks that seem urgent in this new context: an episte-mological reassessment of the historical subject (the first person singular that has been overwhelmed by the voice of objectivity or by that of the narrator and that is so important to many feminists, especially African American feminists); a sim-ilar reassessment of nativeness and native discourse, now barely conceptualized; and a theory of ethnography, now repudiated as the new "false consciousness." And for the time being, at least, we need more ethnographies that raise these issues through concrete cases. Not so much ethnographies that question the author/native dichotomy by exposing the nude as nakedness, but ethnographies (ethno-historio-semiologies?) that offer new points of reentry by questioning the symbolic world upon which "nativeness" is premised. At the very least, anthro-pologists can show that the Other, here and elsewhere, is indeed a product—symbolic and material—of the same process that created the West. In short, the time is ripe for substantive propositions that aim explicitly at the destabilization and eventual destruction of the Savage slot.

That it has not been so in North American anthropology is thus a matter of choice. In spite of a terminology that intimates a decoding of "anthropology as metaphor," we are barely reading anthropology itself. Rather, we are reading anthropological pages, and attention remains focused primarily on the metaphors in anthropology. This recurring refusal to pursue further the archaeological exer-cise obscures the asymmetrical position of the savage-other in the thematic field upon which anthropology was premised. It negates the specificity of otherness, subsuming the Other in the sameness of the text perceived as liberating coopera-tion. "We are the world"?[32]

Anthropology did not create the Savage. Rather, the Savage was the raison d'être of anthropology. Anthropology came to fill the Savage slot in the trilogy order-utopia-savagery, a trilogy that preceded anthropology's institutionalization and gave it continuing coherence in spite of intradisciplinary shifts. This trilogy is now in jeopardy. The time is ripe to attack frontally the visions that shaped this trilogy, to uncover its ethical roots and its consequences, and to find a better anchor for an anthropology of the present, an anthropology of the changing world and its irreducible histories. But many anthropologists only pass near this opportunity while looking for the Savage in the text. They want us to read the internal tropes of the Savage slot, no doubt a useful exercise in spite of its poten-tial for self-indulgence, but they refuse to directly address the thematic field (and thus the larger world) that made (makes) this slot possible, morosely preserving the empty slot itself.

Times have changed since the sixteenth century: One now is innocent until proven guilty. Thus, claims of innocence can take the shape of silence. Somehow, to my surprise, I miss the faithful indignation of a Las Casas.

Chapter 2

North Atlantic Fictions: Global Transformations, 1492–1945

The world became global in the sixteenth century. Europe became Europe in part by severing itself from what lay south of the Mediterranean, but in part also through a Westward move that made the Atlantic the center of the first planetary empires. As such empires overlapped or succeeded one another within the modern world system, they brought populations from all continents closer in time and space. The rise of the West, the conquest of the Americas, plantation slavery, the Industrial Revolution, and the population flows of the nineteenth century can be summarized as "a first moment of globality," an Atlantic moment culminating in U.S. hegemony after World War II.

So couched, this Atlantic moment encompasses five centuries of world history and the shrinking of huge continental masses, including Asia. The designation does not refer to a static space but to a locus of a momentum. The global flows of that era were not restricted geographically to societies bordering the Atlantic Ocean. Spain's conquest of the Philippines, the British conquest of India, and U.S. control of Korea all pertain to this moment. It is no accident that such non-Atlantic ventures took place often enough when the power that launched them claimed partial or total control of the Atlantic Ocean. In short, it is the continuous centrality of the Atlantic as the revolving door of major global flows over four centuries that allows us to speak of a single moment.

Our contemporary arrogance, which overplays the uniqueness of our times, may blind us to the dimensions of what happened before we were born. It may therefore be useful to document the density, speed, and impact of the global flows that made up this Atlantic moment. I will emphasize the earliest centuries for two reasons. First, we are less likely to realize now the importance of these early flows. Second, the evidence shows that the momentum of change was planetary from the start.

The Beginning of Planetary Flows

In 1493 when Columbus returned to the Caribbean island he had named Hispaniola, he was on a different mission than on his first trip. On the deck and in the cargo space of his 17 ships were not only the instruments of conquest that he carried the first time, but also loads of crops, fruits, seeds, and animals, from sheep, pigs, goats, cattle, and chicken to onions, radishes, chick peas, wheat seeds, and grapevine plants. If the image evokes a colonial Noah's Ark, it is in part because Columbus had purposes somewhat similar to those of the biblical patri- arch: He carried these crops and animals for future reproduction in the Antilles (Davies 1991:153–57; Watts 1987:90). Given the tropical climate of the Caribbean, it seems fanciful now that Columbus envisioned the possibility of growing wheat or making wine in what is now Haiti and the Dominican Republic. Yet we need to remember that his successors succeeded quite well in winemaking half a century later in unexpected places such as Chile and California. In that sense, Columbus's second trip prefigured the massive movements of goods, crops, animals, and com- modities that contributed to the Atlantic moment of globality.

Novel also in that second trip was Columbus's certainty that he or others would be able to travel back and forth between the Old and the New World. The contents of his ships were premised on the continuity of planetary flows, both those he wished for and those that he could not predict. They were premised on the fact that others from Christendom would follow his steps. Among the 1,500 men on board that second voyage, in addition to the mandatory soldiers there were also specialists in farming, irrigation, and road building, whose presence pre- sumed back and forth movement between Spain and the Caribbean. Not long after, the Castilian invasion of the American mainland signaled the true beginning of the planetary population flows.

The twentieth century did not invent mass migration. Since the seventeenth century human beings traveled *en masse* to faraway lands for much the same rea- sons as they do today. Except for the early gold rush of the sixteenth century, the major migrations of the Atlantic moment, voluntary or coerced, were generated by the global distribution of labor in the capitalist world system. They included the 12 million enslaved Africans brought to feed the plantation machinery during the three long centuries that the slave trade lasted, and the Europeans—mainly British, French, Spanish, Dutch, Portuguese, or Danish—and white Americans who bought the slaves in Africa, transported them to Europe, or sold and used them in the Americas. After the end of Caribbean slavery, half a million Asians were brought to the area to replenish the labor force. Most came from the Indian subcontinent and went to Trinidad or British Guiana. Yet the areas of origins span the whole of Asia from Japan to Java and Sri Lanka. Receiving areas spanned the Antillean archipelago all the way to mainland territories such as British Guiana and Suriname. At about the same time, more than 300,000 Chinese were moved to Peru, Mexico, and Cuba, which alone took more than two-thirds of the total. By 1927 Chinese were the largest racial minority in Mexico City. During that same era, thousands of Chinese and Japanese also came to the United States and thou- sands of Indians moved to East Africa. In the 1920s and 1930s hundreds of thou- sands of Japanese moved to Brazil and Peru, a flow that did not stop until the 1970s in the latter country.

As North Atlantic states forcibly moved populations all over the world, their own citizens also moved from one continent to another, often between areas with temperate climates. Here again, labor was the main force behind these movements— except that it was rarely coerced. European migration increased tremendously as the nineteenth century came to a close. Between 1846 and 1924, 40 to 50 million European citizens migrated to the Americas. The vagueness of the estimate is itself an indication of the inability of the states involved to control or even measure these flows. We know that most of these migrants ended up in the United States, but millions also went to Canada, Brazil, and Argentina. By 1895, 74 percent of the population in and around Buenos Aires was foreign-born. By 1914, half of the population of Argentina was composed of foreign-born residents and their offspring. No city of that size in the United States, then or now, had such a high proportion of immigrants. Indeed, at the beginning of the twentieth century Argentina, Canada, Australia, and New Zealand had a larger immigration ratio than the United States did either then or now. The coinage of the United States as a nation of immigrants notwithstanding, European migration targeted lands outside of the Americas. Australia, New Zealand, and southern Africa still experience the marks of these early global flows.

As peoples moved so did goods. Massive flows of gold and silver, of crops and spices, of plants and diseases, from tobacco to coconuts, from syphilis to smallpox, and from the mines of Peru to the botanic gardens sprinkled throughout the British Empire, enmeshed world populations into encounters and confrontations unrestricted by physical distance. From the beginning Europeans who came to the New World brought along with their slaves a variety of plants, animals, and other living organisms. Horses, pigs, sheep, dogs, chickens, donkeys, cattle, bananas, plantains, and all their parasites moved to the New World. So did measles, whopping cough, bubonic plague, malaria, yellow fever, diphtheria, amoebic dysentery, influenza, and smallpox. The later alone proved to be a mass murderer of proportions still unmatched for the native population.

While the movement of peoples and animals between the Old World and the New was largely unidirectional, that of crops was not. American crops that spread into Europe, Asia, and Africa included maize, potatoes, tomatoes, peanuts, manioc, cacao (chocolate), tobacco, and many types of peppers, beans, and squashes that were unknown to Europe before the time of Columbus (McNeill 1992).

Other crops and their by-products fully completed the global circle, in the process becoming planetary commodities. Domesticated outside of Europe, they were brought to the Americas by Europeans only to be resold later to Europe or even to African or Asian clients. The first of these was sugar cane. Originally domesticated in New Guinea and introduced to Europe by way of South Asia, in the eighteenth century it became the main export of many Caribbean slave territories, vivifying the European proletariat and the North Atlantic predilection for sweetness (Mintz 1985). Similarly coffee, first domesticated in Yemen and brought to the Caribbean in the eighteenth century, was soon to be resold to Middle Eastern clients of France (Trouillot 1982). The British Admiralty in Africa would later use Caribbean citrus as a protection against scurvy. Bananas, an Old World cultigen, became the main export crop of the Windward Islands, Colombia, and Ecuador. Tobacco, cacao, rice, and to a lesser extent opium and manioc, also became global commodities of this Atlantic moment.

These flows of commodities sustained the life of the North Atlantic both before and after its Industrial Revolution. Economic elites had speculated on the returns from these exchanges, with varying degrees of respect for political boundaries, since at least the sixteenth century. By the seventeenth century, the wheels of exchange had planetary dimensions (Braudel 1992). The history of Holland from the 1592 reopening of the Amsterdam stock market to its crash in 1783 is a textbook story of merchant and finance capital crossing borders, linking continents, and in the process affecting local beliefs and practices. It is also a story of private enterprise dominating states in ways that we often believe unique to our own times. Dutch merchants backed the Spanish colonial enterprise in the Americas, then backed their own fleet against Spanish and Portuguese vessels, then provided credit to France and England while turning Amsterdam into a huge depot for commodities from all continents. In so doing, they accumulated a global power unmatched by any royalty. The Dutch West India Company established warehouses in Brazil, Curaçao, and New York. The Dutch East India Company, the equivalent of a transnational powerhouse using the services of 8,000 sailors, developed a profitable trade within Asia along its own transcontinental axis of spices, selling wood from Timor to China, Indian textiles to Sumatra, and Siamese elephants to Bengal. In short, early on in the first moment of globality, capital, labor, and the commodities they generated circumscribed a world of which the various subparts were increasingly intertwined in ways that we now tend to forget.

The flow of goods and capital across political and geographical boundaries was not always increasing but it did reach a peak in the period immediately preceding World War I. Ratios of export trade to GDP may have been higher in 1913 than in 1973. In 1913–14, Foreign Direct Investment (FDI) was around 11 percent, about the same level as in 1994. Capital flows relative to output were higher during the early decades of the twentieth century than in the 1980s.

In that sense, World War I was aptly named if only because it confirmed the global ties that these figures suggest. The Great War involved the seizure of German holdings in Oceania, Southwest Africa, and Tanganyika. Indians fought on the British western front and Senegalese *tirailleurs* died in France and for France. Eleven years after the war, the great crash of the 1930s tied New York and Vienna together in a downward spiral that sent the prices of agricultural goods from all over the globe plummeting. It was indeed a world depression, soon followed by a second world war.

Changing Practices, Complex Identities

These massive movements of goods, populations, and capital produced abrupt changes not only in the material conditions of the populations involved but also in their practices and in the ways in which they saw themselves and the world around them. We tend to think of our contemporary era as one of swift transformations that challenge our capacity for adaptation, and indeed it is. Yet the first moment of globality was also characterized by speed for many of those who lived it, and it constantly tested their capacity to adapt swiftly. They passed that test more often than we now think.

Again, the sixteenth century gives us a glimpse of the global momentum. Maize most probably went to the Old World during one of Columbus's return trips. By the 1560s it was cultivated in places as distant from the Americas and far away from each other as the West Coast of Africa and the Hunan province of China. At about the same time, Spanish friars were setting up the first wineries of Chile, Peru, and California. Native Mexicans, who did not know cattle before the Conquest, were then working on ranches, some of which counted 150,000 heads of cattle.

Colonialist exploitation was often the motor behind these swift adaptations, especially in the eighteenth and nineteenth centuries when colonial control over production generally became more systematic. Yet direct colonial control was not always a factor. At times the new import provided a clear advantage on its competitors, as did the potato throughout most of Europe. Some Native Americans quickly adopted the horse from flocks that had escaped Spanish ranches. By the time they encountered the first Anglo-Saxon colonists, they had already integrated horseback riding into their daily cultural practices. It took less time for maize to be adopted by Africans on the Angola-Congo coastline in the late sixteenth century than it took espresso to move inland from the two coasts of the United States and become an accessible commodity in the Midwest or the South in the late twentieth. One could argue that maize mush is inherently more agreeable than coffee in its espresso form, but such an argument implies a value judgment on the universal acceptability of edibles, all of which are culturally marked. On surer ground, one could demonstrate that colonial pressures and the political economy of the African coast at the time—including the cost accounting of cereal production, down to individual caloric intake—made the acceptance of maize relatively easy. Africans could swiftly adopt maize because it was practical for them to do so then. That argument immediately relativizes our sense of our own cultural openness.

Such speedy changes affected political and cultural identities and practices and provoked reactions varying from revolt to acceptance to confusion. Not surprisingly, the first moment of globality produced its self-proclaimed hybrids, individuals or groups who saw themselves as belonging to more than one sociocultural unit and as sharing more than one cultural heritage. Seventeenth-century Cambay, a commercial port on the Indian Ocean linking East Africa, the Middle East, and Indonesia, counted a number of Portuguese residents who erected mansions built and furnished according to Portuguese taste. Was it an Indian, Islamic, or Portuguese city? K. N. Chaudhuri (1990:347), who asks that question, answers: "It was all three simultaneously as an abstraction but one or the other according to the viewpoint of its inhabitants." Although Cambay had distinct ethnic quarters, one suspects that the abstraction and the quite concrete presence of each quarter impacted on each group's sense of identity. We know that it was impossible for Dahomeans in Barbados, Japanese in Peru, Javanese in Suriname, or Indians in East Africa to escape the sense of being caught between two worlds. It may have been equally hard for their children to pick any one of the two.

The sense of belonging to many worlds must have also been common among many of the *convertos* (Jews forced to convert to Christianity) who joined the Castilian venture to the Americas. Cultural overlap reinforced by power equally marked the Filipinos first brought under the Spanish umbrella, then forced by the United States to manipulate cultural streams of various densities and provenance. Also hybrids of a kind were the early Americans who discovered they had become "Indians" and were coached to write in Spanish the history of an Indianness that came with the conquistadors. Self-proclaimed hybrids were the mulattos of Cuba, Brazil, Saint-Domingue, and Louisiana, and many Latin American mestizos. By 1815, Simon Bolivar had officialized a narrative of *mestizaje*: "We are . . . neither Indian nor European, but a species midway between the legitimate proprietors of this country and the Spanish usurpers." Clearly the praise of diversity and the celebration of mixed origins are not so new. Nor are their use for political gains. In Latin America as in the Caribbean, the consciousness of mixed origins has been widespread for centuries. Some authors argue that the awareness of cultural *metissage* is inherent in the creolization process as it developed in the Antilles, and thus inherent in Caribbean life. In short, since the early centuries of the Atlantic moment, identities have never been as simple as we are sometimes prone to believe.

The awareness of mixed origins does not mean that individuals can spontaneously retrace the flows that contributed to shaping their current practices and environment. Indeed, the long-term impact of cultural imports is often proportional to the capacity to forget that they were once acquired or imposed. How many Californians routinely ponder the Spanish names of their streets and towns? How many Italians today do not see the tomato as an intrinsic part of their cultural heritage? How many Native American leaders would dare to reject the horse as culturally foreign? In stressing the impact of the plants exported from the Americas to the Old World, William McNeill (1992:34–5) asks us to imagine the Italians without tomatoes, the Chinese without sweet potatoes, the Africans without maize, and the Irish, Germans, and Russians without potatoes. From the record sketched above, we could prolong the list interminably in a number of directions: Latin America without Christianity, India without English, Argentina without Germans, Texas without cattle, the Caribbean without blacks or rum, England without tea, France without cafés, or French fries. The point is obvious. Culturally, the world we inherit today is the product of global flows that started in the late fifteenth century and continue to affect human populations today. Yet the history of the world is rarely told in those terms.

Indeed, the particularity of the dominant narratives of globalization is a massive silencing of the past on a world scale, the systematic erasure of continuous and deep-felt encounters that have marked human history throughout the globe and that I have only sketched here. For sushi in Chicago to amaze us, we need to silence the fact that the Franciscans were in Japan as early as the fifteenth century. For Muslim veils in France to seem out of place, we need to forget that Charles Martel stopped Abd-al-Raman only 300 miles south of Paris two reigns before Charlemagne. To talk of a global culture today as a new phenomenon, we need to forget that Chinese chili paste comes from Mexico, French fries from Peru, and Jamaican Blue Mountain coffee from Yemen.

A central task, then, for historical anthropology is to bring to public consciousness these flows that shaped the world in which we live. Yet the vulgarization of the historical record is not enough. After all, these facts were always part of the available record. That they were rarely accorded the significance they deserve suggests the existence and deployment of mechanisms of silence that make them appear less relevant than they are, even when they are known. The silencing of the past inheres not only in *what* is said but also in *how* it is said (Trouillot 1995).

Thus, a theoretical task parallel to the documentation of these flows is to assess the terms of the dominant narratives of world history—the words used, the concepts deployed, the setting of the plots and subplots, the depiction of the characters and the connections made or ignored between all of the above. We should hold under suspicion any word that describes a chunk of the story while claiming universal relevance. Words such as progress, development, modernity, nation-state, and globalization itself are among those I have in mind. The beginning of this chapter should have raised some doubts about the abuse of the word globalization. The following sections demonstrate further how suspicion toward these master words is well founded by way of an exploration of "modernity," a term increasingly yet differently used by anthropologists (Appadurai 1996; Gaonkar 1999; Knauft 2002a,b).

North Atlantic Universals

Modernity is a murky term that belongs to a family of words we may label "North Atlantic universals." I mean by that words that project the North Atlantic experience on a universal scale that they themselves have helped to create. North Atlantic universals are particulars that have gained a degree of universality, chunks of human history that have become historical standards. Words such as development, progress, democracy, and nation-state are exemplary members of that family that contracts or expands according to contexts and interlocutors. Belonging to that class does not depend on a fixed meaning. It is a matter of struggle and contest about and around these universals and the world they claim to describe. Only time will tell if newly popular expressions such as "globalization" or "the international community" will become North Atlantic universals.

North Atlantic universals so defined are not merely descriptive or referential. They do not describe the world; they offer visions of the world. They appear to refer to things as they exist, but rooted as they are in a particular history they are evocative of multiple layers of sensibilities, persuasions, cultural and ideological choices tied to that localized history. They come to us loaded with aesthetic and stylistic sensibilities, religious and philosophical persuasions, cultural assumptions ranging from what it means to be a human being to the proper relationship between humans and the natural world, ideological choices ranging from the nature of the political to its possibilities of transformation. There is no unanimity within the North Atlantic itself on any of these issues, but there is a shared history of how these issues have been and should be debated, and these words carry that history. Yet since they are projected as universals, they deny their localization, the sensibilities, and the history from which they spring.

North Atlantic universals are always prescriptive inasmuch as they always suggest, even if implicitly, a correct state of affairs: what is good, what is just, what is sublime or desirable—not only what is, but what should be. That prescription is inherent in the very projection of a historically limited experience—that of the

North Atlantic—on the world stage. North Atlantic universals not only prescribe: They seduce. Indeed, they are always seductive, at times even irresistible, exactly because they manage, in that projection, to hide their specific—localized, and thus parochial—historical location. This power of seduction is further enhanced by a capacity to project affect without actually claiming to do so. All ideas come with affect, but a successful universal tends to hide the affect it projects behind a claim of rationality. It makes sense to be modern. It is good to be modern. How could anyone not want to be modern? Similarly, how could anyone not want to join the international community? To be sure, these propositions mean different things to different people. At the same time, the number of divergent voices that use and abuse these words verify their attraction. One might go as far as to say that the capacity to seduce is inherent in such universals.

Their ability to project transhistorical relevance while hiding the particularities of their marks and origins, including their affective load, makes North Atlantic universals as difficult to conceptualize as they are seductive to use. The more seductive these words become the harder it is to specify what they actually stand for, since part of the seduction resides in that capacity to project clarity while remaining ambiguous. Even if we accept the questionable assumption that concepts are merely words, a quick perusal of the popular press in any European language demonstrates that North Atlantic universals are murky references: They evoke rather than define. Furthermore, even that evocation works best in negative form. We have a stronger sense of what modernity may connote when we point to the naysayers—the Taliban of Afghanistan, a native tribe in the Amazon, or whichever figure plays temporarily the good or evil face of the non-modern—than when we investigate those who praise it. The seduction and the confusion are related. Dreams of a democratic future, practices and institutions of a democracy at work, or claims to join and to defend the international community vary in time and place. Even who actually belongs to the international community is a matter of contention, as any debate of the U.N. General Assembly demonstrates. Attempts to conceptualize North Atlantic universals in the scholarly literature reveal little unanimity about their scope, let alone their denotation (Dussel 1993; Gaonkar 1999; Knauft 2002a).

Thus I am quite ambivalent about the extent to which modernity can be fully conceptualized. At the same time, it would be disingenuous not to acknowledge that the word modernity evokes sensibilities, perceptions, choices, and states of affairs that are not easily captured by other words. That is in part why it is a seductive word. But if the seduction of North Atlantic universals also has to do with their power to silence their own history, then we need to unearth those silences, those conceptual and theoretical missing links that make them so attractive. Insisting on such silences, I argue that in its most common deployments as a North Atlantic universal, modernity disguises and misconstrues the many Others that it creates. A critical assessment of modernity must start with the revelation of its hidden faces.

The Management of Imagination

Modernity and modernization each call to mind the necessary coexistence of the two geographies through which the deployment of the West and the deployment of world capitalism take place. As moments and aspects within these deployments, yet figures within two distinctive geographies, modernity and modernization are both discrete and intertwined. Thus, a rigid distinction between societal modernization and cultural modernity can be misleading (Gaonkar 1999:1), especially when it couches them as separate historical developments that can each be judged on its own terms. But the distinction remains useful if we keep in mind that the bundle of facts and processes we package under one label was at any moment of world history, *as a package*, a condition of possibility of the processes and phenomena that we cover with the second. The distinction becomes necessary inasmuch as it illuminates specific historical moments and processes.

To speak of modernization is to put the accent on the material and organizational features of world capitalism in specific locales. It is to speak of a geography of management, of those aspects of the development of world capitalism that reorganize space for explicitly political or economic purposes. We may note among the continuities and markers along that line the French Revolution as a moment in the modernization of the state, as a reorganization of space for political management. We may read the English Industrial Revolution as a moment in the reorganization of labor relations, here again a reorganization of space primarily for economic purposes. Similarly, the wave of decolonization following World War II can be read as a moment in the modernization of the interstate system, one more moment of reorganization of space on a world scale that provides a new geography of management. Closer to our times, what we now call globalization—and which we too often reduce to a concoction of fads and slogans—inheres in a fundamental change in the spatiality of capital (see chapter 3). In short, modernization has everything to do with political economy, with a geography of management that create *places*: a place called France, a place called the Third World, a place called the market, a placed called the factory or, indeed, a work-place.

If modernization has to do with the creation of place—as a relation within a definite space—modernity has to do with the projection of that place—the local—against a spatial background that is theoretically unlimited. Modernity has to do not only with the relationship between place and space but also with the relation between place and time. In order to prefigure the theoretically unlimited space—as opposed to the space within which management occurs—one needs to relate place to time, or address a unique temporality, that is, the position of the subject located in that place. Thus modernity has to do with those aspects and moments in the development of world capitalism that require the projection of the individual or collective subject against both space and time. It has to do with historicity.

I will further expand on that argument both in discussing the work of Reinhart Koselleck (1985) and in discussing features of Caribbean history. For now we may note as markers of modernity historical moments that localize the individual or collective subject while opening its spatial and temporal horizons and multiplying its outside references. The invention of private life in the Renaissance—and the accompanying features noted by Roger Chartier (1989) and others such as the spread of silent reading, personal journals, private libraries, the translation of the Bible into vernacular languages, the invention of the nation and national histories, and the proclamation of the U.S. Bill of Rights, can all be read as key moments in the spread of modernity. Closer to our times, the global production of desire spurred by the unification of the world market for consumer goods expands further the geography of imagination of which modernity is part (see chapter 3).

This last example is telling. That this global production of desire as a moment of modernity parallels globalization as a moment in the spatial history—and thus the management—of capital suggests that although modernity and modernization should not be confused, they are inherently intertwined. One could take the two lists of markers that I have suggested, extend them appropriately and draw lines across them that spell out this inextricability. From the printing press to silent reading, from the political rise of the bourgeoisie to the expansion of individual rights, from the elusiveness of finance capital to the elusiveness of global desires, the geography of management and the geography of imagination are intertwined. Just as the imaginary projection of the West constantly refuels managerial projects of modernization, modernization itself is a condition of possibility of modernity.

Historicity and Alterity: The Modern as Heterology

As part of the geography of imagination that constantly recreates the West, modernity always required an Other and an Elsewhere. It was always plural, just like the West was always plural. This plurality is inherent in modernity itself, both structurally and historically. Modernity as a structure requires an Other, an alter, a native, indeed an alter-native. Modernity as a historical process created this alter ego, which was as modern as the West—yet otherwise modern.

If we follow the line of argument drawn from Reinhart Koselleck (1985) that modernity implies first and foremost a fundamental shift in regimes of historicity, most notably the perception of a past radically different from the present and the perception of a future that becomes both attainable (because secular) and yet indefinitely postponed (because removed from eschatology), we come to the conclusion that modernity requires a localization in space in order to position subjects within the historicity it creates. Koselleck does not reach that conclusion himself, yet those of us who claim that modernity requires a geography of imagination (see chapter 1; Glissant 1989; Mudimbe 1994) are not necessarily at odds with his analysis. As soon as one draws a single line that links past, present, and future, and yet insists on their distinctiveness, one must inevitably place actors along that line. Not everyone can be at the same point along that line; some become more advanced than others. From the viewpoint of anyone anywhere in that line, others are somewhere else, ahead or behind. Being behind suggests an elsewhere that is both inside and outside the space defined by modernity: outside to the extent that these others have not yet reached that place where judgment occurs; inside to the extent that the place they now occupy can be perceived from that other place within the line. To put it this way is to note the relation between modernity and the ideology of progress (Dussel 1993), between modernity and modernism. But there is more to the argument.

In his treatment of modernity, Koselleck insists upon historicity—that is, in part, a relation to time of which the chronologization, periodization, distanciation, increasing speed, and range of affective relations from hope to anxiety help to create a new regime. But if he is correct, as I believe he is, this new regime of historicity also requires a localization of its subject. Time here creates space. Or more precisely, Koselleck's historicity necessitates a locale, a *lieu* from which springs this relation to time. Yet by definition, the inscription of a lieu requires an Elsewhere— a space of and for the Other. That this space can be—indeed, often is—imaginary merely suggests that there may be more continuities than we think between the geography of imagination of the Renaissance and that of the Enlightenment.

Within that geography, elaborations of a state of nature in Hobbes, Locke or Rousseau, as varied as they indeed are between and across these authors, emerge as alternative modernities—places, locales against which we can read what it means to be modern. Rousseau is the clearest on this for two reasons. First, he is not a modernist. He does not believe in either the inevitability or the desirability of linear progress. Indeed, critics wrongly accuse him of naïveté vis-à-vis the noble savage and earlier stages of human history. Second, that critique notwithstanding, Rousseau explicitly posits his state of nature as a structural and theoretical necessity to which the historical reality is largely irrelevant. He needs that fictional time to mark his own space as a modern one. Later observers will be less perceptive. As the line that ties past, present, and future gets more acute and more relevant, as both the momentum behind it and the goal to which it aspires become clearer—otherwise said, as teleology replaces eschatology—from Condorcet to Kant and from Hegel to Marx, the place assigned to the Other may fall not only within the line but also *off* the line. Hegel's dismissal of Africa and Marx's residual "Asiatic" mode of production—maybe his most unthought category—are exemplars of a hierarchy of spaces created through a relation to time. Not only does progress and its advance leave some people "behind" (an Elsewhere from within) but increasing chunks of humanity fall off its course (an Elsewhere on the outside that can only be perceived from within). The temporal-historical regime that Koselleck associates with modernity creates multiple spaces for the Other.

If that is so, modernity necessitates various readings of alterity, what Michel de Certeau (1986) calls an heterology. The claim that someone—someone else—is modern is structurally and necessarily a discourse on the Other, since the intelligibility of that position—what it means to be modern—requires a relation to otherness. The modern is that subject that measures any distance from itself and redeploys it against an unlimited space of imagination. That distance inhabits the perspectival look to and from the painted subject in Raphaël or Titian's portraits. It fueled the quarrel of the Ancients and Moderns in Louis XIV's France. It is crucial to Charles Baudelaire's (re)definition of modern art and poetry as both recognition and rejection of time.

Baudelaire's Shadow

Idiosyncratic as it may be, the case of Baudelaire suggests in miniature the range of silences that we need to uncover for a critical assessment of modernity that would throw light on its hidden faces. As is well known, Baudelaire had just turned 20 when his stepfather forced him to embark for Calcutta. He went only as far as Mauritius and Bourbon (now Réunion), then part of France's plantation empire. That trip inspired—and may have seen the first drafts of—many of the poems that would later be published in *Les Fleurs du Mal*. Back in Paris, Baudelaire entered into a relationship with a "mulatto" actress, better known as Jeanne Duval, widely said to be of Haitian descent. Although Baudelaire's liking of dark-skinned females seems to have preceded that liaison, his tumultuous affair with the woman he called his "Black Venus" lasted over 20 years, during which she was a major source of poetic inspiration for him.

Only recently has the relationship between Mme. Duval and Baudelaire become a central object of scholarly research.[1] Emmanuel Richon (1998) points out that Baudelairian scholarship has not even bothered to verify the most basic facts about Duval, including her actual origins. The many sketches of Duval by Baudelaire, and other portraits such as Edouard Manet's "La maitresse de Baudelaire couchée," only confirm her constant presence in his life. Many visitors recount entering the poet's place to find him reading his unpublished poetry to Jeanne. Literary scholarship has attributed some of Baudelaire's work to a "Jeanne Duval cycle," insisting on her role as "femme fatale" and relishing the assertion that Duval infected Baudelaire with syphilis. Richon demolishes that assertion, convincingly arguing that the opposite was more likely.

But the main lesson of Richon's work goes beyond biographical rectification. His claim that the Indian Ocean trip and especially the relationship with Duval fundamentally shaped Baudelairian aesthetics suggests that Baudelairian scholarship may have produced what I call a "silence of significance" through a procedure of banalization. Well-known facts are recounted in passing, yet kept in the background of the main narrative or accorded little significance because they "obviously" do not matter (Trouillot 1995). Yet can it not matter that Baudelaire was living a racial taboo in the midst of a Paris sizzling with arguments for and against the abolition of slavery and the equality of human races? Slavery was abolished in Bourbon and other French possessions less than seven years after Baudelaire had been there and while he was enthralled in his relationship with Jeanne. Can it not matter that the eulogist of modernity was also Jeanne Duval's eulogist?

The issue is even more intriguing in light of Baudelaire's own disdain for the modernization—the concrete management of places and populations by the French state, republican and imperial as it was—that was a condition of possibility of his own modernity. As in Rousseau, Baudelaire's relation to time, a hallmark of his modernity, does not imply a blind faith in either the desirability or the inevitability of progress. Indeed, Baudelaire is resolutely anti-modernist (Froidevaux 1989). His modernity is founded upon the search for a furtive yet eternal present. The past has no legacy; the future holds no promises. Only the present is alive. With Baudelaire, we are distant from either side of the quarrel between the Ancients and the Moderns and from Koselleck's regime of historicity. Baudelaire's modernity is indeed a new brand that prefigures the postmodern.

How interesting, then, that this new brand of modernity also leads to "the spatialization of time" (Froidevaux 1989:125). Baudelaire's escape from chronological temporality is space—more specifically, the space of the Elsewhere. Here again, time creates space, and here again space generates a heterology. Literary scholars have long noted the importance of themes and metaphors of space and of travel, as well as the role of exoticism, in Baudelaire's poetry. While we should leave to specialists the task of mapping out the many locations in a geography of imagination that links space and time, the Here and the Elsewhere, routine and exoticism, we may want to provoke them to find out the extent to which the modernity of Baudelaire, the critic, establishes itself against the background of an ethereal Elsewhere that Baudelaire, the poet, inscribes somewhere between Jeanne's body and the islands of the Indian Ocean.

Differently Modern: The Caribbean as Alter-Native

I have argued so far that modernity is structurally plural inasmuch as it requires a heterology, an Other outside of itself. I would like to argue now that the modern is also historically plural because it always requires an Other from within, an otherwise modern created between the jaws of modernity and modernization. That plurality is best perceived if we keep modernity and modernization as distinct yet related groups of phenomena with the understanding that the power unleashed through modernization is a condition of possibility of modernity itself. I will draw on the sociohistorical experience of the Caribbean region to make that point.

Eric Wolf once wrote in passing, but with his usual depth, that the Caribbean is "eminently a world area in which modernity first deployed its powers and simultaneously revealed the contradictions that give it birth." Wolf's words echo the work of Sidney W. Mintz (1966, 1971b, 1978, 1983, 1996, 1998) who has long insisted that the Caribbean has been modern since its early incorporation into various North Atlantic empires. Teasing out Wolf's comments and drawing from Mintz's work, I want to sketch some of the contradictions from the Caribbean record to flesh out a composite picture of what I mean by the Otherwise Modern.

Behold the sugar islands from the peak of Barbados's career to Cuba's lead in the relay race—after Jamaica and Saint-Domingue, from roughly the 1690s to the 1860s. At first glance, Caribbean labor relations under slavery offer an image of homogenizing power. Slaves were interchangeable, especially in the sugar fields that consumed most of the labor force, victims of the most "depersonalizing" side of modernization (Mintz 1966). Yet as we look closer, a few figures emerge that suggest the limits of that homogeneity. Chief among them is the slave striker, who helped decide when the boiling of the cane juices had reached the exact point when the liquid could be transferred from one vessel to the next.[2] Some planters tried to identify that moment by using complex thermometers. But since the right moment depended on temperature, the intensity of the fire, the viscosity of the juice, the quality of the original cane, and its state at the time of cutting, other planters thought that a good striker was much more valuable than the most complex technology. The slave who acquired such skills would be labeled or sold as "a striker." Away from the sugar cane, especially on the smaller estates that produced coffee, work was often distributed by task, allowing individual slaves at times to exceed their quota and gain additional remuneration.

The point is not that plantation slavery allowed individual slaves much room to maneuver in the labor process: it did not. Nor is the point to conjure images of sublime resistance. Rather, Caribbean history gives us various glimpses at the production of a modern self—a self producing itself through a particular relation to material production, even under the harshest possible conditions. For better *and* for worse, a sugar striker was a modern identity, just as was being a slave violinist, a slave baker or a slave midwife (Abrahams 1992:126–30; Debien 1974; Higman 1984).

That modern self takes firmer contours when we consider the provision grounds of slavery. Mintz (1978) has long insisted on the sociocultural relevance of these provision grounds, small plots on the margins of the plantations, land unfit for major export crops in which slaves were allowed to grow their own crops and raise animals. Given the high price of imported food, the availability of unused lands, and the fact that slaves worked on these plots in their own free time, these provision grounds were in fact an indirect subsidy to the masters, lessening their participation in the reproduction of the labor force.

Yet Mintz and others—including myself—have noted that what started as an economic bonus for planters turned out to be a field of opportunities for individual slaves. I will not repeat all those arguments here (Trouillot 1988, 1996, 1998). Through provision grounds, slaves learned the management of capital and the planning of family production for individual purposes. How much to plant of a particular food crop and where, how much of the surplus to sell in the local market, and what to do with the profit involved decisions that required an assessment of each individual's placement within the household. The provision grounds can be read not only as material fields used to enhance slaves' physical and legal conditions—including at the time the purchase of one's freedom—they can also be read as symbolic fields for the production of individual selves by way of the production of material goods.

Such individual purposes often found their realization in colonial slave markets, where slaves—especially female slaves—traded their goods for the cash that would turn them into consumers. One can only guess at the number of decisions that went into these practices, how they fed into a slave's habitus, or how they impacted on gender roles then and now in the Caribbean. Individual purposes also realized themselves through patterns of consumption, from the elaborate dresses of mulatto women, to the unique foulard (headscarf) meant to distinguish one slave woman from another. The number of ordinances regulating the clothing of nonwhites, both free and enslaved, throughout the Caribbean in the days of slavery is simply amazing. Their degree of details—e.g., "with no silk, gilding, ornamentation or lace unless these latter be of very low value" (Fouchard 1981 [1972]:43) is equally stunning. Yet stunning also was the tenacity of slaves who circumvented these regulations and used clothing as an individual signature.

Moreau de St-Méry, the most acute observer of Saint-Domingue's daily life, writes:

> It is hard to believe the height to which a slave woman's expenses might rise...In a
> number of work gangs the same slave who wielded tools or swung the hoe during

the whole week dresses up to attend church on Sunday or to go to market; only with difficulty would they be recognized under their fancy garb. The metamorphosis is even more dramatic in the slave woman who has donned a muslin skirt and Paliacate or Madras kerchief... (in Fouchard 1981 [1972]:47).

Moreau's remarks echo numerous observations by visitors and residents of the Americas throughout slavery's long career.

If modernity is also the production of individual selves through patterns of production and consumption, Caribbean slaves were modern, having internalized ideals of individual betterment through work, ownership, and personal identification with particular commodities. It was a strained and harsh modernity, to be sure. Otherwise modern they were; yet still undoubtedly modern by that definition.

One could argue—although the argument is not as easy as it seems—that the selves on which I just insisted may have existed elsewhere without the forced modernization imposed by colonialism. I would readily concede that point if it leads to the realization that the modern individual self claimed by North Atlantic consciousness is not unique to the North Atlantic. At the opposite extreme, one could also argue that the detached individual self is only a fiction of the North Atlantic geography of imagination, an ideological by-product of the internal narrative of modernity. Perhaps surprisingly, I am even more willing to concede that point. In either case, the central issue is not that of an allegedly modern individual subjectivity—whatever that may be—but the insertion of that subjectivity into a particular regime of historicity. Clothing as individual signature may be as old as human society. So too may be the production of identity through labor. At any rate, I doubt that these two features—or any of the markers usually claimed to signify the rise of the modern self—first obtained as such in Renaissance or post-Renaissance Christendom. Intellectual and art history, literature and philosophy may have misled us into overrating these individual attributes of the modern self to the detriment of the historical context within which these selves were fashioned. François Hartog (1988 [1980]) sets the projection of alterity as the context for self-identification as far back as Herodotus. Max Horkheimer and Theodor Adorno see in Odysseus the precursor of the modern subject. Closer to the ground, Georges Duby and his collaborators in the *History of Private Life* project (1988) effectively extend notions of privacy or even intimacy back into the Middle Ages. I suspect that with similar data one could make as potent discoveries outside of Christendom, thus relativizing the narrative that makes the modern individual self such a Eurocentric product.[3]

Necessary as this revisionist narrative is, it is not the central issue. Too often critics of Eurocentrism flesh out their arguments in terms of chronological primacy. They spend much energy demonstrating that such-and-such feature claimed by North Atlantic narratives to have been a European first could actually be found elsewhere before European presence. The mistake here is to forget that chronological primacy is itself a central tenet of North Atlantic imagination. That is, the value of being the first comes from a particular premium on time, a specific take on historicity. The existence of certain social features outside of Europe matters less than the inscription of these features in social and political regimes *in the past*, and much less even than the inscriptions of these same features—as found in Europe then—in North Atlantic narratives *in the present*. From that perspective, the modern self may be less a matter of the content of an individual subjectivity than that of the insertion of that subjectivity into a particular regime of historicity and sociopolitical management. On that latter issue, the most crucial one in my view, the Caribbean story is most revealing.

Modern historicity hinges upon both a fundamental rupture between past, present, and future—as distinct temporal planes—and their relinking along a singular line that allows for continuity. I have argued that this regime of historicity in turn implies a heterology, a necessary reading of alterity. Striking then is the fact that Caribbean history as we know it starts with an abrupt rupture between past and present—for Europeans, for Native Americans, and for enslaved Africans. In no way could the enforced modernization imposed by colonization be perceived by any of these actors as a mere continuation of an immediate past. This was a New World for all involved, even for those who had lived within it before it became new to others.

The consciousness that times had changed, that things were falling apart and coming together in new ways, was both inescapable and yet inseparable from the awareness that others were fundamentally different—different in where they came from, the positions they occupied along any of the intersecting hierarchies, the languages they spoke, the costumes they wore, the customs they inhabited, and the possible futures they could envision. The sensibility to time and the recognition of heterogeneity associated with modernity are inescapable here. Indeed, they have been central themes of Caribbean scholarship (Lewis 1983; Trouillot 1992, 2001b).

Here again the slave quarters are telling. These imposed the sudden discovery of a common African past, but also the awareness that this commonality barely covered fundamental differences. One could not address that Other next door who looked so strikingly similar and engaged at times in practices reminiscent of home, without using a language derived at least in part from that of the masters. Was that not as modern as the vulgate version of the Bible? More modern than the quarrel between seventeenth-century French intellectuals as to whether the King's engravings were best written in French or Latin? If the awareness of one's position in history, not just as an individual but as part of a group and against the background of a social system brought to consciousness, is a fundamental part of what it means to be modern, then the Caribbean was modern from day one, from the very day colonialism imposed its modernization. If the awareness of sociocultural differences and the need to negotiate across such differences are part of what we call modernity, then the Caribbean was modern since at least the sixteenth century—from day one of North Atlantic modernity. But if that is so, the chronological primacy of the North Atlantic falters.

Chronology here is only an index. My goal is not to replace North Atlantic chronological primacy over the rest of the world with a Caribbean chronological primacy over other colonies and postcolonies. Historical particulars made the Caribbean, for better and for worse, the area longest under European control outside of Europe itself and the only one where Europeans moved as if it was indeed empty land, a *terra nullius* to be fashioned along modern lines. Now dominant

North Atlantic narratives—reflecting the world domination of the English language, the expansion of Protestantism as a variant of Christianity, and the spread of Anglo-Saxon and Teutonic sensibilities—reduce the crucial role of Portugal and Spain in the creation of the West. A related emphasis on the Enlightenment and the nineteenth century, and the downplay of the Renaissance as a founding moment, also lead to the neglect of the role of the Caribbean and Latin America in the production of the earliest tropes associated with modernity. That chronological amnesia crucially impedes our understanding of the North Atlantic itself (see chapter 1; Dussel 1993; Trouillot 1991, 1995).

Yet I want to insist that the lessons learned from the Caribbean are applicable elsewhere. As a historical process inherently tied to modernization, modernity necessarily creates its alter-native in Asia, Africa, Latin America, and in all areas of the world where the archetypal Caribbean story repeats itself with variations on the theme of destruction and creolization. Modernity creates its Others—multiple, multi-faced, multi-layered. It has done so from day one: *we* have always been modern, differently modern, contradictorily modern, otherwise modern, yet undoubtedly modern.

I do not want to conclude with this pun on Bruno Latour's famous title, however tempting a *bon mot*. In *We Have Never Been Modern* (1993 [1991]), Latour suggests that the North Atlantic's "modern constitution" rests upon a divide between scientific power, meant to represent things as they are, and political power, meant to represent subjects as they wish to be. Latour sees the formulation of this divide (science/politics, object/subject, nature/culture) as the impossible dream of modernity, since the world so neatly divided is actually made of hybrids. Nevertheless, Latour does admit, almost in passing, that blind faith in this divide also makes the moderns invincible. I am interested in this invincibility. Latour's witty title could be misread as to imply that we could have been modern according to definition. But if modernity is as much blind faith in this narrative as its global consequences, we have long been modern, except that the "we" here is not only the North Atlantic but also the hidden faces of a modernity necessary to North Atlantic hegemony—if not invincibility.

Ultimately, however, the fact that modernity has long obtained outside of the North Atlantic is only a secondary lesson from the Caribbean; it is a conclusion that still makes those outside of the North Atlantic the ones who need to be explained. Yet is the alter-native really what is to be explained? Is the puzzle the female slave who used her kerchief as individual signature, or the laws that repeatedly tried to curb her individual expression? Is the puzzle the resilience of the creolization process under slavery, or the expectation that enslaved Africans and their descendants would be either a *tabula rasa* or mere carriers of tradition (Trouillot 1998)? In short, is not the puzzle within the West itself?

The Caribbean story as I read it is less an invitation to search for modernity in various times and places—a useful yet secondary enterprise—than an exhortation to change the terms of the debate. What needs to be analyzed further, better, and differently is the relation between the geography of management and the geography of imagination that together underpinned the development of world capitalism and the legitimacy of the West as the universal unmarked. Anthropologists need to take further distance from North Atlantic universals as carriers of that legitimacy. As a discipline, we have launched the most sustained critique of the specific proposals rooted in these universals within academe. Yet we have not explored enough how much these universals set the terms of the debate and restricted the range of possible responses. In the context of this much-needed reformulation, the Caribbean's most important lesson is a formidable one, indeed. That lesson, as I see it, is that modernity never was—never could be—what it claims to be.

Chapter 3

A Fragmented Globality

What, if anything, is truly new about our times? The routine answer to that question is globalization. But what is globalization? While the word "modernity" dates back to the middle of the nineteenth century, globalization is a hundred years younger. Yet as a potential North Atlantic universal, globalization is already as murky as modernity. Like modernity, it cannot be all it claims to be. We have already seen that much of the newness it celebrates is fictitious and that this celebration silences much of world history.

We may further relativize its alleged newness with this quote:

> International finance has become so interdependent and so interwoven with trade and industry... that political and military power can in reality do nothing.... These little recognized facts, mainly the outcome of purely modern conditions (rapidity of communication creating a greater complexity and delicacy of the credit system) have rendered the problems of modern international politics profoundly and essentially different from the ancient (Angell 1910).

The main elements of a dominant version of globalization narratives are there: New technology—especially the speed of communication—creates an interdependence that weakens political institutions, and in turn leads to a fundamentally different world. Does this suggest a radical break? Yes, except that the quote is from Norman Angell's *The Great Illusion*, published in 1910. By the first decade of the twentieth century, some knowledgeable observers had already proposed that the main features we associate today with the word globalization fully obtained in the world of finance and politics. Yet we cannot easily discard the word, in part because, just like modernity, it seems to point to phenomena not easily covered by other words. That is because globalization as a word hides as much as it reveals—like the North Atlantic universals that it may eventually join. The task once more is to revisit the story and discover the silences between the lines.

If by globalization we mean the massive flow of goods, peoples, information, and capital across huge areas of the earth's surface in ways that make the parts dependent on the whole, then the world has been global since the sixteenth century. To acknowledge these earlier global flows is not to claim that there is nothing new under the sun. On the contrary, by helping us screen out that which passes for new and may actually be quite old, the reference to a massive empirical record of five centuries highlights the more profound changes of our present. Having discovered the silencing of the past on a world scale, we are better poised to discover the production of silences about our present. We may realize that some of these silences are deliberately and cynically produced, and that what I call "globalitarism" is a dominant ideology of our times, an ideology that aims to propose the teleology of the market as the new master narrative of Western modernity. As we identify the effects of these combined silences on the lived experience of millions of human beings, we may realize the moral duty that the political and scholarly have to establish a critical distance from that ideology and from the visions of humanity that it proposes.

If we approach globalization as naïvely as the recent rise of "a world without boundaries," we find ourselves repeating advertising slogans without knowing how we ended up there. We miss the fact that words like "global" and "globalization" in their most current uses were first broadcast most aggressively by marketing agents and marketing schools. Kotabe Masaki and Kristiaan Helse (1998) locate what they call candidly "the globalization imperative" in the search for new marketing strategies.[1]

Scholarly analysis needs to go beyond the slogans, clichés, and narratives that sustain these strategies. These tropes not only silence the histories of the world, they also veil our understanding of the present—including their own conditions of possibility—by hiding the changing story of capital. Yet changes in the composition and spatialization of capital are crucial in shaping the uniqueness of our present. Henceforth, I reserve the word globalization for the conflation of these changes and their most immediate consequences.[2] In this chapter, three processes will receive special attention: the reshaping of the respective markets for capital, labor, and consumer goods; the ongoing rise of finance capital and the social and ideological ramifications of that domination; and the extravagant increase in inequality both within and across political boundaries.

A New Design for Capital

Capitalism has always been transnational. Crossing political borders is inherent in its historical trajectory. Some analysts have long suggested that capitalism is necessarily prone to cross borders inasmuch as it must find new places to integrate in the sphere of capital (Luxemburg 1951 [1914]). Today as in the past, most firms that operate in more than one country have a distinguishable home base, most often in the United States, Japan, Germany, France, or the United Kingdom. What is new today is not the internationalization of capital as such, but changes in the spatialization of the world economy and in the volume and, especially, kinds of movements that occur across political boundaries.

Recent world history is characterized by a series of fundamental changes in spatialization. Changes in the spatialization of markets—the market for capital (both financial and industrial), the market for labor, and the market for consumer goods—create overlapping spatialities that are not synchronized but together contribute to give the world economy its current shape. Second, and as importantly, the domination of finance capital over the kinds and volumes of global flows now gives the world economy its main directions and trends. Third, predominant among these trends is increased inequality within and across political boundaries.

Three Markets for Inequality

In the last two decades of the twentieth century, the world economy increasingly looked like a Triad (Ohmae 1985), a triangle with three major regional centers as its poles: one in North America (the United States and Canada), one in Asia (with Japan at the epicenter), and one in Western Europe (with Germany as the epicenter).[3] Since then, China's spectacular growth has made it the world's second largest economy, with a 1998 Gross Domestic Product of US$3,846 billion (up from US$821 billion in 1985). That growth increased the intensity of flows both within the Asian pole of the Triad and between that pole and the North American one. Yet since Japan remains China's main commercial partner and since China itself has become Japan's favorite client—second only to the United States—China's growth has not affected the reality of the Triad itself, although it has affected the relative weight of Western Europe in the world economy.

A unique feature of our times is the dynamism of international investments, especially within the Triad. The magnitude of FDI (Foreign Direct Investment)—for instance, capital deployed from one country into branches and subsidiaries located in another country—was reportedly US$317 billion in 1995, dwarfing records from all past eras. Despite yearly fluctuations, notably in 1992 and 1998 after the Asian crisis, as well as in 2002 after the sudden decline of the U.S. stock market due to corporate accounting scandals, the long-term rise seems continuous. Even the risks of temporary recessions in individual countries do not threaten the relative value of FDI within the Triad. Indeed, FDI is becoming the primary form of exchange across state borders, a place traditionally occupied by commerce, and is influencing more than ever the rhythm and direction of international exchanges. This does not mean that capital moves freely across borders. Rather, its spatial distribution is increasingly selective. Most of the world's economic movement, and especially FDI, occurs between or within the poles of the Triad, which alone contained 88 percent of all capital flows in the 1980s. Meanwhile, all but 25 developing countries are excluded from the market for private capital (Passet 2000:136–7). The capital invested across political borders tends to come from six countries: the United States, Japan, the United Kingdom, Germany, France, and the Netherlands, more or less in that order. Investments reach mainly the same countries with the notable addition of China. Of the US$317 billion invested across state boundaries in 1995, US$194 billion stayed in the North Atlantic (within the United States, Canada, and the European Union).[4] Outside of the Triad, exchange tends to take the minor form of subcontracting.

That global exchange remains concentrated among a few countries, mainly within the North Atlantic plus China and Japan, is one of many aspects of the increasing concentration of economic power that characterizes our times—a point to which I shall return. Exchange occurs primarily between the same countries, between firms of the same sectors, between branches of the same firm. Far from moving toward more open markets, the world economy witnessed in the 1980s and 1990s the rise of "private markets," of monopolies and oligopolies that now dominate its most important exchanges, notably that of capital.

Likewise, we have not witnessed the global integration of the price of labor that some optimists promised in the 1960s. On the contrary, the world labor market has become more differentiated. It is differentiated by region, with the highest prices in the North Atlantic and the lowest in rural Asia, Latin America, and especially Africa. A mobile elite has emerged at the very top of every specialization and its visibility often creates the impression that anyone can work anywhere. But while many governments keep the door ajar for members of this elite, the same governments are raising the gates to keep away the vast majority of potential foreign laborers. The speed in communications contributes to reducing the mobility of labor in relation to that of capital, adding to the global differentiation of the labor market. Capital can now find the right laborer in her place of birth and spread the labor process for a single product over countries or even continents. This is true not just for traditional manual labor in agriculture or industry. Credit cards can be processed in a Caribbean country such as Barbados, where literacy rates higher than in the United States guarantee that equal competence can be bought at a lower price. Some Ford cars are now designed simultaneously in a virtual work space by teams of engineers spread over many countries but linked by computers. California-based computer companies that once used to charter flights to recruit programmers and engineers from Bangalore, India, now prefer to subcontract them in situ because salaries are much lower there. Sophisticated communication systems nullify physical distance: Indians and Californians can work together, though with different incomes. The result is increased differentiation across political borders. The material and social prospects of a computer scientist performing the same tasks in Silicon Valley, California, and in Bangalore, India, vary considerably. Finally, labor market differentiation also occurs within political borders. While the prospects for medical doctors or computer scientists vary according to the country in which they live, in no way does the market for agricultural laborers in India compare to that for computer scientists in size, saturation, or life prospects. Few, if any, can cross from one labor market to the other. Only at a lower level, that of consumer products, is the global economy moving at great speed toward a single integrated market. An increasing number of buyers from all continents now have access to some of the cheapest products of the world economy at more or less equivalent prices.

In short, globalization does not mean that the world economy is now integrated into a single space within which capital, labor, and commodities freely flow. Rather, that economy is developing three contradictory yet overlapping modes of spatialization: 1) increased, though selective, flexibility of capital, mainly finance capital within or between the poles of the Triad; 2) differential labor markets within and across national borders; 3) increased yet uneven integration of consumer markets worldwide.

The age of creditors. These changes in spatialization parallel the increasing domination of finance capital, which now tends to impose its own logic on the entire world economy. We have entered an age where rentiers of all kinds, including creditors, are backed by the most powerful governments and institutions of the world, notably the United States, England, and the International Monetary Fund (IMF), and can impose their appetite for quick profits as a natural and irreversible outcome of the human condition. As *The Economist* put it on October 7, 1995: "Financial markets have become judge and jury of economic policy-making." Hans-Peter Martin and Harald Schumann (1997 [1996]:61), who cite these words, rightly add that this new tribunal is also without law and its new dictatorship entails little responsibility. The consequences are awful.

The first is the relative decline of productive investment. Within FDI itself, major transfers have moved away from manufacturing to target "non-productive" assets such as real estate, tourism, department stores, banking, and insurance (Weiss 1997:8). By the late 1990s, among the leading countries only Japan's foreign investments remained relatively high in manufacturing. The major profits, national and transnational, are now in rent-form, notably in the financial markets. As many transnational holdings involved in manufacturing become "financial groups with an industrial concentration" (Chesnais 1994:61–6), the logic of finance capital—which, as both Marx and Keynes warned us, is close enough to the logic of usury—becomes the dominant logic of the system.

The bulk of capital now deployed in the world economy does not target new production. Since the mid-1970s capital accumulation is realized mainly through the annexation of already existing firms via buyouts or fusions. These transactions reached US$411 billion in 1998, an increase of 74 percent over 1997, which was itself an increase of 45 percent over 1996 (Passet 2000:84). To be blunt, capital is not generating new ventures: It combines or reshapes old ones. Enterprises themselves become commodities with indeterminate use values. Their exchange value attracts the raiders who buy them often only to break them down and sell the pieces at huge profits. Similarly, currency transactions, which totaled US$18 billion a day in 1970, climbed to US$200 billion in 1986 and US$1,300 billion in 1995. By 1998, currency transactions had reached the now broken record of US$1,800 billion a day, 60 times more than the exchange value of goods and services (Passet 2000:98). It is as if we have returned full circle to the speculative explosion that accompanied the birth of capitalism, but with the added irony of time lost and gained and the added power garnered through the age-old deployment of capital itself. As merchant capital once defined the direction of deployment only to be overthrown by industrial capital, industrial capital is now being subsumed by finance capital.

Many economists see the mobility of finance capital and the tremendous power unleashed by this freedom as the most important feature of our times. We have entered the age of speculative capitalism. The fragility of unregulated financial markets mixes rumors of immediate doom—and the reality of spectacular crashes, some of which, as we saw in 2002, resulting from the willingness of some corporate managers to engage in deceit on a massive scale—with hopes for extravagant profits. Quick profit, anywhere, by any means—licit or illicit—becomes the explicit ethos of managers. That goal is inherent in the logic of capital, but the increasing domination of finance over industrial capital changes the dynamics of accumulation by introducing a new temporality that now extends beyond the world of finance.

David Harvey (1982) has reminded us of capital's tendency toward acceleration and of the capitalists' strategies to use time against space. Marx—who first exposed capitalism's tendency toward acceleration—and Harvey both insist on this feature as an aspect of industrial capital. The pattern holds even truer for finance capital today. Increasingly freed from bulky physical holdings, further empowered by prompt means of exchange that deny its materiality and challenge our very notion of time, finance capital is picking up the baton from industry because it now epitomizes capital's tendency to erase space. Its new speculative spirit is backed by the increasing speed of information, which it in turn accelerates.

The currency market provides a telling example. Huge amounts of money can be made or lost in a flash. James Tobin's now famous cite of an operator that "my long-term is the next ten minutes" rightly captures the new temporality that finance capital has introduced into the world economy. The logic of finance capital rests on a bet with both time and perception, or better, with perception through time. As an investor I must guess *now* what a majority of people with means will consider *tomorrow* to be a prime source of revenues in an unforeseeable yet dreamable *future*. The point is to buy *now* and to sell *before tomorrow*. Let others wonder about whether the dream was indeed viable and how it will stand up in the long-term future. The more distant and vague the future, the better for me as speculator. Implied in that logic is the need to constantly reduce the gap between now and tomorrow, to play the guessing game faster than the guy next door, while further increasing the distance between near and far futures. In postponing *ad infinitum* the long-term future, yet decreasing the distance between now and tomorrow, the logic of finance capital is accelerating the speed of the world economy, down to those single business firms that must now pay full attention to their short-term performance at the expense of their long-term projects and possibilities. Anything that takes time to show results—research, slow yet reliable growth, calculated yet potentially rewarding risks—become secondary, engulfed by the rapidity of daily stock market assessments.

The cost of that domination is not only economic. It is also social and political. Inflation ranks highest among a creditor's fear, for obvious reasons: As the value of money decreases, time works against the creditor who collects payments of decreasing worth. The domination of creditors means increased pressure against economic recovery programs that risk provoking inflation within a currency sphere, from raises in the minimum wage to massive government projects. Conversely, the political pressure of capital now pushes national governments, especially those in the North Atlantic, to combat inflation notably by keeping wages and salaries low. These pressures to keep wages and salaries low, except at the very top, are not only due to the financiers' fear of inflation. They also reflect the particularities of the relation between finance capital and labor, and the increased distance between human beings when the market place determines the quality of human relations.

The welfare of the labor force was never a high priority of investors. The only relevant exception in the history of world capitalism is—ironically—plantation slavery in the Americas, when masters had some interest in reproducing the labor power of the slaves they had bought, at least until they received a full return on their investments. Yet it is fair to say that the labor movement under industrial capitalism brought a social consensus, backed by most North Atlantic states and quite a few others, in which national populations were seen as both workers and consumers. Unionization, the shrinking of the work day, the recognition of vacation time, differential pay for overtime, and equal pay for women are all part of this consensus about the right of the labor force to reproduce itself. Furthermore, even with flexible production, industrial capital maintains some relations of proximity between those who control—if not those who own—the means of production and the laborers. Capital never had a human face, but with industrial capital at least it wore a human mask.

With finance capital and the intricacies of multi-layered connections in the world economy today, capital takes off its human mask and seems to act with its own merciless logic away from the workplace and the workers. Finance capital emerges as a protagonist in its own right who defines anew the realms and purposes of productive ventures now integrated in its orbit. Yet since finance capital has no particular regard for new productive ventures as such, it has absolutely no qualms about the status of the labor force. This is particularly true in a context where the phenomenal technological advances of the last few decades mean that increased material wealth is now generated with fewer and fewer laborers. Corporate managers can quite honestly speak the depersonalized language of "the market" and reject all responsibility for the human disasters that this language masks. The dominant discourse of political and economic elites projects national populations less as a single potential source of differentiated labor than as differentiated pools of potential consumers. Here again the logic is speculative: Whether or not a number of these laborers starve to death, one is betting that a minority will survive within the targeted consumer pools long enough to purchase whatever one has to sell—at a profit, of course. From this to an ideology of market extremism, the bridge is rather short. Many have crossed it.

The morality of growth. The unabashed defense of the market today flaunts an extremism that Adam Smith himself would not recognize. One of Smith's central arguments is that uncontrolled economic exchange is the only guarantee of growth since the invisible hand of the market is its own regulator. Market extremists today carry that argument to the radical proposition that this regulating function of the invisible hand is at work in all human activities. Uncontrolled economic exchange is the sole guarantee of growth and productivity in all spheres of life. Therefore all the social and cultural preferences eventuating in political controls that may prevent or mediate such exchanges should be abolished. The market is not only the best, but the only reliable social regulator. It does not require political judgment and therefore its activities and the results of such activities do not need to be submitted to political judgment let alone political consensus. Is the educational system of a society declining or nonexistent? Discard political debates on the long-term purpose of education. Reduce government's role in setting educational policy and mid-term goals. Allow entrepreneurs to set profit-oriented schools and universities: The best institutions will survive as parents and students exercise their choice as consumers. With minor variations the formula can be extended to all realms of life: Social harmony will result from the individual decisions of millions of consumers. Politics is out, and with it government intervention. Political consensus need not express itself through government institutions: It expresses itself in the shopping centers. Government's role is to give and protect free access to the malls.

Some observers insist that these extreme positions are coherent with all forms of liberalism (Rosanvallon 1999; St-Onge 2000). Pierre Rosanvallon argues that once we stop thinking of liberalism as a doctrine and assess it as a mode of thinking or a field of vision (*un champ problématique*), economic liberalism, political liberalism, and anthropological liberalism appear as intertwined if not inseparable. Thus the position of market extremists could be read as a logical continuation of the ideas of John Locke or Adam Smith.

This line of argument is relevant only in the field of intellectual history, where ideas can be studied independently of their deployment. I agree that in all three cases liberalism introduces an ontological break between a phenomenon and its context. What could be conceptualized as a process becomes a fixed entity—the market is severed from society, justice is severed from politics, and the individual is severed from history. In their concrete historical deployment, however, economic liberalism, political liberalism, and anthropological liberalism did not always coalesce. Indeed, they often contradict each other. Thus the distinction is crucial to understanding not only times gone by but a present where market extremists are taking the political and ideological lead of the liberal rainbow. There are millions of people today who have not read Locke or Smith, who believe in civil rights and the market, and yet who do not like the idea that one should be able to buy a kidney, a spouse, a child-laborer, a child as sex object, a shot of crack, a uterus, a term paper, a family name, a bag of heroin, rotten meat, biological weapons, or a self-help suicide kit just because someone else is willing to sell them. In short, liberalism also carries its inherent contradictions.

As some critics have noted, carried to the extreme the argument for the market is actually an argument against liberal democracy (Martin and Schumann 1997; Passet 2000). Just imagine political parties selling ballots at the election booth! Yet aberrant as it is, the fundamental proposition behind such a scheme—the social infallibility of the market—is increasingly trumpeted by scholars, corporate lobbyists, and politicians. This repetition has a purpose: To make the aberration sound normal. After all, the strategy worked with some North Atlantic fictions in other times. Thus it may be worth exposing, albeit in schematic form, some of the assumptions behind market extremism. These include:

- A conception of history as preordained and regulated, thus escaping human intervention (i.e., a naturalist view of history).
- A conception of the individual as an atomized self merely placed *in* a socio-historical context, as opposed to a being partly constituted *by* that context.

- A conception of society as a mere addition of such atomized individuals, that is, as an entity in no way greater than the sum of its parts.
- A conception of the social good—the meaning and purpose of specific human collectivities—as the smallest degree of interference between exchanges among such atomized and self-serving individuals.
- A conception of the moral good—what is just, fair, and good for humankind—that does not require any debate about the nature and purpose of humanity as a whole or about the value of any single human life. Growth becomes an end in and of itself, a universal moral value.

Each of these propositions can be proven false both theoretically or by reference to distant or recent history. Even the initial proposition that uncontrolled economic exchange is the sole guarantor of national growth is belied both by the history of the economic take-off of most North Atlantic countries and more recent developments in the world economy. Centuries of political controls over economic flows made North Atlantic countries the world powers they are today. Europe recovered from World War II largely because of the massive state intervention of the U.S. Marshall Plan. The quick recovery of the Asian Tigers at the end of the twentieth century shows that government intervention is not obsolete. They overcame their economic crisis much faster than anyone expected by snubbing the IMF and using massive government intervention to rectify their economy. Argentina, in contrast, took the unregulated route with disastrous results.

Market extremists rarely follow their own prescriptions. The same groups and individuals who argue against government intervention actually constantly solicit that intervention when financial interests are at stake. In 1995, about a dozen powerful individuals, including President Clinton, White House Chief of Staff Leon Panetta, and IMF President Michel Camdessus, raised US$50 billion in record time to back the Mexican peso. A banker from J. P. Morgan described that operation, dubbed "Peso Shield" by the *Washington Post*, as "a bail out for speculators" (Martin and Schumann 1997:41–6). Finally, all the operations of finance capital assume a social structure and a technological infrastructure that are maintained and reproduced by massive government interventions. Since at least the 1980s Savings and Loans debacle in the United States,[5] capital is increasingly socializing its risks and losses while managers loudly denounce government interventions that have social goals.

But economics is not the final frontier in this argument, even if profit is its main rationale. Professional economists continue to argue over the balance of market deregulations and state interventions most likely to generate growth in any society at a specific historical moment. Even more importantly, many argue over the relevance of growth in relation to equality within and across political borders. Thus, in the late 1990s a reader in development economics (Lundahl and Ndulu 1996) fully recast the notion of development in terms that explicitly accounted for the relation between growth and equality. The lead authors write:

Development takes place when the gross national product (or income) per capita grows at a sustained pace over a long period of time *without simultaneously worsening the distribution of income and increasing the number of absolute poor* ... to these requirements should also be added a condition with respect to sustainability.... Growth should not be hampered, but resources must be left to future generations as well (Lundahl and Ndulu 1996:1, emphasis added).

In short, professional economists do know that the study of the economic process is irrelevant without a democratic consensus on its aims. A few even acknowledge that these aims and this consensus are, in the short term, political and, in the long run, moral (Sen 1992, 1999). Such acknowledgments are anathemas to market extremists who claim that their proposals have little to do with ethics or politics.

But if we look closely at the assumptions behind neoliberal extremism, we quickly discover that what we are being sold is not just an economic program. We are being asked to endorse growth as a moral value. We are asked to take as a religious—that is, unquestionable—tenet the proposition that productivity in any domain, anywhere, anyhow is good for humankind as a whole. We are being asked to forget that productivity without a consensus on its distribution is another name for sheer profit and that whenever profit is sheer only a few can collect it. We are being asked to renounce worldviews that suggest the ethical solidarity of humankind. In short, we are being asked to accept a prepackaged formula about what it means to be a good and proper human being in all times and places, to endorse one vision of humanity, and an odd one at that. Visions of humankind are, of course, among the favorite topics of sociocultural anthropologists. We have spent much disciplinary energy over more than a century in showing how such visions vary across time and space. We should have a say in that debate. We should at least demonstrate that this vision of humanity is culturally located.

Nor is that vision politically innocent or morally benign. Behind the unabashed praise of the market as social regulator and growth as a moral value is a total disregard for the rest of humankind. German journalists Martin and Schumann offer a chilling critique of *globalitarism*, the term I apply to the optimistic theory that naïvely posits that the political, economic, and personal interconnections forged over the last 50 years are unprecedented, and that they presage the happy transfer of what were previously state functions to free market mechanisms (see chapter 4). At the 1995 closed-door meeting of the Gorbachev Foundation in San Francisco, members of what has become a global oligarchy calmly agreed that at some point in this twenty-first century only two-tenths of the world's active population would be necessary to sustain the world economy. The middle classes as we know them are likely to disappear. Chunks of humanity will become irrelevant. John Gage and Scott McNealy of Sun Microsystems suggest the motto of that future: "to have lunch or be lunch." And how will the prosperous fifth appease those who may not want to be someone else's lunch? Former U.S. National Security Advisor Zbigniew Brzezinski, the very one who coined the word globalization, provides the most successful answer: *tittytainment*—titty as in tits and motherhood, that is, enough milk for the poor to survive poorly and plenty of entertainment to maintain their good spirits (Martin and Schumann 1997:1–5).

The coincidence in authorship reveals much more than Mr. Brzezinski's talent for neologisms. It suggests that one does not need a conspiracy theory to document the fact that parts of the discourse of globalization are deliberately produced for the management of imagination. There is such a thing as globalitarism as a loosely concerted effort—a gentleman's agreement, though Ms. Thatcher was at the Gorbachev Foundation, to renew faith in a revitalized Western metanarrative against postmodernist despair. The internal limitations of academic postmodernism aside, its rather fast displacement into scholarly discourse—including anthropology—is best read against the background of a public campaign on the benefits of globalization. That this public campaign has been discussed in closed-door meetings at think tanks and in other policy-making centers is more than likely.[6] Yet it is also likely that most of the scholars who contribute unwittingly to that campaign do not even know of such meetings.

The strategies devised at closed-door meetings such as that of the Gorbachev Foundation are backed by public pronouncements such as the increasingly explicit condemnation of the poor as the cause of their own poverty. Revamping old arguments in a new vocabulary, many explanations of poverty now blame the victims of globalization. The poor are poor because they deserve it: They have the wrong culture, the wrong values, or the wrong kind of behavior (Gilder 1993; Harrison and Huttington 2000). The move is again moral—or rather, amoral to the extent that it absolves those with political and economic power from any kind of guilt or responsibility. But by that same token it is also blatantly political. It is a preemptive strike against those who may wonder why, if globalization is so good for humankind, it has created so much misery. Indeed, new to our times is a massive increase in inequality both within and across political boundaries.

Global polarization. Today's world is a polarized one. That polarization takes many forms. Between sellers and buyers, we are witnessing the rise of world oligopolies: A few firms now control the world market for most major commodities. Rather than the level-playing field vaunted by market extremists, this concentration of power eliminates smaller competitors and excludes new entrants. Polarization has also increased between countries. Gone are the developmentalist dreams that assumed all countries to be on the same path. A majority of countries and some continental chunks (notably sub-Saharan Africa) are becoming poorer each day. Even more importantly, their state of affairs is becoming irrelevant to the world economy. Given the declining significance of geopolitics in the post-Cold War era, this means quite concretely that chunks of humankind are seen as superfluous to world political and economic leaders. The global map has increasingly large black holes.

Striking is the concentration of resources of all kinds in a few hands, most often in the North Atlantic. In 1998, 74 of the 200 top international corporations were based in the United States, 41 in Japan, 23 in Germany, 19 in France, and 13 in the United Kingdom (Clairmont 2001). The turnover for only half of them then exceeded France's national product and dwarfed that of Mexico by a ratio of six to one. Whatever the domain, from communications to energy, from transportation to biotechnology, from cereals and bananas to clothing, a smaller number of actors seem to hold most of the cards, and these actors are usually located in the North Atlantic or in Japan.

This massive concentration of economic power, and the polarization, fragmentation, and related increase in inequalities of all kinds that accompany it, rarely make headlines. A rare and eloquent warning was raised in the pages of the usually conservative magazine, *The Economist*, by guest commentator Robert Wade of the London School of Economics. Wade's presentation of the data on purchasing power parity (PPP), drawn from two World Bank studies, is worth quoting at length. He writes (2001:72):

> The distribution has two poles. One, at the bottom end, is at an average income of less than $1,500 a year. It contains the populations of most of Africa, India, Indonesia and rural China. At the other pole, with average PPP income of more than $11,500, are the United States, Japan, Germany, France, Britain and Italy. Some of the space between $1,500 and $11,500 is occupied by countries such as urban China, Russia and Mexico. But notice the strange "missing middle": relatively few people live in countries with average PPP incomes that fall between $5,000 and $11,500.

Increased polarization of incomes between countries now characterizes the world. To start with, the very poor and the very rich tend to live in different countries. The president of Morgan Stanley collected US$14 million in bonuses in 1996 alone, more than many Third World countries received in aid from the United States in the same year. In 1993, the salary of the chief officer of the Disney corporation was 325,000 times higher than that of the average Haitian worker toiling for Disney subsidiaries, and by 1998 the three richest personal fortunes in the world were higher than the national product of the 600 million people living in the 48 poorest countries of that same world (Passet 2000:138–9; see also Clairmont 2001).

The figures that tell these tales of tycoons and scions are so indecent that their trumpeting in the likes of *People* magazine may actually distract from the geographical distribution of global inequality. Few readers of this book can hope to make US$14 million in a year. Thus many North Atlantic residents may feel that they are also on the other side of global richness. That is simply not true. Where one lives today makes the most crucial difference for what one's income is likely to be, *both* in absolute and in relative terms. Since at least the mid- 1980s, the richest ten percent countries have been getting richer at a faster pace and the poorest ten percent have also been getting poorer at a faster pace, furthering trends inherent in the development of world capitalism. The ratio of per capita income between poorest to richest countries was only 3 in 1820, and 11 in 1913, but already 35 in 1972. It has more than doubled to 72 by 1992. The per capita income of 80 countries was lower in 1998 than ten years before (Passet 2000:138). Some economists estimate that it will take 40 to 50 years for most countries in sub-Saharan Africa—but Haiti or Honduras also come to mind—to reach the mediocre levels of real income they enjoyed in the 1970s. Furthermore, as Eric Toussaint (1999) puts it, "an infernal spiral of debt" tremendously increases the woes of the countries of the South. The restrictions and regulations imposed together by the IMF, the World Bank, the Paris Club (comprised of the North Atlantic states in their capacity as creditors), and the London Club (which regroups the most important private lenders) put peripheral countries in the absurd situation of having to fill a bottomless barrel. As Toussaint (1999) shows, between the 1982 debt crisis and the late 1990s, peripheral countries had, together, reimbursed more than four times what they owed. Even so, the sum of their external debt was four times greater in 1998 than it was in 1992. Interest payments on the debt, low ratings of currency, low wages, and structural adjustments imposed from the outside are among the many factors that contribute to the increased poverty of the South and the increased richness—in both real and relative terms—of the countries within the Triad. More than ever before, both richness and poverty have a geographical face. Citing the work of the World Bank's Branko Milanovic, Wade writes: "By 1993 an American of the average income of the poorest ten percent of the population was better off than two-thirds of the world's people." By virtue of being born in the United States, even a poor American is likely better off today than two thirds of humanity. By virtue of being born somewhere else, say in sub-Saharan Africa or in rural India, one is also automatically targeted for poverty. Not surprisingly, the gap between the median and the poorest ten percent countries is also widening (Wade 2001:73–4).

At least some economists argue that inequality is also on the rise *within* countries, although the evidence of a long-term trend remains disputable. Wade sees the gap between urban and rural sectors in both India and China as wide enough to warrant treatment of these two countries as four different entities. Indicators of polarization also obtain in the North Atlantic where the percentage of families with middle-class incomes is decreasing. In Québec alone it decreased from 60 percent of the population in 1973 to 41 percent in 1996 (cited in St.-Onge 2000:30). According to the former U.S. Secretary of Labor Robert Reich (1991), by the early 1990s one-fifth of the population of the United States was doing increasingly well while the remaining four-fifths were on a downward path. By the end of that decade, the 2.7 percent richest Americans owned as much as the poorest 100 million of their fellow citizens (Passet 2000:127). Socialist-oriented programs have slowed similar trends in Europe, but they are under serious political attacks from big business and their allies. The United Kingdom, where the political power of business has most eroded the role of government as regulator and redistributor of wealth on that side of the Atlantic, has registered one of the most serious increases in inequality in Europe. It has also seen one of the highest increases in corporate profits. There as here, the debate continues about the number of citizens who will fall on the bad side of the gap. Some economists insist that polarization within countries remains rare and quite temporary. For Alberto Figueroa, "the empirical evidence shows an increase in the degree of inequality between countries but a viscous change in inequalities within countries in the long run" (personal communication 2001). Still, the public acknowledgment that populations within the same industrialized countries might be headed in different directions is itself a new feature.

The possibility of multiple and divergent futures increases a political apathy already premised on the distribution of inequality. In a context where the average of the most poor in the United States still has more purchasing power than two-thirds of humanity, it becomes much harder to motivate the population of this country about the woes of citizens elsewhere. If these woes are presented as both inevitable and irreversible, dictated by the laws of nature—the inevitability of the market as social regulator—rather than as the consequences of ongoing deployments of power, then quite understandably the average American citizen would rather not hear about them. She has her own uncertain future in mind. To make matters worse, academic, political, and corporate leaders throughout most of the world have joined in what Linda Weiss (1997, 1998) calls "the political construction of hopelessness," telling citizens that they cannot do anything about the social consequences of globalization. Once unequivocal assumptions that citizens of Western democracies had some control over the fate of their neighborhoods, towns, or children are now being questioned. Right-wing populism feeds on that despair, silencing the fact that social polarization was not handed down to us by an anonymous world market but is the partial and predictable result of conscious political decisions made by North Atlantic states since the Reagan-Thatcher era.

We are far from the idyllic vision of a global village where everyone is connected to everyone else. Rather, our times are marked by the growing awareness of global flows among ever more fragmented populations. World histories and local histories are becoming both increasingly intertwined and increasingly contradictory. Homogenization is at best superficial. The world is global indeed; but it is also more fragmented than ever.

To be sure, a few corporations from the United States, Japan, Italy, and France now seem to share global cultural control through the distribution of entertainment and clothing. The planetary integration of the market for cheap consumer goods does tie world populations into a web of consumption in which national ideals are becoming closer even as the means to achieve them wither for a growing majority. The integration of that market, the speed of communications, and the oligopolies in media and entertainment contribute to projecting the same image of the good life all over the world. Prompted by global media, more human beings than ever before share similar lists of the products they need to consume and the objects they need to possess in order to achieve individual satisfaction. In that sense we are truly witnessing for the first time, especially among the youth, a global production of desire.

This global production of desire and the integration of the market for consumer goods upon which it rests have lured many analysts into two related illusions. The illusion that a single-market society is both desirable and possible rests on an emphasis on the development of a global market for consumer goods and a total neglect of the processes of differentiation unleashed or reinforced by the financial and labor markets.[7] The related illusion of a single global culture builds upon that emphasis. It singles out the most obvious similarities in consumer behavior and reduces culture, at worst, to consumption patterns, or at best to style. The concentration of economic power and the integration of the retail market within the clothing, food, and entertainment industries provide the empirical basis for this latter illusion.

Yet even the integration of the global market for consumer goods does not produce harmonious borders, let alone harmonious directions. The very same processes that link populations often provide them with the means to affirm differences that crisscross political, economic, and cultural fields. There is no theoretical ground to claim and no empirical evidence to suggest that similar consumption patterns necessarily lead to cultural or political homogeneity. Nor can we assume that economic exchange alone necessarily fosters social integration, even when that exchange takes the form of face-to-face encounters. Thus, for instance, the proportion of individuals born in Senegal and living in France or in Italy today as compared to earlier times is less significant than the perception of that presence as an invasion—a perception enhanced by the visibility of the few Senegalese peddling cheap wares on the street. Proximity here does not mean automatic acceptance on the part of the natives. Nor does it imply a desire on the part of the Senegalese-born residents to become French or Italian as defined by most natives. Indeed, equally significant is the immigrants' increasing refusal to blend and disappear culturally into France or Italy, and their material capacity to sustain that refusal. To be sure, a vision of the good life in France and Italy was what attracted them there in the first place, but their material capacity to both accept and reject parts of France or Italy is reinforced by a number of global processes, including the development of a global market for consumer goods that includes the airline tickets they bought as well as the Chinese-made watches that many of them sell on the streets of Turin or Paris.

To put it more simply, the market economy itself prevents the rise of a global market society because, contrary to the philosophical assumptions of market extremists, human beings everywhere have had and will have goals that are not market-oriented. These goals and the moral values, cultural codes, and social ideals that sustain them ensure that the effects of economic processes can never be reduced to the economic sphere.

From Islamic fundamentalists and Christian evangelicals to the followers of Reverend Moon and of the Church of Scientology, the late twentieth century abounds with individuals who engaged in economic practices to fulfill what they saw as primarily religious goals. Even when the decision to engage in such practices stems primarily from immediate material needs, economic returns are deployed in all spheres of life. Market women from Haiti who buy cheap goods in Florida or St. Marteen to resell in Port-au-Prince or elsewhere in the Caribbean may use substantial parts of their otherwise meager profits to restore vodoun temples in their village of origins. Profits made in Turin, Nice, or San Francisco through the global network of the Mourid followers of Cheik Amadou Bamba help launch small ventures in Dakar, from taxicabs to food stalls and tourist shops. The global economic strength of the Mourids reinforces their socioeconomic power at home. Their increased influence on the local Senegalese scene reinforces ethnic, religious, and cultural divisions that could eventually threaten the Senegalese state itself.

While the integration of the market for consumer goods and the global production of desire enforce homogenization, both also contribute to the exacerbation of tensions through the differential use of opportunities, the social polarization noted above, the unequal means available to satisfy new desires, and the always-specific discrepancies between global models and local ones. There is no global cultural model to attenuate those discrepancies in part because there is no agreement on the long-term meanings of social life—a point to which I shall return. Within and across state boundaries, polarization and entanglement now create new ways of perceiving distance—temporal, spatial, social, and cultural—thus shaping a new horizon of historicity that is an inherent part of the "fragmented globality" that marks our times.

There is a paradox in that coinage, but ours are times of paradox and irony. On the one hand, the global village cliché rings true for a larger proportion of the world population that is increasingly aware of global flows and their impact on daily routines. At the same time, most human beings continue to act locally, albeit with less confidence that their actions might affect the global order. This perceived powerlessness simultaneously accentuates cultural openness and chauvinism. World histories and local histories are perceived as intertwined and contradictory at once. The twenty-first century is likely to be marked by the speed and brutality of these contradictions as the global village becomes an ever more constant, yet more elusive presence.

Living in a Fragmented World

The perception of powerlessness. Even the most sublime narratives of globalization cannot easily reconcile their glorification of the present and the perception of individual powerlessness that they themselves help to nurture. Because "the market" is said to have become one of the most powerful actors on the world scene today, albeit still an invisible one, prominent individuals, from corporate leaders to chiefs of state, now routinely claim their inability to control events. Commenting on Operation "Peso Shield," IMF President Michel Camdessus voiced his own powerlessness vis-à-vis the financiers, claiming, "the world is in the hands of these guys" (Martin and Schumann 1997:45).

More often than not these claims are convenient shields for choices that protect capital accumulation (Weiss 1998). Political decisions made by elected leaders of the North Atlantic between 1972 and the late 1990s led to a situation where financial markets appear all powerful and where humanity is controlled by a rising class of anonymous global speculators. Even now that the domination process has gained its own momentum, the powerlessness of political leaders remains a choice. But claims of powerlessness from the mighty ring true to millions of individuals all over the world who feel that they have little control not only over their own destiny, but also over the terms under which to negotiate their present. In spite of the rosy promises of globalization, for an increasing number of human beings ours are times of uncertainty. For the poorest, some of that uncertainty inheres in the economic polarization described above—because they are on its wrong side. The increased impersonal nature of life outside the household, the increased weight of institutions—indeed, the increasing need for institutionalized forms of organization, public or private—and the related growth of government bureaucracies reinforce the sense of vulnerability for many poor and not so poor. But there is more to the story.

We have seen earlier that human beings were surprisingly swift in adopting materials, crops, animals, and customs during the first moment of globality.

Yet nothing could have prepared our predecessors for the dazzling speed at which information moves today. That I am able to write these lines in the south of France, have my research assistant in Chicago verify facts and references, and—given her diligence—receive the correct citation and incorporate it in my text all within half an hour is something few of them could have imagined, especially before the mid-nineteenth century, as Jules Verne's works remind us. It is unlikely that even these futurists could envision the back-and-forth flow of information that I just described as a routine part of their life. From the time of the Roman Empire down to the nineteenth century, news moved at speeds that look sluggish today. At the beginning of the sixteenth century it took four days to deliver a message from Nuremberg to Venice. From the 1490s to the 1730s, the average distance one could cover by any means of transport in 24 hours was about a hundred kilometers (Braudel 1967:318). Historian Fernand Braudel, who provides this estimate, adds: "Mail took weeks, months, to reach its destination" (1967:416). Extraordinary advances in sea travel "created a global network of communications" (Braudel 1967:415) but only in determining how far people could go, not how fast they could get there. And since information moved at the same rhythm as its human carriers, it moved slowly. News of the Haitian Revolution, important and silent as it was, took five weeks to reach Europe by way of Jamaica. News of the French Revolution, thought then as it is now to be a most important event, moved slowly through Europe and even through France itself. According to Eric Hobsbawm (1962:10), "the news of the fall of the Bastille reached the populace of Madrid within thirteen days; but in Peronne, a bare 133 kilometers from the capital, 'the news from Paris' was not received until the 28th."

In the midst of that revolution, the linking of Lille and Paris by way of the Chappe brothers' optic telegraph in 1793 first broke the tie between the speed of human travel and that of information. But the real impact of both the optic and electric telegraphs started to be felt only in 1857 when the first underwater transatlantic cable linked Ireland to Newfoundland. Thirteen years later, an underwater cable linked Brest to Duxbury. The spread of radio, telephone, air travel, and television considerably accelerated planetary flows of communications in the twentieth century and made transcontinental information accessible daily to millions of individuals. Since the last quarter of that century, satellite communications and related developments such as the spread of the Internet signaled the beginning of another era. Even when the old means of communications seem unchanged, new technology makes them more efficient, and thus faster or cheaper. In 1990 dollars, the cost of the same phone call between New York and London went down from US$245 in 1930 to US$3 in 1990. By 1999, it was a mere 35 cents (Passet 2000:83).

The individual use of these means remains extremely unequal. By 1997, three-quarters of the world's telephones were concentrated in the eight richest countries. At about the same time, nearly 80 percent of all Internet users were in the North Atlantic (57 percent in North America and 20 percent in Europe). This inequality both reflects and reproduces the economic polarization that divides continents, countries, and populations. In the United States alone, where individual access to the Internet dwarfs figures for the entire world, ethnic minorities have much less access to computers than whites both within and across income categories. Thus the fundamental change is not in the number—or even the proportion—of individuals who have direct access to these new means of communications, even though such numbers are increasing everywhere. Rather, the magnitude and velocity of planetary flows of information now affect routine practices of millions of individuals who themselves are not necessarily wired. In so doing, they contribute to the fragmented globality of our times. A major consequence of the magnitude and velocity of these flows is an increasing difficulty to reconcile time and space—not only analytically but also ethnographically and phenomenologically—in the lived experience of ordinary human beings.

If I am correct that massive global flows have been part of world history since the sixteenth century, it follows that millions of human beings before us had to negotiate various temporalities and spatialities. As we have seen, efforts to locate, define, and come to terms with modernity all have to do with probing or redefining relations between time and space. While such explicit efforts engaged mainly theorists and philosophers, the majority of individuals routinely faced these issues on the ground. With limited modifications to the work of Braudel and other historians associated with the *Annales*, one could generate models that would account for time-space convergence and divergence in different historical eras, compare the velocity of particular flows, identify what sorts of durées or microdurées applied to particular aspects in life, find out how long particular news from certain areas took to reach others, and how the locals assimilated this information. Whatever the results of this exercise, we know enough from the historical record to suggest that most individuals and groups reconciled *bon gré mal gré*[8] these divergences in their lived experience through adjustments that were possible in part because of the practicalities of daily life. I will draw once more from the history of plantations to sketch an example.

A resident plantation owner in seventeenth-century Barbados, eighteenth-century Saint-Domingue, or nineteenth-century Brazil, Mauritius or Ceylon was necessarily enmeshed in multiple spatialities and temporalities. The space of the colony, the space of the empire, the space of the plantation itself, the rhythm of the market, the rhythm of the work process, and the temporariness of his own presence, often exacerbated by the desire to be in the metropolis, were all necessary parts of his lived experience. Fortunately we have enough journals and personal testimonies from such planters to suggest that they made sense of these fragments by tying them together around what we may call a dominant space-time unit.

To simplify a complex story, for that resident plantation owner the space of the plantation and the rhythms associated with it not only came to dominate the daily routine, but often also provided the terms under which to reconcile, however temporarily, other otherwise irreconcilable spaces and times. The reconciliation of multiple temporalities and spatialities was accomplished through their partial reduction in or around a central space-time unit, a phenomenological one, which in this case we can call, for short, "plantation life." The family or household may have played that same role in other contexts or for other individuals, just like the work place, the village, the neighborhood, the city, or the nation do in other contexts.

The deployment of this dominant space-time unit was made possible by the necessary delays that obtained between the appearance of events and processes in other—more distant—units and their intrusion in the dominant space of lived experience. However much of our plantation owner's attention may have been pulled towards price changes on the global markets for tropical commodities in Bordeaux or Liverpool (Braudel 1992:96, 141, 229), or the fluctuations of the Amsterdam stock market, there was a necessary delay between the advent of such news in Europe and its reception and integration by that planter. The local gained some of its phenomenological coherence because of the necessary distance between it and other space-time conflations that constituted the global. To put it differently, at the level of lived experience the global remained in the background of the local, even when it was structurally determinant. The lived geography of place reconciled different spaces and times and reduced the individual's sense of fragmentation.

Today, this reconciliation is increasingly difficult for at least two reasons. First, the growing instability of all the social spaces within which the individual once found reassurance—matrimony, career, neighborhood, civil associations, or extended family—makes the construction of a dominant phenomenological unit much harder. Simplistically put, if the family as we used to know it appears increasingly shaky, how can we take refuge in it against the world?

Second, even when that dominant unit remains relatively stable the speed at which flows of capital, goods, but especially information travel today and their related impact—sometimes simultaneously—on different space-time units reduces the capacity of that dominant unit to act as a buffer. Events happening or processes eventuating elsewhere are part of the news of the day in the lived experience of people who do not inhabit in any immediate manner the space-time units within which these events or processes originate. The speed of reactions therefore also increases and can affect individuals or collectivities that were not part of the news of the day, or did not even hear about those events.

News of gun battles in the streets of Kingston, Jamaica, in 2001 provoked immediate reactions from the U.S. State Department by way of a warning that affected North American travel agents, who in turn cautioned many potential tourists to stay away from the island. It mattered little that the north of Jamaica, the island's main tourist area that is served by a separate airport, remained calm throughout the fighting. The foreign tourists who were there then did not face any greater danger than they would have on the streets of Miami or Los Angeles. Yet it is likely that the livelihood of a few local Jamaican workers was affected by the speed with which the news rebounded in Washington and provoked reactions in Miami and Los Angeles. It is even probable that some of these Jamaican workers appraised the impact of the fighting on their chances of employment only after hearing the news from a hotel manager who watched the events on CNN. Although my argument rests on the increased role of world media and the Internet, it does not require the naïve illusion that a majority of people spends their day glued to CNN or surfing the Web. Rather, it suggests that the individuals, groups, and agencies that have privileged access to particular kinds of flows—notably information—can use that privilege in ways that reinforce an already uneven distribution of power.

Even those with greater power may not reconcile the space-time units phenomenologically better than others. Behold this hotel manager in Jamaica glued to CNN, attentive to the daily weather in Chicago throughout the winter, paying special attention to the virulence of armed conflict around Bethlehem at Christmas, anxious about the purchasing power of the dollar or the viability of the Euro the next spring. In many ways, his capacity to reconcile these various times and spaces is greatly diminished when compared to the plantation owner who may have sat in the same spot 300 years before. The structural components are comparable: The two enterprises are inscribed in the world economy in similar ways. As foreign-oriented ventures in a dependent peripheral area of the world economy, both rely on metropolitan dwellers as suppliers, intermediaries, and customers. Both are extremely vulnerable to fluctuations among any one of the foreign groups and markets on which they depend. The problem of the hotel manager as opposed to the plantation owner is that, thanks to technology, he receives all the information that registers his dependency at once. Thanks to technology, he must also digest it at once. Speed is an intrinsic component of his competitiveness. The global penetrates the local phenomenologically and the distance between the two vanishes within lived experience. That penetration accentuates both the sense of connection and a feeling of distantiation, since the individual is both increasingly aware of the impact of events happening elsewhere, yet relatively powerless to affect them. The financial operator's statement that the long-term is the next ten minutes can thus be read as a dual acknowledgment. On the one hand, it boasts of his capacity to manipulate the next 600 seconds and possibly cause millions of dollars to change hands. On the other, it acknowledges his lack of power beyond that short temporal frame.

The possibility remains that people who otherwise exercise some amount of power claim their own powerlessness not as a conspiracy or as an intended deception, but because they cannot fully reconcile within their lived experience the contradictions of different spaces and times. This can be documented only with ethnographies of the global elite, including the global academic elite. Yet if substantiated, that ambivalence would be one more irony of our fragmented globality, namely that globalization deceives the very people who believe in it and make it possible. But that irony only masks another deception. The very discomfort of the global elite may be not only a privilege of that status, but also one of the many factors that make its deceptive narrative believable not only to itself but to others. I can easily imagine our hotel manager, a travel agent, a stockbroker, or a State Department official lamenting the impact of these global flows over which they feel they have little control while praising the virtues and promises of the global village. These are indeed deceptive times.

The death of utopia: historicity for our times. This deception is in part self-inflicted, rooted in the difficulty of admitting that the tributaries of the Enlightenment may have run their course and that we are entering a new regime of historicity. While we find it hard to take distance from these conceptual tools—the vocabulary and especially the imaginary first proposed by the Renaissance, formalized by the Enlightenment, and institutionalized by the nineteenth century—few of us can deny that this imaginary has lost its appeal. While the world today reproduces more than ever the institutional forms inherited from the nineteenth century, these forms are increasingly empty shells void of the historical drive that once made them so attractive.[9] A central newness of our era is a new relationship with history, or more properly, with historical time. We are at the threshold of a new regime of historicity that implies a different relation with the past and, especially, a new relation to the future. This new historicity fundamentally challenges the right to define utopia that was always essential to the legitimacy of the West. We might as well acknowledge that and face the consequences.

The new relation with the past is marked by the awareness of irreversibility. Of course, the irreversibility of the past is an old-age notion not restricted to the post-Renaissance North Atlantic. Even there, it coexisted for centuries with the possibility of decadence or with notions of historical cycles that until recently made rebirth a possibility even for intellectual and political leaders. Today, however, historical irreversibility—whether perceived or actual, since we cannot in any case accurately predict the future—is on the rise, but with the added effect that it evokes damages rather than possibilities. While good times may not return, injuries may be permanent. Nowhere is that clearer than in our changing relationship with the natural world. It is likely that generations before us have inflicted irreparable damage to the environment. What is new to our times, since at least the 1972 declaration of the Rome Club, is the spreading knowledge in the North Atlantic that nature is not an unlimited good and that many of the damages we inflict upon it are irreversible. This is no big news outside of Europe and North America. However, as a Western-driven pressure group, the ecological movement stands as the clearest manifestation of a new sense of historical irreversibility.

The impossibility of recapturing old times does not apply only to nature, nor is it acknowledged in the North Atlantic alone. The horrors of the Chinese Cultural Revolution and of the killing fields of Cambodia were both premised in part and in different ways on the possibility that rural-urban migration could somehow be reversed. Some alternative development programs also flirted with that possibility. Now most scholars, governments and especially peasants assume that rural-urban migration is irreversible. Yet at the same time, just as for the environment, solutions to the problems created by this trend are unclear. No one knows how to best deal with the growing flow of urban poor. Rural-urban migration is one example of a larger phenomenon. At the United Nations, the World Bank, and in most major countries—with the possible exception of China—policy increasingly eschews any assumption of reversibility. Irreversibility marks our present, yet without the promises of the nineteenth and twentieth centuries, misguided as they were.

Irreversibility creeps again, quite perversely, into the numerous calls for apologies and reparations for historical damages that are peculiar to our times. What propels these calls is in part a desire to repair despite the knowledge that the damage is irreparable. The move is akin to that of a parent who sues for malpractice after the loss of a child. No amount of money and no acknowledgment of guilt can actually compensate for that loss, yet the reparative gesture becomes necessary to the actor exactly because the damage is so great and so irreparable. The impossibility for descendants of victims or descendants of perpetrators to envision a future that is altogether common, desirable, and attainable is one of the many reasons why historical apologies are increasingly in demand and yet remain abortive rituals (Trouillot 2000).

Our new relationship to the past hinges upon a more fundamental shift in our relationship to the future. The shift is most clear when we acknowledge the temporal features of progress as outlined by a number of writers. Thus Reinhart Koselleck (1985:17) writes: "Progress opened up a future that transcended the hitherto predictable, natural space of time and experience, and thence—propelled by its own dynamic—provoked new, transnatural and long-term prognoses." Progress thus both produced and relied upon the capacity to envision a long-term that was simultaneously credible but unprovable.

Yet in times of progress there was also implied a mid-term future, that Koselleck notes only in passing and that also required credibility beyond the immediate experience of the actors. The nineteenth century made most obvious this mid-term that stretched the limits of experience. Augusté Comte based his whole sociological enterprise on that temporal range and its predictability. The joint belief in that mid-range and in the capacity to foresee beyond immediate experience made possible both the massive investments in industry and the institutionalization of the social sciences in the nineteenth and twentieth centuries. Until recently political science, economics, and sociology basked in the glow of this mid-term and related claims of control. Relying on analyses often nurtured in academe, planners who set government policies for road construction, education, and immigration acted upon this capacity to both predict and orient behavior beyond the immediate experiences of single actors. Likewise, for the duration of the Cold War the United States and the Soviet Union engaged in a chess game predicated upon the abilities of both to manage the mid-term.

This mid-term is now fading. The future as we knew it is now increasingly fractured into two new parts: a near-present that challenges our technical mastery, and an aftermath, out of real time, that our imagination has yet to seize. While the distance between now and tomorrow shortens, that between tomorrow and the long-term becomes increasingly inscrutable. Worse, the exigencies of this near-present now seem to reduce our grip on a long-term forever postponed. The content of that long-term is open to question. This temporality recalls the accelerated rhythms of finance capital but expands way beyond economic life. The need to adapt quickly to tomorrow's exigencies, yet the inability to envision beyond them, is now part of the lived experience of an increasing number of human beings.

The new long-term future is not only farther, its contents are murkier. Here again, the difference between the temporality of the Enlightenment and our times is palpable. Koselleck (1985:15) writes: "The future of this progress is characterized by two main features: first, the increasing speed with which it approaches us, and second, its unknown quality." Yet until the end of the twentieth century the planning of the mid-term future helped to slow the speed of progress's future. Hope and expectations acted as the affective connections between the mid-term of the planners and credible long-term prognoses. Although the long-term future could not be predicted, it could be both invoked or evoked, and such evocations and invocations contributed to shape a "horizon of expectation" (Koselleck 1985) that embraced the possibilities of utopia.

Striking today is that the speed of that long-term future has become indeterminate while the speed of the short-term has accelerated—as if the momentum of the once long-term had been transferred to the next ten minutes of our financial operator. The urgency of the short-term—the future as the next ten minutes, now the norm in the world of finance—penetrates all aspects of life. The long-term has also lost its evocative power. That latter proposition was put forward best by Pierre-André Targuieff, whose opus, *L'Effacement de l'avenir* (2000), describes what we may call a *futur sans avenir*, a future without prospects.[10] Targuieff builds on the distinction, lexically marked in French between *le futur* as a temporal frame that may be empty of content, and *l'avenir*, which fills that temporal frame with a usually positive substance.[11]

I read Targuieff as one of the most explicit writers to suggest with apprehension that our historicity today is marked by the death of utopia, by the increasing gap between possible and desirable futures. Today we are neither able nor willing to evoke or invoke the long-term future of progress underscored by Koselleck. Humans all over the world renounce the old nostalgia for times yet to come that colored North Atlantic historicity since at least the writings of Thomas More and on which rested the entire package of the Enlightenment. Recall that the West, as a project first sketched during the Renaissance, required utopia. Recall that Western claims to global legitimacy rest in part on the capacity to project North Atlantic dreams of possible futures as beneficial and necessary to the entire human species. In light of this trajectory, the twentieth century ended with an irony. Once a North Atlantic right to propose a dreamable future to the rest of the world, utopia died just as the world rediscovered globality.

Lest my argument be misunderstood, let me insist that I am not suggesting that scholars or intellectuals should abandon the Enlightenment project, let alone its most generous promises. Rather, I am suggesting that we do not have that choice anymore.[12] The voluntarism of a few intellectuals and the posturing of a few politicians are not enough to make this project appealing or meaningful to the majority of humans today. The geography of imagination of the West as we know it cannot function without utopia, yet a major shift in historicity has made the future impervious to utopian prognoses.

The demise of communism stands as a marker of this shift. In the late 1970s, communism was still an ideology tuned to the future, an evocation of things to come—the promise of hell for its opponents, the promise of justice and peace for those who believed in it. Fifteen years later communism had become an ideology irrevocably turned to the past. To everyone's surprise less than a decade after the fall of the Berlin Wall, market democracy—the winning alternative—did not fare much better. As a prospect or as an achievement, global market democracy is neither presented nor lived as a utopia, if only because as an idea or an ideal it cannot reach the transcendental plane on which utopias function. More people were willing to die in the name of fascism, communism, nationalisms, and separatisms of all kind than are willing to die for globalization today. The individuals more likely to take personal risks on the globalization issue are those who protest against it in the streets. Yet even the growing grassroots movement against globalization has yet to propose a long-term future that seems altogether common, desirable, and attainable. The tens of thousands of demonstrators who challenged the agenda of the World Trade Organization on the streets of Seattle in 1999 and the two hundred thousand who challenged the G8 meeting on the streets of Genoa in 2001 share a rejection of the present as offered by the apostles of globalization rather than a common vision of the long-term. As the numbers of demonstrators and grassroots movements that challenge globalitarism keeps growing, a consensus may be reached on a positive agenda.

Chances are such an agenda will not emerge easily. Meanwhile, a majority of humans is losing faith in what were, up until the last quarter of the twentieth century, the most convenient roads to utopia. Science, religion, and politics are losing their power not only as possible futures but also as imagined means to these long-term futures. The connection between science and utopia is now shattered. Condorcert's loud and blind faith that knowledge—if not science itself—necessarily brought social and moral improvement to the whole human species now looks like a foreign religion.[13] World organized religions, especially monotheist ones, no longer provide temporal havens from which to envision the future of humankind. The utopic role of the major churches now falls to religious sects whose appeal registers a need now unfilled, rather than a renewed global vision.

That the roads to utopia are narrowing is even clearer when we look at the third traditional means to a dreamed future: fundamental institutional change as envisioned by Thomas More, globalized by the French Revolution, renewed by Marx, and popularized by revolutionary movements until the end of the twentieth century. With the demise of the Soviet bloc, North Atlantic societies in general and the United States in particular have found it increasingly difficult to generate a unified meaning and purpose to social life for their own citizens, let alone agree on an ideal that they can sell to others (Laïdi 1993, 2001; Resch 1992). The few societies outside of the North Atlantic that once flirted with that pretension—notably the semiperipheral leaders of the defunct non-aligned movement—have abandoned any claim to global modeling. Various mixes of politics and religion in countries such as Afghanistan before the 2001 war with the United States, Iran, or Saudi Arabia no longer rest on the pretense of a global vision to be shared with the rest of humankind. On the contrary, they flaunt their exceptionalism—even when it is couched in terms of an alternative universal vision for humanity.

Thus postmodernism did identify a central feature of our times, the fall of grand narratives and the increasing difficulty in generating alternative visions of the long-term future. But to the extent that it refuses to acknowledge that its own nostalgic mood and negative affect takes for granted the narratives that it mourns, postmodernism itself can be read as one of the latest ruses of a modernity entrapped in its own production (Harvey 1989; Targuieff 2000). It is a solution that still refuses to question the primacy of the West's geography of imagination.

Unfortunately, most other solutions so far, regardless of the tone with which they are proposed, do not question this primacy (Bessis 2001). Thus with a triumphant tone quite different from that of the postmodernists, globalitarists today try to restore faith in a Western metanarrative centered around the market as the ultimate human value. As this book suggests, the results are mixed since the undeniable appeal of globalism keeps bumping into the lived reality of local spaces.

More subtle and less ambitious solutions abound, not all of which I can mention. Remarkable among them is the recent revisionist reading of "Western civilization" as a "Judeo-Christian heritage," not withstanding the continuity of anti-Semitism in the North Atlantic from the Middle Ages to the present and the fact that the West built its universalism in part on the back of the Jew conceived from the beginning as its savage from within (Bessis 2001). Noticeable also is the renewed praise of a modernity without prospects, the nonchalant applause of movement for movement's sake, symbolized in academic circles by the glorification of Baudelaire's perfect flaneur and by neo-nihilist readings of Walter Benjamin. Even subtler, yet of more direct interest to anthropology, are moves—not always conscious—to restore the Savage slot without reference to utopia, manifest in what I call the eulogy of Otherness.

In praise of difference. In the preceding chapter I made much of the adoption of maize by the Chinese and Africans as compared to the adoption of espresso coffee in North America in order to temper our enthusiasm about the alleged cultural openness of our times. There is no way to prove that U.S. citizens in the twentieth century were more open to foreign items and practices than Africans were in the sixteenth. The very idea that somehow the cultural openness of human groups can be measured on a single scale and that it actually progressed along such a scale from the Renaissance to our times is among the illusions inscribed in North Atlantic narratives of world history.

Since legalized discrimination is immediately measurable, we know that many of its blatant manifestations have declined here and elsewhere, and this is not a bad thing. Nor is it inconsequential that scientific racism is on the regress almost everywhere as an official ideology and as a serious intellectual proposition, for that regress makes it harder to legitimate discrimination. Most legal systems throughout the world—especially in the North Atlantic—increasingly recognize individual liberties in ways that affect not only the citizens and practices once banned, but improve the moral and political life of the entire country. I do believe that the United States is a better society for having taken laws against cross-racial marriages, illegal in some states as late as the 1960s, off the books, and for at least thinking about eliminating the remaining sodomy laws that barely mask the forceful discrimination against gay sexual practices. I do believe that Germany is a better country now for recognizing the right of children born on German soil to be German citizens. There have been major institutional changes in the sociopolitical arena that we can only label as positive. I also believe that there are quite a few developments in the opposite direction, here as elsewhere, but my main concern here is not a simple balance sheet, positive or negative, of sociological and political markers.

Indeed, more peculiar to our times than any sociopolitical improvements is an acute concern for a balance sheet that is not only sociopolitical, but fundamentally moral, and the accompanying claim that we are now somehow more culturally open, more diverse, more welcoming of alterity today than ever before, especially in the North Atlantic. Even more peculiar is the way that latter claim is played out.

Whether or not we accept or reject difference, but especially when we claim to welcome it, we value ourselves publicly for doing so and we expect others to pass similar judgment. This moral premium on difference, accepted or rejected, lauded or attacked, yet increasingly projected as a universal value good or bad, seems on the increase. It is on the increase among the extremists who loudly reject foreigners, Jews, Africans, Muslims, gays—or any other marked population—on the basis of an alleged purity threatened. They also think that "we" are more open than ever before; in fact, they argue that we have become "too open." But the moral premium is most visible among those who loudly welcome this growing openness. Often the premium on difference takes a doubly flattering form—praise for the Other and for the self who praises. I want to question this indiscriminate eulogy of alterity. One of its most perverse results is the reproduction of the Savage slot—and therefore of the West—good intentions notwithstanding.

The convenience of the unmarked. The wholesale praise of Otherness pushes us to accept the sociohistorical equivalence of all manifestations of alterity and therefore the political equivalence of all forms of discrimination and redress. It reproduces a main feature of the Savage slot, the erasure of the Other's historical specificity. All others are Others and they are so in the same way. Except for gender, minority status becomes a mere attribute of demography. Alterity is extracted from the sociohistorical contexts that give it birth and the ones within which it is renewed and continues to operate. It is striking, for instance, the way race is projected as a subset of ethnicity, especially in the United Sates. Striking also is the equation of all sexual minorities which, when carried to its extremes, actually silences the history of gender inequality. Taken out of this equation of all differences is the added value of the power—always specific and different, and therefore historical—that was deployed and felt in the production and reproduction of these numerous others. One did not become gay the way one became woman or the way one became black. One did not become a gay male even the way the one became a lesbian. Neither did one become black in the United States the same way others became *beurs* in France or blacks in Britain, for that matter. The physical and symbolic violence exerted to create and enforce these categories in specific times and places, and the identities tied to them, were always and remain both different and incommensurable. The needs and the means to redress the inequalities so produced cannot be the same.

More perniciously, redress is often a secondary—when not altogether a superficial—issue in this eulogy. The push toward the sociohistorical equivalence of manifestations of alterity parallels a move toward the moral and political equivalence of all forms of contact with the Others so produced. Exceptions are made for contact that is explicitly derogatory or physically violent. Language is purified to the point of silliness—hence the vacuous debates about the faults and virtues of political correctness that further mask both sociological inequalities and differences in symbolic power. One does not vilify the Other on radio or television. One does not call the Other names. One does not attack the Other with bare hands or stones, although bombing can be permitted if approved by Washington.

These exceptions aside, the premium is on the presence of that Other, however mediated—or better yet, on the mere fact of contact with the Other rather than on the relations between the Other and us. It does not matter, therefore, if that relationship reproduces the Other's otherness, a point to which I will return. Strategies of diversity in the United States—in government, academe, urban planning, and the private sector—best reflect this premium on contact for contact's sake. Yet we should be aware that the U.S. model, first developed around black-white relations in the midst of desegregation and the civil rights movement, is being praised and introduced elsewhere in part because it has claimed more visible results than many others. But it has also produced bigger problems and more disappointment than others exactly because it has reduced re-presentation to presence, or more precisely, attendance.

Pushing to the extreme the strategy based on the illusion that the mere presence of the Other is a sign of better relations, in the beginning of this century the presidency of George W. Bush managed to produce a historical first, the most "diverse" and yet the most conservative leading team in the history of the United States since the end of World War II. However, before we turn conservatives into scapegoats we may want to remember that this strategy was first devised by whites and blacks who saw themselves as political liberals. I vividly remember being among a group of academics—all indisputably left-leaning and mostly feminists—the day that Madeleine Albright was named as the first female Secretary of State in the United States. The question was genuinely raised whether we should celebrate the event. At that time none of us knew anything about Albright. We had no idea how her political views might affect the foreign policy of the United States, including relations with countries where governments enforce blatant practices of discrimination along gender lines. The mere fact of her presence was taken as a positive sign, a step toward reducing alterity.

Yet the entire history of colonialism, slavery, and racism could easily teach us that contact and proximity have never been the panaceas that the eulogy of Otherness claims them to be. The love affair between Thomas Jefferson and Sally Hemmings—if indeed that's what it was—did not erase either her slavery or her blackness. But Jefferson never claimed that it did. Publicly, at least, he never claimed that the world was better because of that relationship. That illusion is quite peculiar to our times.

Illusions not only mask certain realities. They also allow other realities by enabling certain practices. It is not enough to claim that the social and historical equivalence of all forms of alterity and the moral and political equivalence of all forms of contact are mere illusions. We need to ask: What kinds of practices do these new illusions enable, and what are the major consequences of these practices today?

The first of these consequences is the increased convenience of the unmarked. If contact is always good, if the mere proximity of the Other is a sign of diversity, then whoever is not an Other has greater latitude than before in defining the character of that relationship. Individuals or groups who are in the unmarked category of any alterity (whites, heterosexuals, males, citizens by birth, etc.) have greater power in defining the form, the nature, and the meaning of contact, and therefore what it means to be "sensitive," "diverse," "open," or indeed "non-discriminatory."

If in addition all alterities are equivalent, then the more I belong to the unmarked categories of a specific locale, the more I can choose among my many Others which ones to embrace and how to embrace them. Alterity is additionally convenient for me as an unmarked: I define it, I decide how to overcome it, and I alone decide that it has been defeated. Then I demand recognition for all of the above.

Numerous surveys on the progress of racial integration in the United States expose this convenience of the unmarked. Again and again, a majority of whites overestimate the income of blacks, their level of education, the closing of the gap between these and other socioeconomic indicators and those of whites. The mis-reading is not only sociological. With these underestimates also come feelings and beliefs that racial inequality is on the wane, that equality has been achieved, or that "we have done enough for them." At the opposite end, most blacks know that their situation—or that of those with whom they are associated—has not improved as much as thought by the unmarked. Not only do they not understand the feelings of satisfaction that comes with this tale of Otherness vanquished, their resentment increases toward those who broadcast this false news and want to take credit for it. One must insist that this disagreement is not only about sociological facts and their political interpretation, although sociology is its inescapable ground. Nor is the disagreement merely ideological, although racial ideology and mutual mistrust play a role. The moral aspect is defining: The unmarked are broadcasting a morality play in which *they* are the good guys. On the other side of alterity, the Others take moral offense at that fraud even more than they are disturbed by their own social dejection.

Lest we think of the United States as the sole locus of deception, we need only to turn to the equally numerous surveys—some more serious than others—that publicize the misunderstandings across gender lines especially—though not only—throughout the North Atlantic. Again and again, in the household and in the work place, males display their astonishment at claims of gender inequality, dis-crimination, or harassment while females are genuinely appalled that they should somehow be satisfied with the current situation. The scenario repeats itself with Arab immigrants and their immediate descendants in France, with Pakistani in England, with dark-skinned Cubans or Brazilians at home, or with women in many Middle Eastern countries that claim to have modernized. On the one hand, we hear versions of the "We have done everything we could," on the other, "You have done nothing." This "nothing" rarely indexes a sociological measurement. Rather, it expresses the moral rage of the Other at the convenience of the unmarked.

Restrictive identities.   While moral and political convenience defines the situation of the unmarked, the eulogy of alterity further restricts the margins of maneuver of both the token Other and the population that she supposedly represents. An even more perverse consequence of the eulogy of Otherness is the production of restrictive identities that give most Others few choices in defining themselves or in changing the terms of their relations with the unmarked. This production of restrictive identities for minorities is the flip side of the convenience of the unmarked.

Every time a *français de souche* (a white French citizen endowed with Frenchness since times immemorial) claims to have North African, black, or even Eastern European friends—and implicitly expects recognition for that deed—he also verifies his right to be both French—and therefore universal—yet open to diversity. This claim further locks the "friends" who become merely—at least for the moment—instances of Otherness and thus, by definition non-universal. Every time a corporate executive, a university dean, or a building owner in the United States, Canada, or Australia points to the number of "minorities in residence," he reinforces the symbolic power of the boundaries that created and reproduce these minorities. Most of these acts stem from genuine desires to reduce some of the most damaging gaps within and across populations. I have too many friends of all shades and definitions who agonize about these issues to doubt their sincerity. Yet with all due respect to these friendships, I am arguing without apology that good intentions often produce perverse results, and that in this particular case the reinforcement of restrictive identities is one such result. Often, the reinforcement of such identities is the only durable result of such acts.

Even more unfortunately, the minorities so defined further entrap themselves in these confining self-definitions. The attraction is understandable. How can one refuse to represent or defend the very group that supposedly makes us not only what but whom we are? How could one be blind to the inequalities of which one bears the mark? Yet the role comes with a price and the other side always sets that price. Sometimes that price is bearable—although never acceptable. In some cases the challenge is worth facing. But often that price includes an implicit or even explicit restriction: The Other is forbidden to claim expertise, control, or relevance outside of a Savage slot suddenly eulogized in ways that deny its universal potential. This separatist division of labor reaches its caricatured extremes on some North American campuses where black professors claim—or are afforded—a monopoly on "black" topics, gays a monopoly on homosexual themes, and women faculty a de facto veto on gender issues, unaware or unwilling to admit that the price for this monopoly is the inability to branch out and claim relevance outside of it. Praise for the occupants of the slot masks the fact that the territory is restricted and that a curfew has been set upon it. One understands the frustration of those conservative politicians who are most likely to protest against being someone else's minority in residence. But their solution, which implies a different denial of history and historicity, is no more acceptable. They are, indeed, someone's minority: The status is not theirs to choose or to reject. Restrictive identities are imposed from the outside.

The dilemma is thus quite real, especially for those whose identities are most restrictive. If they reject such identities, they become turncoats. If they turn them into badges of pride, they gain in self-respect but also confirm their classification into the Savage slot and further legitimize the symbolic restrictions imposed on them. The dilemma is no less real for those among the unmarked who seek the equality of the Other, since most solutions to date seem to go through at least a minimum reproduction of the divides they wish to erase. I am not sure that anyone can find a universally applicable formula, as its attractiveness may only hide other traps. Thus I am sympathetic to the argument, advanced by many states—most notably the French one—that racial categories in statistical data often help perpetuate negative images. Well-publicized statistics on crime rates among minorities in the United States confirm the worth of that argument. Yet I am also open to the argument that statistical data using ethnic or racial categories could increase the awareness of the French majority about the sociological inequalities that keep most French citizens of Caribbean, sub-Saharan, or North African descent from enjoying the privileges of being part of the republic, just as I do not want to dismiss the idea that the absence of detailed data on socioeconomic inequality across color lines in Brazil reinforced the Brazilian myth of color blindness. The dilemma—as it presents itself today—is truly unique to our times.

I suspect that the way out of this dilemma involves lifting off some of the rigid constraints imposed on the most restrictive identities, although I have no systematic plan on how those restrictions are best lifted. To get there, we need at least the collective will to establish more critical distance vis-à-vis the eulogy of Otherness. The point is not to avoid forcefully and publicly challenging racists and bigots of all kinds. We should challenge them. But in many ways that job is the easiest one. For although their discourse is often more potent and their political clout stronger than many naïve observers realize, that discourse is in many ways anachronistic: It does not define our times, hence the many contortions that public figures who espouse the most racist or exclusivist ideologies engage in to not lose their moral legitimacy. It takes more political courage to question publicly the blind eulogy of alterity, but such courage is much needed, especially since the equivalence of all alterities also help disguise the contortions I just mentioned. We also need more ethnographic studies of how restrictive identities are produced and reinforced by both the unmarked and the Others that they define. I am not taking the usual academic escape route that "we need more research." Rather in admitting that we need to flesh out how this dilemma is perceived by various individuals and groups at the level of lived experience, I am also admitting that, to a certain extent, we are all trapped by it.

The reproduction of the west. But we are trapped to a certain extent only. At the end of the day, some of us are still more trapped than others. Even among minorities, some identities are more restrictive than others. Some are more restrictive because the unmarked against whom they stand has greater reach and power as a default category. Gender matters here, but so do race and religion. Other identities are more restrictive because they are attached to populations that are more restricted in socioeconomic terms. The fault lines between them and their respective unmarked have such historical, social, and economic depths that their place in the geography of imagination closely parallels their position in the geography of management. Class matters here, and so do the inequalities between countries noted earlier.

Let us suppose that race and class tend to overlap for an individual or a specific group, that the fault lines of global inequality parallel those of race and religion for another, or that race and gender define a third. Then the material and symbolic restrictions noted above do not simply multiply with the number of fault lines. We see this most clearly at the individual level. To be Muslim and female in France is *not* to be a double minority. More often it is to be incapable of claiming whatever remains of the symbolic power of the two subaltern locations to which one belongs sociologically. One may find no refuge in Islam against Frenchness. Yet one may find even less comfort from Islam in French feminism. To be black and gay in the United States is to experience a symbolic restriction that most gays who are not black and most blacks who are not gay cannot begin to imagine, restrictions that make it harder not only to escape the identity so imposed but even to locate its actual position with strategic certainty. Some of James Baldwin's work, aspects of his life, as well as his declared need to physically escape the United States in order to just breathe make that point poignantly.

Keep in mind the poignancy of this vulnerability imposed on the individual by the overlap of restrictive identities. Keep in mind that a consequence of globalization is an increased economic inequality and that the knowledge of these inequalities itself is increasing worldwide. Recall that this grand scale division between the haves and the have-nots is happening at a time when grand narratives of development or Marxist-inspired narratives of revolution have lost their persuasiveness. Fewer human beings are convinced today than, say, in the 1960s that the whole of humanity is heading in the same direction. Now add to this the not so hidden fact that the greatest number of those who are thought to not be moving, not moving fast enough, or are condemned to never move are also those likely to be described as non-Westerners, whether or not they live—or were born—in North Atlantic countries. The result is a stunning renewal of the symbolic power of the West on the global stage. This renewed global power repairs and revitalizes the Savage slot and resonates in local arenas down to individual encounters.

The least restrictive identities are imposed on those Others whose status as Westerners is unquestioned and unquestionable, even though they may fall on the dominated side of a specific alterity (e.g., gender, sexual identity). Feminists of color, especially in the United States, have long made a similar point, although it has often been misread—and at times misstated—as a mere claim of belonging to multiple minorities. The closet of shame in which most gays once hid perversely makes that same point, as does their sizeable coming out in recent times in North Atlantic countries. So does their greater difficulty at coming out outside of the North Atlantic. The ability to define and affect the many choices and permutations just evoked is disproportionately shared by the universally unmarked, that is by a majority of these people whose status as Westerners is unquestioned and unquestionable. To simplify the argument by way of an easy yet poignant example: White gays in North Atlantic countries have a power to reproduce the markedness of blacks disproportional to the power of blacks over the markedness of sexual orientation. The eulogy of Otherness not only helps to reproduce the Savage slot, it also further reduces the power of the universalized Others and their capacity to get out of that slot.

***

Both the perception of powerlessness and the moral premium on difference exacerbate tensions and increase confusion within and across state boundaries. Both contribute to hiding what is actually new in this moment of world history. Both make it harder to understand the relations between the global and the local. As such, both are constitutive of the fragmented globality that marks our times.

This multilayered fragmentation is further increased by the growing inability of national states to function as uncontested cultural containers. Indeed, another distinguishing mark of our times and an increased source of confusion is the changing figure of the state, to which I turn in the next chapter.

Chapter 4

The Anthropology of the State in the Age of Globalization: Close Encounters of the Deceptive Kind

Sociocultural anthropology often arises from the banality of daily life. I will start this chapter with three banal stories.

In January of 1999, Mr. Amartya Sen, Nobel Laureate in economics, was stopped on his way to a conference in Davos, Switzerland, at the Zürich airport for entering Switzerland without a visa. Never mind that Mr. Sen was carrying credit cards, as well as his U.S. resident greencard. Never mind that he claimed that the organizers had promised him a visa to be delivered at the airport. North Americans and West Europeans can enter Switzerland without a visa, whether or not on their way to a conference. Mr. Sen, however, uses his Indian passport. The Swiss police were worried that he would become a dependent of the state, as Indians are likely to be. The irony of the story is that Mr. Sen was on his way to the World Economic Forum. The theme of the Forum that year was "Responsible Globality: Managing the Impact of Globalization."

Less funny but no less ironic is the story of the fourteen-year-old "Turk" who was sent *back* to Turkey by the government of Germany—when in fact he had never set foot in Turkey, having been born and raised in Germany. This was less funny, yet as banal, because similar occurrences are not exceptional. The French and U.S. governments routinely expel "aliens" whose school-age children are citizens by birth.

Less funny still was the encounter between one Turenne Deville and the U.S. government in the 1970s. At the news that the Immigration and Naturalization Service was to send him back to Haiti, Mr. Deville hanged himself in his prison cell. A tragic yet banal story, to the extent that Mr. Deville's suicide is no more dramatic than the wager of hundreds of Haitian refugees who continue to dive—both literally and figuratively—in the Florida seas, betting that they will beat the sharks, the waves, and the U.S. Coast Guard.

Are these encounters with the state? In all three cases, we see a government—or a government agency—telling people where they should or should not be. If, as James Scott (1998) among others argues, the placement of people, including their enforced sedentarization, is a major feature of statecraft, the encounters I just described do seem to be cases in which state power was yielded to enforce physical placement.

My three stories speak of borders, of the space between centralized governments with national territorial claims where encounters between individuals and state power are most visible. Yet millions of banal and not so banal encounters of the same kind also occur within national or regional boundaries: a car owner facing state emission laws in California; a family facing school language in Catalonia, India, or Belize; a couple dealing with a new pregnancy in China; a homeless person deciding where to sleep in San Francisco, Rio de Janeiro, or New York; a Palestinian in the Occupied Territories having to decide which line to cross and when; or a citizen of Singapore or Malaysia having to conform to prescribed behavior in a public building.

Behind the banality of these millions of encounters between individuals or groups and governments, we discover the depth of governmental presence in our lives, regardless of regimes and the particulars of the social formation. The opening statement of Ralph Miliband's (1969:1) opus on the state still rings true: "More than ever before men now live in the shadow of the state." One can even argue that the penal state has actually increased in size and reach in a number of countries since Miliband wrote—notably in the United States, with the increase of prison space and the routinization of the death penalty.

This, however, is only one side of the story. Indeed, while signs of the routinization of governmental presence in the lives of citizens abound everywhere, the turn of the twenty-first century also offers us images of governmental power challenged, diverted, or simply giving way to infra- or supra-national institutions. From Chiapas and Kosovo to Kigali and Trincomale, separatist movements have become increasingly vocal on all continents. On a different scale, a growing number of analysts suggest that globalization renders the state increasingly irrelevant, not only as an economic actor but also as a social and cultural container. They point to the significance of practices that reject or bypass national state power—such as the "new" social movements—or to the power of trans-state organizations from NGOs and global corporations to the World Bank and the International Monetary Fund as concrete signs of that relative decline.

Thus this century opens with two sets of contradictory images. The power of the national state sometimes seems more visible and encroaching, and yet sometimes less effective and less relevant. This chapter explores how anthropologists can make sense of that tension and fully incorporate it into our analysis of the state. To do so, we need to recognize three related propositions: 1) state power has no institutional fixity on theoretical or historical grounds; 2) Thus, state effects never obtain solely through national institutions or in governmental sites; and 3) these two features, inherent in the capitalist state, have been exacerbated by globalization. Globalization thus authenticates a particular approach to the anthropology of the state, one that allows for a dual emphasis on theory and ethnography.

If the state has no institutional or geographical fixity, its presence becomes more deceptive than otherwise thought, and we need to theorize the state beyond the empirically obvious. Yet this removal of empirical boundaries also means that the state becomes more open to ethnographic strategies that take its fluidity into account. I suggest such a strategy here, one that goes beyond governmental or national institutions to focus on the multiple sites where state processes and practices are recognizable through their effects. These state-effects include:

(1) *an isolation effect*, that is, the production of atomized individualized subjects molded and modeled for governance as part of an undifferentiated yet specific "public";
(2) *an identification effect*, that is, a realignment of the atomized subjectivities along collective lines within which individuals recognize themselves as the same;
(3) *a legibility effect*, that is, the production of both a language and a knowledge for governance, of theoretical and empirical tools that classify, serialize, and regulate collectivities, and of the collectivities so engendered;
(4) *a spatialization effect*, that is, the production of boundaries—both internal and external—of territories and jurisdiction.

This chapter is an exploratory formulation of that strategy.

Thinking the State

Exploratory though it may be, this exercise requires a conceptual baseline. We need to determine at what level(s) to best conceptualize the state. Is the state a concrete entity, something "out there"? Or is it a concept necessary to understand something out there? Or is it an ideology that helps to mask something *else* out there, a symbolic shield to power, as it were?

Unfortunately, sociocultural anthropologists have not given these questions the attention they deserve. In a major review of the anthropology of the state, Carole Nagengast (1994:116) wrote: "Insofar as anthropology has dealt with the state, it has taken it as an unanalyzed given." Interestingly, Nagengast's own treatment of the state in the context of her assessment does not attempt to turn this unanalyzed given into an object of study.[1] Indeed, is there an object to study?

The anthropologist A. R. Radcliffe-Brown answers this question with a resounding "no" that should give us food for thought even if we disagree with its extremism. Introducing Meyer Fortes's *African Political Systems* in 1940, Radcliffe-Brown wrote:

> In writings on political institutions there is a good deal of discussion about the nature and origin of the State, which is usually represented as being an entity over and above the human individuals who make up a society, having as one of its attributes something called "sovereignty," and sometimes spoken of as having a will (law being defined as the will of the State) or as issuing commands. The State in this sense does not exist in the phenomenal world; it is a fiction of the philosophers. What does exist is an organization, i.e. a collection of individual human beings connected by a complex system of relations... There is no such thing as the power of the State...
> (1955 [1940]: xxiii).

One could call this death by conceptualization inasmuch as Radcliffe-Brown conceptualizes the state into oblivion.

To be sure, that answer carries the added weight of both empiricism and methodological individualism. Yet Radcliffe-Brown is not simply saying that "army" is merely the plural for "soldiers." Nor is he saying that the state does not exist because we cannot touch it. Governmental organizations have different levels of complexity even if for sake of functionality, when not for the sake of functionalism. Thus, a generous reading of Radcliffe-Brown, which would prune out the added philosophical baggage of his school and times, still leaves us with a powerful answer. The state is neither something out there nor a necessary concept. Each and every time we use the word, words such as "government" would do the conceptual job, and they would do it better.

I do not agree with that answer, as I hope to make clear. However, it seems to me that anthropologists cannot continue to ignore it. Radcliffe-Brown's answer to the state question contains a warning that anthropologists should keep in mind. Since the state can never be an empirical given, even at the second degree (the way, say, particular governments can be thought to be), where and how does anthropology encounter the state, if at all? What can be the terms of our analytical encounter with the state? What can we possibly mean, for instance, by an ethnography of the state?

In an important article, written in 1977, Philip Abrams revives Radcliffe-Brown's warnings. Abrams provides a sophisticated demonstration of the reasons to reject the existence of the state as an entity and he raises some serious doubts about the analytical purchase of the state concept. He writes (1988:76): "The state ... is not an object akin to the human ear. Nor is it even an object akin to human marriage. It is a third-order object, an ideological project. It is first and foremost an exercise in legitimation. ... The state, in sum, is a bid to elicit support for or tolerance of the insupportable and intolerable by presenting them as something other than themselves, namely, legitimate, disinterested domination."

Contrary to Radcliffe-Brown, Abrams admits an object for state studies: the very process of power legitimation that projects the image of an allegedly disinterested entity, "the state-idea."[2] As stated, Abrams's "state-idea" is not immediately conducive to ethnography but it does provide a warning that balances Radcliffe-Brown. Something happens out there that is more than government. The question is what.

Theorists have provided different answers to that question that I will not survey here. For the purposes of this discussion, let me only say that my own evolving view of the state starts with the "enlarged" notion of the state first put forward by Antonio Gramsci. I also find extremely fruitful Nicos Poulantzas's reworking of Marx and Gramsci. I continue to gain also from various writers such as Ralph Miliband (1969), Louis Althusser (1971 [1969]), Paul Thomas (1994), James Scott (1998), and Étienne Balibar (1997).[3] All this is to say that I do not claim to provide an original conceptualization. Rather, I hope to make a contribution to an ongoing dialogue with an eye to the kind of research best performed by sociocultural anthropologists (see also Trouillot 1997).

Most of the writers I have mentioned insist that the state is not reducible to government. In Miliband's (1969:49) words, "what 'the state' stands for is a number of particular institutions which, together, constitute its reality, and which interact as part of what may be called the state system." Miliband's overly socio-logical treatment of that system needs to be backed by Poulantzas's and Gramsci's more elaborate conceptualizations of the state as a privileged site of both power and struggle. Gramsci's insistence on thinking state and civil society together by way of concepts such as hegemony and historical bloc is fundamental to this approach. I read Gramsci as saying that within the context of capitalism, theories of the state must cover the entire social formation and articulate the relation between state and civil society. One cannot theorize the state and then theorize society or vice versa. Rather, state and society are bound by the historical bloc that takes the form of the specific social contract of—and thus, the hegemony deployed in—a particular social formation. "A social contract is the confirmation of nationhood, the confirmation of civil society by the state, the confirmation of sameness and interdependence across class boundaries" (Trouillot 1997:51). Yet even that phrasing needs to be qualified lest it seem to reinforce the nineteenth-century homology of state and nation.

As institutionalized in degree-granting departments in a context where faith in progress was unquestioned, nineteenth-century social science built its categories on the assumption that the world in which it was born was not only the present of a linear past but the augur of an ordained future. For most of its practitioners, the world may not have been eternal but the referents to the categories—if not the categories themselves—used to describe that world were eternal. Nineteenth-century social science generally assumed the ontological fixity of the boundaries it observed. State boundaries were prominent among those. They provided the natural frameworks within which the processes studied by social scientists occurred (Wallerstein et al. 1996:80). In its simplest form, their methodological assumption, shared equally by literary scholars, ran along the following lines: France was obviously a nation-state. It had, therefore, a single economy, a single history, and a single social life, all of which could be studied by the appropriate discipline, all of which were also fundamentally circumscribed within the distinct political territory called France.

Thus the conflation of state and nation was naturalized because it seemed so obvious within that present—evidence to the contrary notwithstanding. But what if the correspondence between statehood and nationhood, exemplified by the claimed history of the North Atlantic and naturalized by its social science, was itself histori-cal?[4] Indeed, there are no theoretical grounds on which to assert the necessity of that correspondence, and there are some historical grounds for questioning it.

If we suspend the state-nation homology as I suggest we should, we reach a more powerful vision of the state, yet one more open to ethnography, since we discover that, theoretically, there is no necessary site to the state, institutional or geographical. Within that vision, the state thus appears as an open field with mul-tiple boundaries and no institutional fixity—which is to say, it needs to be con-ceptualized at more than one level. Though linked to a number of apparatuses, not all of which may be governmental, the state is not an apparatus but a set of processes. It is not necessarily bound by any institution, nor can any institution fully encapsulate it. At that level, its materiality resides much less in institutions than in the reworking of processes and relations of power so as to create new spaces for the deployment of power. As I put it elsewhere (Trouillot 1990:19): "At one level the division between state and civil society has to do with content.... At another level it has to do with methodology in the broad sense." The consequences of that position are crucial to the understanding of the changes that define our times.

Changing Containers

The idea that the state was a natural container—and indeed, the only legitimate one—of populations and of their defining practices was first proposed in most vigorous terms by the government of the Franks under Francis I. Though absolutist France tried to put this idea in practice through the forceful Frenchicization of the hexagon from Francis I to Louis XIV to the Revolution, its success was only partial. Linguistic history alone makes the point: The language of Isle de France, which later evolved into modern standard French, was not the mother tongue of the majority of French citizens at the time of the French Revolution (Calvet 1974:166). It took a little Corsican man whose first language was not French—and who was born less than a year after the French army took control of his island—to fully nationalize the French state. It also took, of course, the political and cultural hegemony of the French bourgeoisie.

The lesson is clear: The conflation of state and nation is a process that requires time, constant intervention, and much political power. The Napoleonic reforms of French institutions and their successive corrections up to World War II came close to achieving the dream of a somewhat culturally unified France. But even then, reality introduced its inevitable discrepancies. In his autobiographical writings, 1947 Nobel laureate André Gide (1929), who was raised as a Protestant in that most Catholic country, recalls his own multilingual childhood and his own lack of national roots. He threw this absence of ruins as a badge of honor in his famous response to right-wing nationalist Maurice Barrès, whose novel *Les Déracinés* (1897) called for a new appraisal of French roots.[5] Still, one can argue that nineteenth-century bourgeois governments were more able to enforce—and nineteenth-century bourgeois societies more willing to accept—the idea of the state as a natural container. Indeed, in an amazingly short time the naturalization of the nation-state has become one of the most powerful and pervasive fictions of modernity, an essential part of the North Atlantic narratives of world history.

The problem with this narrative today is that it has become suddenly less persuasive, though we are not entirely sure what, if anything, should replace it. Changes in the functions and boundaries of national states generate confusion even among social scientists in part because globalization now produces spatialities—and identities—that cut through national boundaries more obviously than before, and in part because the social sciences have tended to take these very same boundaries for granted. Social scientists argue about the declining relevance of the state, politicians and activists debate about the extent to which the state should be multicultural, and reactionaries all over the North Atlantic vociferate about the need to secure their borders from unwanted immigrants.

The pattern should now be familiar: it echoes others exposed throughout this book. An idea first proposed in forceful yet indistinct terms by the European Renaissance becomes quickly institutionalized by the nineteenth century, and with that institutionalization gains the power of a necessary universal, only to be questioned by the changing experiences that singularize our times.

My proposed solution should also be familiar. First, we need to take distance from the nineteenth century and reject the restrictive terms under which it framed the legacies of the Renaissance. We are best equipped to assess the changes that typify our times if we approach these changes with a sober awareness that the national state was never as closed and as unavoidable a container—economically, politically, or culturally—as politicians and academics have claimed since the nineteenth century. Once we see the necessity of the national state as a lived fiction of late modernity—indeed, as possibly a short parenthesis in human history—we may be less surprised by the changes we now face and may be able to respond to them with the intellectual imagination they deserve.[6]

Second, we need to reject the temptation to search for a unique linear trend that would account for all the changes that mark our times, the temptation to suggest that states everywhere are gaining or losing power in the same way and at the same time. Claims of the declining relevance of the state along globalitarist lines are at best premature, if only because they presume such a continuum.

There are other problems with various assertions about the growing irrelevance of states. First, they often rest on an illusion of the political as an analytically distinct sphere, a proposition questioned long ago by Talcott Parsons (1951:126ff.) and explicitly rejected by most of the state theorists I have used here, notably Gramsci. A second theoretical slip is the illusion that states are equivalent to governments. Since many of the kinds of intervention traditionally thought to be within the purview of governments are not as easily achieved or simply impossible today, globalitarists conclude that the state has declined. A third theoretical rejoinder to the declining relevance thesis is that the state and the international system of states—without which each state is, in turn, unthinkable—are necessary conditions of possibility for globalization.

In reality, globalization is not theoretically or historically conceivable without a number of strong states and, most especially, without a strong international state system and constant state intervention. Whether we date the new freedom afforded to finance capital to the termination of the Bretton Woods system by the United States in 1971, or to the deregulations imposed by the Reagan and Thatcher governments in the 1980s, the economic landscape of globalization is the fruit of a number of governmental decisions systematically calibrated to produce a terrain most favorable to finance capital. In two decades, North Atlantic governments led by the United States and the United Kingdom broke down the centuries-old institutions that regulated the operations of finance capital (Labarde and Maris 1998:100–5). If politics appears irrelevant today, the state of affairs that brought on this irrelevance was the product of concerted political decisions.

This state of affairs—where states are supposedly irrelevant—is maintained through the background presence and the constant interventions of very powerful states that help maintain the interstate system. Never before have states punished other states so often and so systematically through economic sanctions and embargos than in this era of alleged state irrelevance. Yet while embargos, however routine, could be explained away as anomalies of the system, the freedom of finance capital—the backbone of the system—can be guaranteed only by the military power of the strongest states and by the recognized rules of the interstate system. Corporations that move freely across political borders do so because they rely on state protection within these borders. Without that political—and military—protection, the freedom of economics vanishes in thin air. The proper behavior of each individual state relies upon the enforcement power of the international state system. In practice as in theory, in historical as well as in structural terms, globalization is a political phenomenon inconceivable without state intervention.

As suggested in chapter 3, ours are times of dislocation, polarization, and fragmentation. It is against the background of this fragmented globality that we can best evaluate changes in the effectiveness of the national state as a primary site for economic exchange, political struggle, or cultural negotiation. These changes cannot be measured quantitatively on a singular scale. Even if we were to reduce states to governments, a quick comparison of Iran, Mexico, India, France, Iraq, and the United Sates within and across their recognized borders suggests that one cannot measure governmental power on a continuum. The changes that typify our times are not unilinear, but multiple, and as I suggested earlier, sometimes contradictory (Comaroff and Comaroff 2000). I will note only a few among the most significant ones.

First, and directly related to globalization as defined here, the domains of intervention of national governments are rapidly changing. Caution is necessary lest we exaggerate our empirical markers. Private companies and individuals have often exercised what boils down to state power or taken over state functions since at least the fifteenth century. I already mentioned the transnational power of Amsterdam merchants who towered above most European kings in the seventeenth and eighteenth centuries (see chapter 2). Long before that, in 1453, the town of Genoa had turned over political and administrative control of the island of Corsica to the bank of Saint George, a commercial and financial firm. Much later, in 1892, the postmaster of the United States, acting as a private citizen-broker, bought the entire foreign debt of the Dominican Republic. Between these dates we could find many such examples.

A central difference today is the extent to which a dominant global discourse pushes governments all over the world to relinquish domains of interventions that in the nineteenth century and most of the twentieth had been firmly established as state-controlled. This new construction of state powerlessness relative to private efficiency—which one must insist is a political choice—eases the transfer of jurisdictions and responsibilities.

Second, and quite important for sociocultural anthropologists, national states now perform less well as ideological and cultural containers, especially—but not only—in the North Atlantic. Third, new processes and practices that seem to reject or bypass the state-form—such as the new social movements—creep into the interstices so opened. Fourth, state-like processes and practices also increasingly obtain in nongovernmental sites such as NGOs or trans-state institutions such as the World Bank. These practices in turn produce state-effects as powerful as those of national governments.

To complicate matters, none of this means that national governments have stopped intervening in economic or other walks of life. The number of sovereign states has more than quadrupled between 1945 and the end of the last century. But the kinds of intervention national governments perform have changed—at times considerably. As Terry Turner (2002) acutely notes, we can see in retrospect that since the end of World War II military intervention within the North Atlantic has become obsolete as the means to capture the leadership of the capitalist world economy.[7] More recently, changes in the composition and spatialization of capital have rendered government interventions in international commerce both less necessary and less effective.[8]

Most crucial for sociocultural anthropologists, the national state no longer functions as the uncontested social, political, and ideological container of the populations living within its borders. To be sure, it was never as solid a container as we were told to believe. However, in the North Atlantic at least, and to a lesser extent in the American states that saw the first wave of decolonization, it often secured the outer limits of political struggle, economic exchange, and cultural negotiation. Their performance notwithstanding, national governments were often expected—and often pretended—to act as cultural containers. Now neither citizens nor governmental leaders expect the state to play that role effectively.[9]

That is due in part to governments' inability (especially in the South) or unwillingness (especially in the North Atlantic) to deal with the increased inequality ushered in by globalization and, more importantly, to deal with the citizenry's perception of that mixture of inability and unwillingness. That is due also to the increased inability of national governments, from Iran and China to France and the United States, to play a leadership role in the shaping of cultural practices, models, and ideals. Almost everywhere both the correspondence between the state system and what Louis Althusser (1971) calls the "ideological state apparatuses" have declined as these apparatuses increasingly reflect rather than deflect locally lived social tensions, notably those of race and class.[10] The fiction of isolated national entities built by nineteenth-century politicians and scholars no longer fits the lived experiences of most populations.

Cracks in the fiction appeared soon after World War II. In the North Atlantic, the declining relevance of war as the path to global economic leadership also meant a decline in the use and effectiveness of nationalist rhetoric—partly masked and delayed, especially in the United States, by the existence of the Soviet bloc. The deep tremors experienced in Africa and Asia during the second wave of decolonization[11] augured badly for presumed national homogeneity. Where and how to delineate the borders of new African and Asian polities proved often enough to be an unforeseen predicament. Partition by decree, in cases as varied as India-Pakistan, Israel-Palestine, and French and German Togo, exposed the artificiality and the use of power inherent in border-making practices. Cases such as Algeria's *pieds noirs* suggested that even the distinction between home and elsewhere was not as easy as once thought.

From the 1950s to the 1990s, the Cold War, in spite of its rhetoric, also brought home the relevance of events happening in other regions of the globe. In North

America, Vietnam—and later the taking of hostages in Teheran—played a key role in ushering in that understanding. In the 1970s and 1980s citizens throughout the North Atlantic discovered their partial dependency on foreign imports after most OPEC countries assumed ownership of their oil fields.

One can safely suggest, however, that geopolitical and economic changes on the world scene were less crucial in breaking the fiction of impermeable entities than the manner in which those changes have affected the daily lives of common citizens in the North Atlantic since the 1970s. To give but one example, the objective degree of U.S. involvement in Indochina in the 1960s was arguably less than that of Spain in seventeenth-century Mexico, that of France in eighteenth-century Saint-Domingue/Haiti, or that of Britain in nineteenth-century India. That involvement might not have contributed to changing North Americans' imagination if not for the fact that television made the Vietnam War a daily occurrence in their homes, just as television would later make the Iran-U.S. confrontation a matter of nightly routine. Even more than television, refugees knocking at the door, new patterns of immigration, and the reconfiguration of the ethnic and cultural landscape in major North Atlantic cities brought the elsewhere to the home front. The speed and mass of global flows—including the flow of populations deemed to be different and often claiming that difference while insisting on acceptance—profoundly undermined the notion of bound entities, and not just on an abstract level. The barbarians were at the door, which was bad enough; but they were also claiming that "our" home could be theirs.

North Atlantic natives both rejected and accommodated that daily presence. Segregationist practices notwithstanding, the commodification of exotic customs and products, from Zen and yoga to Mao shirts and dashikis, facilitated a guarded cultural acceptance. Food played a major role in that process. "Korean" vegetable shops in the United States and "Arab" groceries in France provided needed services. A wave of "ethnic" restaurants swamped Paris, London, Amsterdam, and New York beginning in the 1970s and now brings couscous, curry, or sushi to inland cities once thought impermeable to Third World cultural imports. The daily presence of the Other, mediatized, commodified, tightly controlled, yet seemingly unavoidable—as Other—on the screen or on the street is a major trope of globalitarist ideology. That trope functions at least in part because it illustrates for local populations the growing difficulties of the national state functioning as container even within the North Atlantic. There are plenty of other such tropes. The consolidation of "ethnic" votes in the United States is among the most blatant.

Lest the argument be misunderstood, let me reiterate that it does not adhere to the dominant theses of the declining relevance of the state. I fully agree that the European Union makes sense only against the background of national states that remain as powerful as ever. Their surrender of part of their traditional power to the construction of Europe also allows them to increase their reach at home. I also agree that in many areas of the world, from Eastern Europe to South Asia and the Caribbean, states cling ever more to their role in defining citizenship and the ethnic or cultural content of that citizenship. Assessing Benedict Anderson's influential work (1983), I suggested over a decade ago that the nation is not an imagined political community but an imagined community projected against politics, more specifically against state power (Trouillot 1990:25–26). Thus, I do not think that national states have become irrelevant as containers for the English or the French—the opposed poles of the Union—or as projects for Palestinians, Kashmiris, Kurds, Nevisians, Basques, Martinicans, Puerto Ricans, Corsicans, or Gypsies, to cite only a few. National liberation movements of all kinds remind us of the potency of the appeal. That they are now often labeled "separatist" also reminds us that this appeal is based on a North Atlantic fiction that became universal, albeit one for which we do not yet have an alternative. We do not need to formulate a specific alternative in order to acknowledge the fact that both the efficiency of these containers and the desirability of these projects now face qualitatively new obstacles. On the contrary, the more we acknowledge the contradictions that mark our times, the better we can pierce through its fragmented globality and the more likely we are to find imaginative solutions to the dilemmas that differentiate us from previous eras.

For An Ethnography of the State

None of the above means the declining relevance of the state, if by state we mean more than the apparatus of national governments. If the state is a set of practices and processes and the effects they produce as much as a way to look at them, we need to track down these practices, processes, and effects whether or not they coalesce around the central sites of national governments. In the age of globalization state practices, functions and effects increasingly obtain in sites other than the national but that never fully bypass the national order. The challenge for anthropologists is to study these practices, functions and effects without prejudice about sites or forms of encounters. I will note the possibilities of that approach by sketching further the state effects mentioned at the beginning of this chapter as ground for an ethnography of the state.

Nicos Poulantzas (1972) identified what he called the "isolation effect"—which I read as the production of a particular kind of subject as atomized member of a public—as a key feature of statecraft. Through the isolation of socio-economic conflicts, notably class divisions, the state guarantees not only its own relative autonomy vis-à-vis dominant classes, but also produces atomized, individualized citizens who all appear to be equal within a supposedly undifferentiated public sphere. Modern states produce subjects whose consciousness and agency it channels through restrictive individual forms. Ultimately the individual is isolated—alone in the voting booth, in the tribunal, or in the tax collector's office—and theoretically equal to all such individuals. Thus the isolation effect separates individuals from the very social history that produced them as distinct individuals in the first place.

In many societies today, the national public sphere is fractured differently than when Poulantzas wrote. At the same time, the relative rise of judicial power in almost all North Atlantic countries suggests that individual atomization is going on while mechanisms of homogenization also take new forms. Identity politics notably signals new configurations of the citizenry. Rising notions of universal human rights and the global spread of North Atlantic legal philosophy and practices produce isolation effects, in both the North and South, and at times with the backing of national governments or with the still timid support of transnational state-like institutions. The isolation effect—including the masking of class divisions, the joint production of a public, and the atomized subjects that comprise it—still obtains, but the processes and practices—and hence the power—that produce it are being deployed in unexpected sites.

Following Poulantzas's approach and terminology, we can identify a number of state-effects on which he did not insist by name. To the isolation effect we can add, as suggested earlier, an identification effect, a legibility effect, and a spatialization effect. In all these cases we observe a *déplacement* of state functions, a move away from the state-system as described by Miliband, or even from the state apparatuses described by Althusser. State power is being redeployed, state effects appear in new sites, and in almost all cases this move is one away from national sites to infra-, supra-, or trans-national ones. An ethnography of the state can and should capture these effects in these changing sites.

We may call "identification effect" that capacity to develop a shared conviction that "we are in the same boat" and therefore to interpolate subjects as homogenous members of various imagined communities (Balibar 1997; Poulantzas 1972; Scott 1998; Trouillot 1997). This homogenizing process, once thought a fundamental purview of the national state, is now shared by the national state and a number of competing sites and processes including region, gender, race, and ethnicity. Identity politics helps redefine the national for better and—often—for worse. The so-called "new" social movements also have become sites for accumulating, redirecting, or deploying social and political power that often tries to bypass or challenge national states, albeit with limited success.[12] Many are both parochial and global, with multiple boundaries.[13] Few—not even the U.S. Michigan militia—see national borders as the sole line of demarcation for their activities.

The national state also produces what I call a "legibility effect," following James Scott's (1998) development on legibility practices. The tools that enable government planning, practices ranging from the production of a language and a knowledge for governance to the elaboration of theoretical and empirical tools that classify and regulate collectivities, produce such effects. From income or age groups to voting districts, governments measure populations in serialized units that gain a life of their own through these enforced divisions and in the process become manageable targets of state power. However, as Scott himself suggests, governments are not the only actors who "see like a state." In the South notably, NGOs and trans-state institutions from the World Bank to the IMF now act in this way—at times better than states themselves—and produce similar if not more potent legibility effects. UNESCO or ILO statistics are more reliable than those of quite a few national governments. NGOs' capacity to plan effectively at the local and regional level all over the South, and the World Bank and the IMF's power to envision and promote everywhere a future based on their assessment—however questionable—of the present, have moved a number of state practices away from the national. For better and for worse, these are all, analytically, state-like institutions.

Since most state effects can be captured in part through the subjects they contribute toward producing, ethnographers are well poised to follow this worldwide *déplacement* of state functions and practices. Part of the difficulty of studying the state today stems from a single-track methodology that followed the trail of state practices, which were assumed to be immediately observable as such, from government institutions to civil populations. In a context where institutions are increasingly not acting as expected, this single-track methodology leads either to impasses or to the rediscovery of the obvious. By focusing on state effects through the lived experience of subjects, we can build an ethnography of the state up from the ground. We can discover when and how some of these effects obtain, their conditions of production, and their limits.

To give one manifest example, we are well equipped to follow NGOs "on the ground," to evaluate their capacity to interpolate specific populations and the conscious acceptance or rejection of that interpellation. Kamran Ali's ethnography of a family planning campaign in Egypt—which involves USAID, internationally funded NGOs and the national government—suggests that one of the potential outcomes of the campaign is the production of newly atomized "modern" subjects (Ali 1996, 2000). I read Ali as saying that nongovernmental and governmental practices combine today in the production of quite new yet quite "Egyptian" citizens. Similarly, NGOs attempting to reform "street children" in Mexico City are also producing new yet Mexican subjects, with different mixtures of accommodation and resistance on the part of the citizenry so shaped (Magazine 1999). The extent to which emerging subjects recognize the state-like nature of nongovernmental organizations and other institutions vary, but there are indications that the awareness of their roles is increasing. Beatrice Pouligny (personal communication) reports that some Haitians say in reference to NGOs: "*yo fè leta*" (literally, "they make the state"). In the Haitian language (where the word *leta* can mean "state" or "bully"), the phrase suggests that at least some citizens see NGOs as a site of power equal to and capable of challenging the state, but also as potential bullies.[14]

NGOs are only the most obvious cases begging for an ethnography of state effects. We need to note, however, that they fit within a more general movement of privatization of state functions (e.g., Hibou 1999; Gill 2001) of which the rise of privately run prisons, the proliferation of private armies in Africa and Latin America, and the privatization of public enterprises worldwide are other evident manifestations. Only careful ethnographies will tell us the extent to which these— or other less visible emergent manifestations—produce state effects.

Postcolonial Chaos

Ethnographies of state effects—as registered in the lived experience of subjects— are most urgent in postcolonial societies. There national institutions never produced such effects as successfully as in most industrialized countries, and the *déplacement* produced by globalization encounters much less resistance. Unfortunately, the common knowledge that independent states emerged in the periphery of the world economy as replacements of colonial polities has not generated the much needed debate about either their specificity or that of the colonial state itself (but see Alavi et al. 1982; Comaroff 1997; Coronil 1997; Trouillot

1990). Not only does the postcolonial state bear many colonial scars, it also developed characteristics of its own that make the encounter with the forces of globalization significantly different than that of the North Atlantic. Drawing on my previous work on the postcolonial state (Trouillot 1990), I will note some of the features that deserve closest attention today and prompt ethnographies that do not rely on the obviousness of national institutions.

Given their insertion into the interstate system upon which they depend for their viability, their reproduction, and their capacity to claim jurisdiction, all states are to some extent outward looking. Isolation imposed from the outside or isolationist rhetoric generated from within barely attenuate this centrifugality, but throughout the North Atlantic outside connections, indispensable as they may be, provide the necessary background against which state effects obtain at home by way of local institutions. By contrast, in the periphery the centrifugal forces inherent in political and economic dependency gather enough strength to significantly challenge the centripetal direction of the state. Peripheral polities are not only outward looking, their home priorities can be set and achieved only in light of the country's subaltern position in the world economy and the interstate system. Dependency sets the peripheral state apart from industrialized countries.

In many postcolonial societies the disjuncture between state and nation, often masked with partial success in the North Atlantic, expands to such an extent that it may become a feature of daily life (Trouillot 1990). The fiction of homogeneous entities never obtained in the South or Eastern Europe. The peripheral state never produced an identification effect as competently as did the state in France, Britain, Germany, or the United States. Just like dependency, this greater disjuncture between state and nation predates political independence. In an important essay on the specificity of the colonial state, John Comaroff (1997:15) notes that unlike European polities, "colonies were never places of even tenuously-imagined homogeneity." In the postcolonies successive governments not only had to impose homogeneity through violence, as they did for centuries in Italy, France, Germany, and the United Kingdom, they had to do so with fewer resources and much less time to reap the expected results. Success was rare and many nationalist governments saw their homogenizing projects meet armed resistance. Given the stakes, others did not even try, contenting themselves to rule over national patches.

The uneasy interface between state and nation in the periphery is tied to a similar discrepancy between political and economic power, exacerbating features inherent in the deployment of state power. Contrary to the most simplistic analyses of orthodox Marxism, state power is never synonymous with class domination (Trouillot 1990:27). In the periphery, where dominant classes tend to be those with the strongest ties with international capital and most open to foreign influence, state power and—consequently—the legitimacy of national governments require a deepening of that distance. The nationalist stance became a necessary feature of state politics, the guarantee of a small room to maneuver for most political leaders vis-à-vis the dominant classes, the ultimate justification of political independence. Nationalist populism often emerged as the mixture that best combined the individual aspirations of local leaders and the multiple reactions of various parts of the citizenry with the visibility of economic dependency.

Given the limits of this populism, its inability to modify either the class structure at home or the structures of dependency within the world economy, it often blossomed around messianic figures. From Nehru's India and Peron's Argentina to Aristide's Haiti, the Third World has produced a spectacular range of messianic figures whose popularity at home was matched only by their relative powerlessness vis-à-vis the structures of dependency.

Globalization, as defined here, has changed the rules of the game to such an extent that the nationalist stance is increasingly harder to maintain, especially in populist and messianic forms. First, flexible production and the domination of finance capital have increased the economic dependency, the overt prominence of which is now part of the political landscape. IMF officials give direct and public orders to many heads of peripheral states whose messianism now looks like an empty pose. Meanwhile, many among the middle classes abandon the symbols of a cultural nationalism of which they were, until the second half of the twentieth century, the most resilient advocates.

Second, Third World messianism always stood in a symbiotic relationship with North Atlantic utopias. Political messiahs promised or were expected to uplift their nations, to devise a magical leap that would help their people either bypass the hurdles imposed by North Atlantic modernization, or reach their own home-made versions of modernity. In either case, these prognoses and promises relied implicitly on North Atlantic visions of progress and utopia, even if only as counterpoints to a homemade future. They always assumed a linearity to world history, whether it was to be joined, broken, or bypassed. With the crumbling of North Atlantic utopias, Third World messianisms lose the ability to harness state power through a prophetic drive because they lack a universalist narrative against which their prophecies make sense as visions of an alternative future.[15]

Today, the identification effect—the production of subjects who recognize themselves as part of overlapping collectivities, nationality remaining the dominant one for about a century—increasingly escapes the purview of the peripheral state. The fragmentation that accompanies globalization further saps the legitimacy of that state and reduces the impact of nationalist discourse on the routine of daily life. Outside of events deemed exceptional (such as armed conflicts with a traditional foreign enemy), individuals in the postcolony are ever more likely to identify with an ethnic or linguistic group, a religion, a sect, a political movement, or even a village or a gang, than to cling to a national identity that claims to encompass all citizens equally yet provokes no representative spark in their political imaginary. It is also less likely that the main leaders of such gangs, sects, or movements with which individuals identify will gain state power in their own name, or if they do, that they will gain legitimacy in the interstate system. Some of the religious groups that now provide powerful interpellations to a fragmented citizenry—from the Falong Gong in China to U.S.-based evangelical sects in Latin America and the Caribbean—claim to have no interest in direct political power. These claims may change as their numbers grow. Regardless, with separatist, ethnic, and factional tensions feeding on and reproducing national fragmentation, the probability of internecine conflicts increases within countries outside of the North Atlantic. So does the probability of border conflicts that help cover, albeit temporarily, the internal weaknesses of the state. Globalization has made explicit a congenital weakness of the peripheral state: its inherent difficulty in producing identification effects. Ethnographies centering on the lived experience of subjects will have to demonstrate when such effects are produced, through what institutional clusters, and explore the consequences of this *déplacement*. As this discussion suggests, the political stakes are high enough to warrant such research. So are the intellectual ones.

The weakening of the peripheral state—most obvious in the identification of subjects—reproduces itself with regards to all the effects highlighted in this chapter. I have already mentioned the increased power of NGOs, of trans- and supranational institutions in producing both the isolation and the legibility state-effects in peripheral societies. International organizations, private or state-sponsored, now help to fashion throughout the periphery an incipient public sphere that expands beyond national confines. For better and for worse, this new arena incorporates North Atlantic dominant tropes from the language of the ecological movement and the discourse on individual human rights to the rhetoric of ethnic or racial preferences. The knowledge necessary for the management of local populations in the postcolony increasingly accumulates in foreign hands, both private and state-sponsored. Such recent developments only confirm the need for detailed ethnographies that document the extent of the *déplacement* and reveal whether or not it entails the production of fundamentally new subjects and fundamental changes in the reach and potency of state power.

Are national governments in the postcolony obsolete reminders of fictitious histories? Are they everywhere mere survivals from times gone by? Or are they left only to watch borders—and ineffectively at that? The three stories with which I started this chapter suggest that government still performs a gate-keeping role.[16] Regardless of the relative effectiveness of governments at border patrol, the national state still produces—and quite effectively among most populations—a spatialization effect. Citizens all over the world may be less likely to buy the slogan that all nationals are in the same boat, but they remain aware that "we" (however defined) do live in a place usually defined in part by a political border.

While the spatialization effect may also be produced in other sites, national governments are less likely to let go of their power in this domain. With the spectacular exception of the European Union—a truly innovative and changing formation, of which we cannot even guess the long-term political consequences inside or outside of Europe—national states are likely to retain their power to define political boundaries. First, in a context marked by the obvious incapacity of national states to function as cultural containers the protection of borders becomes an easy political fiction with which to enlist support from a confused citizenry. Second, the right to define boundaries remains a fundamental component of sovereignty to which national governments must cling in an age where many state functions obtain elsewhere. To put it bluntly, national states produce countries and countries remain fundamentally spatial. Globalization itself produces inequalities that are also fundamentally spatial. The economic prospects of most individuals, their access to health, to education, their life expectancy, their very ability to express themselves both as individuals and as citizens, depend primarily on the country within which they reside. Hence it is quite understandable that emigration has become a favored venue of individual improvement. As befits our speculative age, the world economy has taught most individuals the three rules of real estate: location, location, location. Yet most human beings continue to act locally most of the time, even though many claim to think globally. One of anthropology's many challenges for this century may be to pay deserved attention to the tensions inherent in that contradiction.

The respatialization of various state-functions and effects occurs today in a context already marked by the differential respatialization of markets. These incongruent spatialities inevitably produce tensions in the location of state power and in citizens' perception of and reaction to its deployment. An anthropology of the state may have to make these tensions a primary focus of its research agenda. These tensions will be found not only in organized politics but also in the many practices through which citizens encounter not only governments, but also a myriad of other state-like institutions and processes that interpolate them as individuals and as members of various communities. Anthropology may not find the state ready-made and waiting for our ethnographic gaze in the known sites of national government. Government institutions and practices are to be studied, of course, and we can deplore that anthropology has not contributed enough to their study. However, anthropologists are best suited to study the state from below through ethnographies that center on the subjects produced by state effects and processes. We may have to look for these processes and effects in sites less obvious than those of institutionalized politics and established bureaucracies. We may have to insist on encounters not immediately transparent, and we must further insist that our colleagues in other disciplines recognize their importance. We may indeed have to revert to the seemingly timeless banality of daily life.

Coda

This banality is a matter of perspective. As all perspectives, it is revelatory only under certain circumstances. As we move closer to matters of ethnography and to methodological issues, we may want to pause and make more explicit some of the lessons learned in this exploration of the state.

The critical reading of both Radcliffe-Brown and Abrams, among others, should warn us that concepts are neither words nor definitions; they are not terms that can be simply replaced by a more or less equivalent gloss. Government and state may or may not be interchangeable words. But to decide that they are not—as I have argued—depends on one's conceptualization, on a particular theoretical construction of the object of study. Whether or not we agree with the various and overlapping conceptualizations of the state put forward by Gramsci, Poulantzas, Abrams, or others—the virtues of which I have tried to integrate—we can agree that these virtues boil down to framing the object of study in ways that open it to investigation—notably, but not always or only, empirical observation.

A related lesson from reading many of the authors cited here, from Radcliffe-Brown to Abrams, from Gramsci to Poulantzas by way of Althusser, becomes almost unavoidable. If concepts are not words and if conceptualizations provide the theoretical frame that helps to construct the object of study, then this object of study can never be what is given to the naked eye, however sharpened its vision. The object of study cannot be the object of observation.

To these three theoretical lessons—the necessary distance between concepts and words, the necessary construction of the object of study, and the necessary gap between the object of study and the object of observation—we may want to add the need to establish distance from the state-centrism of nineteenth-century academic production. This state-centrism heavily influenced anthropology's approach to its objects of study, including the early deployment of the concept of culture in North America, which is the topic of the next chapter.

Chapter 5

Adieu, Culture: A New Duty Arises

> A new duty arises. No longer can we keep the search for truth the privilege
> of the scientist.
>
> —Franz Boas

Culture Matters

The conceptual kernel behind "culture" as deployed in North American anthropology provides a useful and fundamental lesson about humankind. Yet the word culture today is irretrievably tainted both by the politics of identity and the politics of blame—including the racialization of behavior it was meant to avoid. Contrary to many of the critics usefully reviewed by Robert Brightman (1995), I do not see the concept as inherently flawed on theoretical grounds. Thus I agree with Richard Shweder (2001) that something akin to a culture-concept remains necessary not only to anthropology as a discipline, but also to social science in general. Nevertheless, the distinction between concept and word is central to my argument. So is the related emphasis on the sites and processes of deployment and the modes of engagement that mediate between concepts and words. If concepts are not just words, the vitality of a conceptual program cannot hinge upon the sole use of a noun. We can abandon the word and be better off politically and theoretically. Without that shorthand, we will have to describe specific traits ethnographically and evaluate analytically the distinct domains we previously compressed into it. We could then better pursue a practice rooted in the concept.[1]

Culture's popular success is its own theoretical demise. Its academic diffusion has generated new institutional clusters on North American campuses: Cultural— and Multicultural—Studies. Outside of academe, culture has entered the lexicon of advertisers, politicians, business people, and economic planners up to the high echelons of the World Bank and the editorial pages of the *New York Times*. Thus the "Asian miracle" of the 1980s could be attributed in varying degrees to Japanese, if not Asian, culture—whatever that may be. So could Latin America's failure to follow suit. Culture now explains everything—political instability in Haiti, ethnic wars in the Balkans, labor difficulties on the shop floor of Mexican *maquiladoras,* race tensions in British schools, and the difficulties of New York's welfare recipients on the job market.

As the explanatory power of culture increases, many anthropologists react negatively to what they see as the abuse of one of their favorite categories by the general public, journalists, and especially colleagues—reserving their most emotional attacks for practitioners of Cultural Studies.[2] Occasional and acute irritation aside, most academic anthropologists have a limited awareness of both the extent of this abuse and the extent to which it now serves politically conservative causes. I confess a triple weakness: The narrative and the solutions sketched here are valid only to the extent that we have both a conceptual problem and a *public*—therefore political—problem, that these problems are intertwined and urgent, and that the massive exportation of essentialized and racialized views of culture(s) from the United States increases both their theoretical and political urgency.

The massive diffusion of the word "culture" in recent times awaits its ethnographer, but even the trivia is revealing. One Internet search engine produced more than five million *pages* on "culture," even after exclusion of most references to cultivation and agriculture. When culture was coupled with anthropology or ethnography, the total went down to 61,000 pages. While the search engine of a major Internet bookseller produced more than 20,000 titles with the word culture, the list went down to 1,350 titles when culture was coupled with anthropology or ethnography in the subject index. Culture is out there, but anthropologists have no control over its deployment.[3]

Prominent among those 20,000 titles is *Culture Matters* (Harrison and Huttington 2000), an anthology praised by the *Wall Street Journal, Time* magazine, and political heavyweights such as Patrick Moynihan and the president of the World Bank. The underlying argument of most of the volume's essays, as is explicit in Harrison's introduction, is that culture explains the state of affairs in the world today, especially economic inequalities between countries and even continents.[4] Culture matters, indeed, but in ways few anthropologists would recognize.[5] Yet the success of the word is in part a reflection of the corporate success of anthropology in the United States, and to that extent we may wonder if the anthropological critique of culture's deployment should not start at home.

Words are not concepts and concepts are not words. Words and concepts intertwine in complex ways, sometimes overlapping, sometimes canceling each other out. The same word can express various conceptualizations. A conceptualization can survive the demise of the word that once encapsulated it. Conceptualizations, whether or not encapsulated by a single word, take full significance only in the context of their deployment.

That context is inherently multilayered. It certainly extends beyond the walls of academe. It not only includes other concepts, including academic, lay, and political deployments of key words (Williams 1983), but the very social milieu that is a condition of possibility of any conceptualization. Theories are built on words and with words, but what ties those words together is always a specific moment in the historical process. In short, conceptualizations are always historically situated.

So historicized, the North American trajectory of the concept of culture seems to offer a contradiction. The kernel of the conceptualization teaches fundamental lessons about humanity that were not as clearly stated before its deployment and that cannot be easily unlearned. Yet the deployment of the word "culture" today, while evoking this conceptual kernel, carries an essentialist and often racialist agenda outside and especially within the United States.

The connection between these two states of affairs is not the misappropriation of an otherwise "clean" concept by non-anthropologists. Rather, North American anthropology's theoretical disregard for the very context of inequality—and specially the racism—that allowed the emergence of the conceptualization also doomed its deployment. This only appears to be a contradiction if we take concepts as disembodied truths. If we turn to context as a condition of possibility of any conceptualization, a different story emerges—that of a political move in theory that denied its own conditions of possibility. The trajectory of culture is that of a concept distancing itself from the context of its practice. As it did so, a concept created in part as a theoretical answer to an American political problem lost both its theoretical bite and its progressive political potential—and in so doing, also lost its universalism.

For purposes of this narrative, I choose to distinguish two contexts: academe and the society at large. Within the first, the culture-concept appears as an anti-concept, *a political move in theory*, the benefits of which become increasingly restricted by the status of anthropology as a discipline, the state-centrism of the human sciences, and micro-practices of reproduction such as the doctoral thesis. Within the second, the culture-concept appears as *a theoretical move from politics*, that is, a theoretical practice that silences its own conditions of possibility.

A Political Move in Theory

Two substantive propositions are central to the conceptualization of culture as it is deployed in North American anthropology:

(1) Human behavior is patterned. There exist within historically specific populations recurrences in both thought and behavior that are not contingent but structurally conditioned and that are, in turn, structuring.

(2) Those patterns are learned. Recurrences cannot be tied to a natural world within or outside the human body, but rather to constant interaction within specific populations. Structuration occurs through social transmission and symbolic coding with some degree of human consciousness.

These two propositions are indispensable to the most influential definitions of culture proposed by anthropologists in the United States—with the possible exception of Leslie White.[6] These two propositions are likely to be agreed upon as being a central point of departure to their practice by a majority of individuals who earned anthropological degrees in the United Sates. Yet they are not unique to North American anthropology, or even to anthropology as a discipline.[7] The first is necessary to Machiavelli's politics and fundamental to Montesquieu's socio-cultural geography. The second echoes European thinkers from Machiavelli, Montaigne, or Montesquieu to Kant and Vico. Nor do these two propositions exhaust all anthropological definitions of culture. As conceptual foundations of North American anthropology, they precede by a decade at least—notably in

Franz Boas's writings—the routine use of the word that came later to embody them.[8]

So stated, *this conceptual kernel does not impose an essentialist reading on either the definition or the use of the word culture.* It certainly does not predispose a racialist interpretation. How culture found itself on the essentialist track with a racialist bent is much less about definitional truth than about context, much less about intellectual history than about the history of power that the concept itself was used to silence. Central to that context is race and racism.

North American anthropologists love to claim with no small pride that Boasian anthropology's answer to American racism was its theoretical drive to separate race, language, and culture. If that claim is true, as I believe it is, the culture-concept is not just an intellectual product remotely connected to society—if indeed such a thing could exist—but an intellectual maneuver against the background of a social, political, and intellectual context. I will describe that maneuver as a political move in theory.

In its initial context of deployment, culture is first and foremost an anti-concept. It is inherently tied to race, its nemesis. Culture is race repellent—not only what race is not, but what prevents race from occupying the defining place in anthropological discourse that it otherwise occupies in the larger American society. Within that privileged space, the culture-concept can limit the impact of notions and descriptions linked to biological inheritance. When Boas wrote in 1930 that "human cultures and racial types are so distributed that every area has its own type and its own culture" (Boas 1940:265), it was to insist that race (by which he meant the distinctive biological inheritance of a group) had no influence on culture. Boas's constant movement between anthropomorphic exercises and programmatic articles on cultural research similarly highlights a race-culture antinomy (Baker 1998; Cole 1999; Darnell 1997, 1998; Stocking 1974, 1982 [1964]).

The consequences of that positioning are far reaching yet unavoidable. As an anti-concept, the peculiarity of culture in North American anthropological theory stems less from its possible German predecessors or its distance from Malinowski's abstractions than from the peculiarity of North American notions of race and practices of racism. What makes culture unique in the U.S. academic context is not a definitional feature or a combination of such features, but its deployment in a society with a peculiar one-drop rule (Harris 1964), where either of the Dumas would have been a "black writer,"[9] and where black blood becomes not only a thing—that is, as Marx would say, an objectified relation—but also where that relation supercedes other such sets. What makes Boasian and post-Boasian "culture" peculiar and necessary is the white American gaze on blackness—the centerpiece of American racial consciousness—that justifies its gate-keeping function.[10]

Unfortunately, culture's academic career only reinforced the gate-keeping qualities that made its birth possible and necessary. Launched as the negation of race, culture also became the negation of class and history. Launched as a shield against some of the manifestations of racial power, culture eventually protected anthropology from all conceptual fields and apparatuses that spoke of power and inequality. Culture became what class was not, what evaded power, and what could deny history. How it became so has much to do with context. The political move in theory was further restricted by anthropology's position within the human disciplines and by its practitioners' temptation to mimic the state-centered social "sciences." Its essentialist potential was also enhanced by micro-practices of reproduction within the discipline itself. "Culture" was part of the price sociocultural anthropology paid to gain a legitimate foothold in North American academe.

The Price of Power

I formulated earlier two propositions that constitute the substantive kernel of the culture-concept. But the career of the concept was also tied to a third proposition, both epistemological and methodological, which propelled if not required the use of the word "culture" and its cognates. One can summarize that proposition as follows: Cultural analysis is a legitimate lens of observation that relates to a distinguishable domain of human activity. Culture is a way to look at populations, the same way economics is.

So stated, *this methodological proposition is no more essentialist than the substantive propositions at the core of the conceptualization.* One can derive from it strong positions against both essentialism and philosophical empiricism. At best the domain of culture is a cut practiced by the analyst but does not exist independently in the phenomenal world. That reading is a legitimate interpretation of the work of Franz Boas and his followers up until the second decade of the twentieth century. Yet as early as perhaps the 1910s, but most certainly by the 1920s and especially in the four ensuing decades, culture had shifted from a domain of analysis to something "out there" (Stocking 1982 [1964]).

I am less interested in retracing all the steps of that history than in highlighting some prominent features of the academic context of deployment. In that context, the theoretical possibilities of what I have described as a political move in theory became increasingly restricted much less by theoretical arguments than by practices that allowed anthropology's solidification as a degree-granting discipline.

In the second half of the nineteenth century, the new discipline brought to the Savage slot some of the methodological assumptions shared by the fields that studied the North Atlantic, such as history, sociology, and economics. One such assumption was that of the state-centrism addressed in chapter 4. Anthropology easily avoided that assumption when it turned its attention to ancient times, studying such massive and transcontinental movements as the spread of cereals or domesticated animals. Yet when it came to the study of its contemporary "primitives," anthropology mimicked the state-centrism of the other social sciences, often assuming a waterish version of the nation-state, the borders of which were alleged to be as obvious and as impermeable as those of the North Atlantic entities.[11]

Since that watered-down polity was only a copy, and a bad one at that, it could not provide either the methodological stability or the naturalness of borders that made North Atlantic countries appear to be obvious units of analysis. From the 1890s to the 1950s, anthropologists increasingly made up for that fuzziness. In France and Britain notably, they emphasized the rigidity of such concepts as the "total social fact" or the "social structure," each of which supposedly brought to the observer's mind a closure otherwise difficult to demonstrate on the ground. In the United States, "culture" provided an even thicker closure.

The solidity of that closure came less from the methodological proposition sketched above than from the way it was used. Culture as a domain became what North American anthropologists could cling to in contradistinction to, say, sociologists or economists (Cole 1999; Darnell 1997, 1998; Stocking 1982 [1964]). But the emphasis on the distinction also entailed the acceptance of a model: the production of self-evident units of analysis of the kind produced by those "harder" social sciences, and the implicit acknowledgement of an essence within these boundaries. Culture became a thing in the footsteps of other thing-like entities such as the market, the economy, the state, and society.

As culture became a thing, it also started doing things. Parodying the market and the model set by economists, culture shifted from a descriptive conceptual tool to an explanatory concept. The more it explained, the more rigid and reified it became, just like the market or the state. In the process, North American anthropologists grafted an essentialist notion of culture that reproduced the state-centrism of the other human sciences unto the self-evident units of the Savage slot. Just as France or the United States obviously had one economy, one history, and one social life, the Iroquois, the Samoan, the Dobu, the Zuni, or the Japanese for that matter, could have only one of each. The extent to which their economy or their history mattered depended on the interests and benevolence of the observer. The extent to which inequality among them mattered was partly silenced by the liberal aversion toward Marxism and by the preconditions of the Savage slot, which made the people without history "classless societies." Culture functioned as an anti-concept, just like the Savage had functioned as an anti-concept in earlier times. For Columbus as for Montaigne, savages were those who had no state, no religion, no clothes, and no shame—because they had nature. For North American anthropology, primitives became those who had no complexity, no class, and no history that really mattered—because they had culture. Better still, each group had a single such culture whose boundaries were thought to be self-evident. Thus North American cultural anthropology reconciled the Boasian agenda with both the state-centrism of the strong social sciences and the taxonomic schemes (Silverstein, n.d.) of the even stronger natural sciences, notably zoology and biology.

Not every anthropologist welcomed the essentialist turn. Some, notably Edward Sapir, rejected it quite loudly (Brightman 1995; Darnell 1997). Many acknowledged outside influences (Stocking 1982 [1964]).[12] Their deep knowledge of history often led early anthropologists to recognize diffusion and thereby at times circumvent the borders they had erected around culture. In an impressive chapter on "The Spread of Culture," Clark Wissler (1923) recalled the early history of the horse, and then demonstrated how that animal, whose advance in the Americas often preceded that of the Europeans who had introduced it into the New World, became fully integrated into a number of Indian tribes. Similarly, Wissler (1923:13) easily conceded that identities were not always fixed. It was quite conceivable that as Europeans moved along the Alleghenies "a man could have lived part of the year as an Indian and part as a colonist." Yet the same Wissler went on to say that we should dismiss such cases because they are not so common, and proceeded to find in the area that became the United States "six hundred separate cultures...one for each tribe," grouped into seven cultural types, provinces, or areas. That this taxonomy replicated the model honed at establishing racial divisions may not be accidental, as we will see later.

As acknowledged, Boasian anthropology overemphasized the concept of culture not only to inscribe its space within academe but also as a response to biological determinism. Yet its noblest goals notwithstanding, as North American anthropology became more powerful and more popular, cultural centrism—if not determinism—obscured the finer points of the intellectual program for the public and graduate students alike.[13]

Increased specialization made it impossible for single writers or even groups of writers to maintain the back and forth movement between race and culture that characterized the early work of Boas. Boas's definition of race now looks faulty, but it did play against culture and vice-versa. Culture and race then spoke to one another in the restricted context of anthropological discourse and "Man" remained a physical being.

Increased specialization, however, facilitated a mind/body dualism. Man the symbol maker was freed from the physical realities of his being and of his world. Culture was left on its own even within anthropology. Its boundaries became thicker; its negative reference to race blurrier. Increasingly the history of "contact," "change," or "acculturation"—including the history of power that led to these contacts—was dealt with separately, in specialized books or distinct chapters, when not completely silenced.[14] Diffusionism, a school that made serious indents in the United States and especially in Germany in the nineteenth century by tracing the movement of traits and artifacts, practically disappeared from cultural anthropology. Anthropologists such as Ruth Benedict (1959 [1934]) and Ralph Linton (1955) emphasized the "wholeness" of distinct cultures, a theme later revived by the work of Clifford Geertz (1973).[15]

Slanted as it became toward closure, *theory alone would not have sufficed to sustain the notion of cultures as isolated wholes.* Extreme isolationist pronouncements such as those of Benedict or Linton did not necessarily gain unanimity within the discipline (Brightman 1995; Darnell 1997). Archaeological data kept reminding sociocultural anthropologists of the extent of diffusion in ancient times and under more difficult conditions of contact. Daily field activities constantly questioned the myth even among those inclined to accept it on faith. Anthropologists in the field met people who did not follow the rules, did not share the dominant beliefs, did not reproduce the expected patterns, and had their eyes wide opened on the Elsewhere. The anthropologists' own presence in the field and the support system that made their research possible belied the possibility of a cultural quarantine.

Yet whatever individual doubts emerged from field practice crashed against the corporate wall of institutionalization. Institutionalized disciplines necessarily impose rites of passage that ensure and confirm professionalization. As anthropology gained demographic and institutional power, the ethnographic monograph became a major proof of professionalization in France, England, and especially the United States where fieldwork support was more available. The production of at least one such work became the easiest—and soon enough the privileged—rite of access to the profession. In the North American context, it became the sole credential unanimously recognized for entry into the guild (Cohn 1987).

The institutionalization of the monographic tradition, primarily through doctoral dissertations and publications by university presses, in turn reinforced what I call the ethnographic trilogy: one observer, one time, one place. Since what is accessible to the gaze of a single observer who stays in one place for a limited amount of time is inherently limited, the ethnographic trilogy, as inscribed in a rite of passage, invited practical closure.

Contrary to recent critics, I do not see this closure as inherent in fieldwork, as indeed I will argue in chapter 6. Rather, on theoretical grounds, a naïve epistemology strongly influenced by empiricism predisposed anthropologists to fetishize fieldwork—first and most importantly by blurring the necessary distinction between the object of study and the object of observation, and second by avoiding the issue of the epistemological status of the native voice (Trouillot 1992). Furthermore, on practical grounds, in the first half of the twentieth century, procedures of acceptance within the guild provided additional corporate and individual incentives to fetishize fieldwork. To put it bluntly, at some point in time one has to close the book and the easiest way to do so is to claim to have exhausted the territory. Doctoral theses claimed—not always implicitly—to put between two covers all that was essential to know about "the culture" under study. The monographic tradition may have had more impact on the closing of culture within academe than theory, exactly because it enforced the practice even among those who did not necessarily believe that cultures were integrated and isolated wholes.[16] At any rate, by the middle of the twentieth century these units of analysis were most often taken as natural, obvious, and for all practical purposes, impermeable on both sides of the Atlantic, and "culture" in the United States became the impenetrable boundary of these units.

A Theoretical Refuge

The story described so far is academic in most senses of the word. It happens within academe. Its consequences may seem commonplace both within and outside of that context. The parallel with the deployment of terms such as economy, state, or society is evident. Each of these three words has been as thoroughly reified as culture. There is a difference, however: None of these terms today suggests the exact opposite of what it was originally intended to mean, and naturalizes what it was meant to question. The paradox of culture promoted by North American anthropology is unique. A word deployed in academe to curb racialist denotations is often used today inside and outside of academe with racialist connotations. A word intended to promote pluralism often becomes a trope in conservative agendas or in late liberal versions of the civilizing project. The story of how that happened is not merely academic. It is the story of a move away from politics, the story of a conceptualization whose deployment denied its very conditions of possibility.

The political move in theory described earlier was not necessarily fatal, even with the limitations mentioned. Within academe culture could be read as a step back from politics, but this step backward could have been healthy if the privileged space it created became one from which to address power, even if indirectly. Unfortunately, the pendulum never swung back. The privileged space became a refuge. Culture never went out to speak to power.

I am not suggesting that sociocultural anthropologists should have become political activists. Nor am I blaming them for avoiding the correct political positions. As far as academic organizations are concerned, the American Anthropological Association has taken quite a few positions that can be described as politically progressive. I am willing to concede a lot on mere political grounds. But my contention is that within the terms of its own history of deployment, the culture-concept failed to face its context. What I see as a move away from politics inheres in that deployment and the silences it produced. Those silences on which I insist are not political silences as such—though there were enough of those also. They are silences *in theory* that shielded theory from politics or, better said, from *the political.*

Two of them are most telling: first, the benign theoretical treatment of race, and second, the failure to connect race and racism in the United States and elsewhere along with the related avoidance of black-white relations in the United States as an ethnographic object.

Race for Boas was a biological fact. It did not need to be conceptualized, but it had to be documented. It is between that careful documentation—in the terms of the times, to be sure—and the development of a program of cultural research that the race-culture antinomy plays out in Boas's work (Darnell 1998; Stocking 1982 [1964]). Yet as biological determinism seemed to fade out of public discourse with the decline of scientific racism, as nineteenth-century definitions of race became questioned in academe, and as anthropologists themselves sub-specialized further within the discipline, culture and race went their own ways (Baker 1998:168–87). The result is that today there is more conceptual confusion about race among anthropologists than there was at the beginning of the last century.

After a careful survey of anthropological textbooks at the end of the twentieth century, Eugenia Shanklin (2000) argues that "American anthropologists deliver inchoate messages about anthropological understandings of race and racism." Echoing the pioneering work of Leonard Lieberman and associates (1989, 1992), she documents inconsistencies and lacunas that combine to make anthropology "look ignorant, backward, deluded, or uncaring" about race and racism.[17] Should we be worried? Sociocultural anthropologists have also proposed myriad definitions of culture, perhaps their most favorite category. That they would not agree on definitions of race should come as no surprise.

Yet this response to Shanklin's judgment makes sense only if we reduce conceptualizations to mere definitions. If we return to the conceptual kernel I sketched earlier, the two cases are diametrically opposed. Behind the definitional differences about culture there is a core understanding of the notion shared by most

sociocultural anthropologists. Definitional debates about culture are in fact battles over control of that conceptual core.[18] The opposite is true as far as race is
concerned. Definitional divergences reveal the lack of a conceptual core.

The absence of a conceptual core is verified—at times inadvertently—by
numerous entries in the *Anthropology Newsletter* on and after October 1997, when
the American Anthropological Association (AAA) presented its chosen theme for
1997–1998, "Is it 'Race?' Anthropology and Human Diversity." Both the statement
that announced this theme and the debates following it confirmed what we could
already have concluded from Lieberman: Something of the order of the kernel
sketched above for culture is blatantly missing.[19]

I read both Lieberman's and Shanklin's research as confirming my intuition
that few within anthropology want control over a concept of race, except for a few
politically naïve or conservative biological anthropologists. It is as if North
American anthropologists—especially, perhaps, those who see themselves as
politically liberal—were worried about stating bluntly what race is, even as a matter of intellectual debate. From Shanklin's survey as well as from the *Newsletter*
entries, we learn much more what race is *not* than what it is. If there were a majority opinion about a working concept, it would boil down to the following statement: Biological inheritance cannot explain the transmission of patterns of
thought and behavior. Culture (and/or social practice) does, including the transmission of the belief that biological inheritance plays such a role.

That may seem good news. And indeed, it is. In a context marked by racism
that statement is worth repeating loudly and as often as possible, as both Shanklin
and Yolanda Moses, who drafted the AAA statement, insist. Still, against the background of the deployment of culture as an anti-concept, that statement brings us
back to our starting point. We have gone full circle so far as the race-culture antinomy is concerned. We have restated our belief in the conceptual kernel. But in
spite of that kernel, within the antinomy itself culture is what race is not and race,
in turn, is what culture is not. We have gained absolutely nothing *conceptually* on
the race-culture relation, the original tension that propelled the conceptualization. Worse yet, in another way culture has been freed from its original milieu of
conception, from the political tension that made its deployment necessary. It can
function alone. It has become a theoretical refuge.[20]

Some may object to the apparent harshness of that judgment. Have we not
learned that race is a "construction?" Indeed, we may have. Yet this catchword only
states that race is a proper research interest for sociocultural anthropologists, like
other kinds of constructions such as language, history, marriage, ritual, gender, or
class. It says little about how to conceptualize this particular construction, about
the specific mechanisms of its production or its special modes of operation.[21] To
put it most simply, if race does not exist, racism does; and the mere coining of race
as a construction gives us little handle on racism.

Shanklin's work verifies that conclusion. Mentions of racism seem to be more
rare than mentions of race in North American textbooks. The dominant trend
here is not divergence, but neglect. While disagreeing on what race is, North
American anthropology often overlooks practices of racism. That outcome was
predictable. Studies of racism by anthropologists in North America are extremely

rare. To be sure, as Roger Sanjek (1994:10) recalls in introducing the anthology that he edited with Steven Gregory, there are some anthropologists "who never turned away from [race] in their lives or their scholarship." Sanjek's (1998) own work, as that of Gregory (1998) and others, are obvious exceptions. But exceptions they are. So are works on blacks in the United States, though here again one can point to a few shining titles, notably Melville J. Herskovits's *Myth of the Negro Past* (1958). Yet Herskovits's own move from the proposition that "[Negroes] have absorbed the culture of America" to the celebration of a distinct Afro-American culture (Mintz 1990) poignantly reveals the political dilemma of cultural essentialism and augurs the recapture of culture by race.

The fact that anthropologists traditionally study people in faraway places is not enough to explain these low numbers. Native Americans have long been favorite objects of anthropological enquiry. In a fascinating article, unfortunately unavailable in English, Sidney W. Mintz (1971a) juxtaposes North American anthropology's aversion toward the study of the black victims of white domination and its predilection for the "red" ones. Mintz has a number of suggestions to explain this bizarre polarity. I would like to insist on one of them, lest it be lost between the lines. Indians fitted quite well the Savage slot. Black Americans fit less well. The combined reasons are theoretical and political in the way addressed here. Whereas each "Indian culture"—enforced isolation abetting—could be projected as a distinct unit of analysis, it is impossible to describe or analyze patterns of thought and behavior among the people who pass for blacks within the United States without referring to racism and its practices. Without that reference, anthropology will continue to look irrelevant to most blacks.[22] With that reference, the pendulum would swing back. Culture would have to address power.

A Liberal Space of Enlightenment

Why does power seem to provide the stumbling block to anthropological theory at almost every point of this story? I contend that a recurring assumption behind the difficulties and silences we have encountered here about both culture and race is the illusion of a liberal space of enlightenment within which words-as-concepts can be evaluated without regard for their context of deployment.

On the front page of the October 1997 *Anthropology Newsletter* is another title: "AAA Tells Feds to Eliminate 'Race'." The Association recommended to the Office of Management and Budget to eliminate race from Directive 15, the Race and Ethnic Standards for Federal Statistics and Administrative Reporting. The rationale was that race and ethnicity are indistinguishable and commonly misunderstood and misused. Therefore the Census bureau should stop classifying Americans on the basis of race. Restating proposals first made by Ashley Montagu (e.g., 1974 [1942]), the AAA suggested first coupling race and ethnicity and then phasing out race all together.

The coupling seems awkward: native informants are likely to feel that one is not African-American the way one is Italian-American, especially since a reconsolidation of whiteness occurred soon after Montagu's initial proposal

(Jacobson 1998). This reconsolidation makes it both easier to claim the equivalence of all alterities and to subsume race under ethnicity (see chapter 3). Yet as I stated elsewhere (Trouillot 1995:133): "All hyphens are not equal in the pot that does not melt. The second part of the compound—Irish-*American*, Jewish-*American*, Anglo-*American*—always emphasizes whiteness. The first part only measures compatibility with the second at a given historical movement." Only when that compatibility is confirmed does one become "ethnic" in the U.S. context.[23] In the United States, as elsewhere, ethnicity and race need to be conceptualized together (Williams 1989), not evened out empirically or theoretically. Shanklin (2000) rightly castigates textbook authors who subsume race under ethnicity. Moses herself rightly implies that the change of labels may prove meaningless as long as "white" remains an unquestioned category. But can we really erase whiteness with a mere stroke of the pen?

A major contention of the AAA official 1997 position is that the public is misusing ethnic categories and especially the concept of race. Thus anthropology, which may have been silent on race, has to reclaim it and provide a better and unified concept in order to enlighten that public. The only way we can accept this solution as the primary response of the discipline is to assume a liberal space of enlightenment—a space blind to the world, isolated from the messiness of social life, within which the concept of race would go through its own intellectual cleansing and whence it would emerge with the purity to edify a world all too social and political.[24]

Left out of the discussion of Directive 15 are the practices within which these concepts and categories are mobilized and reach full realization. The problem with these concepts is not one of scientific exactitude, of their purported referential relation to entities existing "out there." The crux of the matter is the use to which these categories are put, the purposes for which they are mobilized, and the political contests that make this mobilization necessary in the first place. Here the academic, lay, and political lives of concepts (Williams 1989) intertwine.[25] Not to address this overlay boils down to assuming the imperviousness of the privileged space. That is a huge assumption. Yet it is a common assumption in anthropological practice, indeed the very one that overlays the deployment of the culture-concept itself.

In separating race and culture, Boas consistently notes "the errors" of racialist theories. Contrary to many followers, he does mention race discrimination in his academic writings as well as those directed at a popular audience (e.g., Boas 1945). Yet the fundamental strategy is to disconnect race and culture in anthropology, not to connect race and racism inside or outside of anthropology. It is within that space of enlightenment—and the politeness it guarantees—that Boas critiques the "ambitious attempt of [Count Arthur de] Gobineau to explain national characteristics as due to racial descent" (1940:263).

The evidence is overwhelming that Franz Boas, the individual, wanted to go beyond that space and its rules of engagement. His activism and his efforts to bring the results of his research into public space are well known (Hyatt 1990). At the end of his life, scarred by institutional fights within academe and appalled at the horrors of Nazism, Boas seems to question the very idea that truth produced within academe can be simply projected onto the public without a different form of engagement that might imply a theorization of the relation between concepts and the world.

When read chronologically and against the background of *Anthropology and Modern Life* (Boas 1932), the essays collected posthumously in *Race and Democratic Society* (Boas 1945) hint at a dual progression rather than a fundamental break. From about 1925 to 1941, the themes—as well as a gradual shift in vocabulary—register a move from the description of politically neutral states of affairs (e.g., race 1925, race feelings 1932) to *inherently political categories* (e.g., prejudice 1937, racial injustice 1937, and racism 1940). The introduction and the concluding essay interrogate the purported isolation of academic institutions—and thus their mere role as exporters of good concepts. Boas wonders to what extent academic knowledge is influenced by "demagogues" and by both the prejudices and the institutional structure of the society at large. "A bigoted democracy may be as hostile to intellectual freedom as the totalitarian state" (1945:216). To be sure, "the ice-cold flame of the passion of seeking the truth for truth's sake must be kept burning. . . . But a new duty arises. No longer can we keep *the search for truth* the privilege of the scientist (1945:1–2; emphasis added). If this is not a full agenda, it is the closest anthropology came to the real thing in the first half of the last century.

As a rule, however, theory in sociocultural anthropology never followed that direction. Perhaps the political will was missing in—or poorly channeled through—the discipline as an institutional site.[26] Many of those individuals least willing to accept anthropology as refuge—St. Clair Drake, Otto Klineberg, Allison Davis, or Eugene King—never became its tenors. Perhaps the need to establish anthropology as an objective "science" limited the terms of engagement. It would be futile for us today to divide anthropological ancestors along Manichean lines. Ruth Benedict's pamphlet on the *Races of Mankind* (1943), co-authored with Gene Welfish, who was later a victim of McCarthyism, was banned by the Army as "Communist propaganda" (di Leonardo 1998:196). Yet in spite of her anti-racist activism, Benedict rarely questioned the implicit evaluation of white advancement. Worse, *Races* neatly reproduced some dominant ideological tenets of the times in separating "real" races (Negroes, Caucasians, and Mongoloids) from the not so real (Celts, Jews, etc.), most of which were comprised of whites.[27] Boas himself never went as far as Montagu (1974 [1942], 1946, 1964) whose 1941 claim that race was a complete fallacy made its various constructions a necessary topic for sociohistorical research. At any rate, the study of "race relations" relinquished by anthropology remained a purview of sociology—often with the unfortunate premise that race is a biological given. Sandwiched between *Races of Mankind* and *Race in a Democratic Society*, the publication of Gunnar Myrdal's much more influential *An American Dilemma* (1944) signaled both the absorption of culture by race and their twin capture from anthropologists in the public arena. Myrdal saw "American Negro culture" as a pathological distortion of the general (i.e., white) American culture.

The public resonance of Myrdal's thesis only verified an old division of labor within academe rarely acknowledged by historians of anthropology (but see Baker 1998). Anthropology's monopoly on both the word and the concept of culture obtained only when the use of either was restricted to the Savage slot. When it came to black savages in the cities, white immigrants, or the majority population, other social scientists, such as political scientists or sociologists—notably of the Chicago school—took the lead. Their varying notions of culture challenged the Boasian race-culture divide at times. But even when non-anthropologists accepted the Boasian divide, the politics of race and assimilation and the belief in American exceptionalism led these scholars to emphasize the "white American culture" that Myrdal assumed.

To say that sociologists coined the wrong concept or distorted the right one for a general public obsessed by race is to miss the point. The political persona and professional career of Clark Wissler illustrate how much these public developments came from anthropology's own theoretical ambiguities. After a Ph.D. in psychology, Wissler turned to cultural anthropology and became an important figure in the field with ties to Boas, Kroeber, Lowie, and Mead, whose research he helped to fund.[28] His writings on culture-areas and "American Indian cultures" fit broadly within the Boasian paradigm.

When Wissler turns his gaze to "Euro-American culture," however, his conceptual handling reveals the extent to which conceptual and political ambiguities overlap. He identifies three "main super-characteristics" of "our [American] culture," one of which is the practice of universal suffrage and the belief that the vote is one of the "inalienable and sacred rights of man" (1923:10). Strange on many grounds, the proposition becomes suspicious when we recall that Wissler wrote these lines at a time when about forty states had laws against miscegenation and when grandfather, poll, and literacy laws—among other features of the Jim Crow apparatus—kept most blacks from voting throughout the U.S. South.

Wissler's position becomes both conceptually stranger and politically clearer in his discussion of the race-culture relationship—a topic "where everyone should watch his step." He backs his reserve toward miscegenation by evoking this major tenet of "our" American culture, universal suffrage. He writes: "if it can be shown that negroes may under favorable conditions play an equal part *in the culture of whites*, it is yet proper to question the social desirability of such joint participation" (emphasis added). The first issue is amenable to "scientific treatment." The second depends only on "the preferences of a majority of the individuals concerned" (Wissler 1923:284–87). In other words, miscegenation it is not a topic for anthropological study but a political matter best left to universal suffrage.

It may not be surprising that the same Wissler, who thanks members of the Galton Society in the preface to his book on culture for "many illuminating suggestions," also sat on the Executive Committee of the Second International Congress of Eugenics in 1921 and on the Advisory Council of *Eugenics, A Journal of Race Betterment* up until at least 1931.[29] He was most likely the influence behind the presence of Melville J. Herskovits in the pages of *Eugenics*, where Herskovits provided a rather polite rebuttal to those who saw interracial mixture as a recipe for undesired mutants (Davenport et al. 1930).[30]

I am not arguing that Wissler was a standard representative of the Boasians—if there was such a being.[31] I am arguing that his positions demonstrate not only the inability to produce a clear *theoretical reply to racist practices* from the space carved by the Boasians, but also the possibility to short-circuit culture as an anti-concept both from within (Wissler/Benedict) and from without (from

Davenport and Myrdal to Murray and Harrison). The space Wissler used between politics and "science" was carved by the two moves described here, which fully isolated culture (best approached from within academe) from issues of power, including racism, and made it relevant only to the world around the Ivy walls.[32] Wissler's position could be made theoretically consistent with most of Boasian anthropology, just as racist practices today can very well accommodate the belief that "race" is a construction.

A political climate that mixed nativism and exceptionalism is also part of the story of culture's road to essentialism.[33] Although North Americans have no monopoly on exceptionalism or essentialism, there is a specific mixture of the two in North American social science. Drawing from Dorothy Ross (1991), I read the American particularity as the confluence of three trends: a methodological reliance on natural science models, a political reliance on liberal individualism, and an ideological reliance on American exceptionalism. Liberalism and exceptionalism permeate Benedict's dismissal of racism as an aberration of North American democracy.[34]

Variously prompted by the confluence of those trends, Boas's successors contributed to reinforcing the isolation of the space that he carved for culture, especially as the discipline of anthropology solidified. Current reactions among many anthropologists about what they see as the misuse of the culture-concept rely on the same assumption. Worse, they nurture it. The quite common statement that anthropologists should recapture the word culture encourages a belief in that impervious space. If only culture could get back where it belongs, the world would be edified. But who is to say where culture belongs?

The desire to occupy a privileged space of enlightenment is a frequent feature of both philosophical and political liberalism, though not unique to them. It echoes dominant ideologies of North American society, notably the will to power. Liberalism wishes into existence a world of free willing individual subjects barely encumbered by the structural trappings of power. The dubious proposition follows that if enlightened individuals could indeed get together within their enlightened space, they could recast "culture" or "race" and, in turn, discharge other free willing individuals of their collective delusions. But is racism a delusion about race? Or is race made salient by racism? That is the crux of the matter.

Albert Memmi (2000 [1982]:143) may have been the first scholar to loudly proclaim that "racism is always both a discourse and an action," a structuring activity with political purposes. Semantic content and scientific evidence thus matter less than the denunciation of that purpose, argues Memmi.[35] Along a somewhat similar line, Étienne Balibar (1991 [1988]) asks how we can eliminate some of the practices of power rooted in ambiguous identities when we disagree with the politics of these practices. Balibar argues that we cannot get rid of these practices by repression, that is, by forbidding some kinds of thoughts or speech. He goes on to say that we cannot get rid of these practices through predication, either, that is, by the mere infusion of new kinds of thoughts and new kinds of speech.

One need not put a low premium on the value of thought and speech to recognize that the primary solution anthropological theory has tended to propose to the problems that many anthropologists genuinely want to solve is the infusion of new kinds of words.[36] From the early Boasian wager to the recommendations about either race or culture, the reduction of concepts to words has worsened—hence the fetishization of "culture" to the detriment of its conceptual kernel. The distance has increased between theory and its context of deployment, and not only within anthropology. The pressures are much greater now than they were in Boas's time to find refuge in a privileged space of enlightenment where words are protected and in turn protect their writers (see chapter 6).

That space does not exist. Once launched, the concepts we work with take on a life of their own. They follow trajectories that we cannot always predict or correct. We can place them into orbit, design them with a direction in mind that we know will be challenged inside and outside of academe. Even then, there is no guarantee that the final meaning will be ours. Yet without such prior attention to the wider context of deployment, the words that encapsulate our concepts are most likely to become irretrievable for us. That, I think, is what happened to "culture."

Out of Orbit?

The debate continues about how much distance anthropologists can take from their own milieu. We need not accept the often essentialist terms of that debate to recognize that the culture-concept, as summarized here, is not uniquely North American but quite universalist in both its assumptions and pretensions. We must also acknowledge that its deployment echoes a voluntarism quite distinctive of liberal ideologies that permeate U.S. society. As anthropologists debated on culture within their privileged space, the word and the concept were placed into orbit in the world outside—mostly by non-anthropologists.

That possibility was premised in an academic deployment that denied the historicization of the object of study. If culture had remained tied to the race-culture antinomy even as circuitously as with early Boas—therefore maintaining an engagement with biology and biological anthropologists—or, more importantly, if its anthropological deployment compelled references to sociohistorical processes—such as mechanisms of inequality—it would have been more difficult to displace. Launched on some conceptual path, it still could have been nabbed in orbit. But as a self-generating, singularized, and essentialized entity, it was literally up for grabs.[37]

The complexity of the Boasians's private debates (Brightman 1995; Darnell 1997) was not immediately accessible to the general public. Even within the discipline, groups of specialists integrated different parts of an increasingly vast corpus and inherited only sections of an increasingly wide agenda. While some cultural anthropologists have successfully questioned biological determinism as far as group behavior is concerned, some biological anthropologists may have reinforced biological determinism as far as individual behavior is concerned.[38] The separation of race and culture heralded by Boas, which was the major public purpose of the culture-concept, filtered down quite slowly to parts of the citizenry (Baker 1998). By then it had become, for all practical purposes, a mere matter of terminology. Not only racism survived the Boasians; it survived them quite well. Worse, it turned culture into an accessory.

While the culture-concept helped to question the theoretical relevance of race in some learned circles, it has not much affected racism in the public space. At best, the racism that evokes biological determinism simply made room for a parallel racism rooted in cultural essentialism. At times the two forms of racism contradict one another. More often they reinforce each other inside and outside of academe. The biological determinisms of a Charles Murray or a Vincent Sarich both imply an essentialist notion of culture without which the biological package does not hold. Many of the chapters in *Culture Matters* imply an essentialist take on racial, religious, or geo-ethnic clusters projected as cultural isolates. Instead of the culture versus race effect that Boas expected, many in American society now espouse a culture *qua* race ideology that is fast spreading to the rest of the world.[39]

Culture has become an argument for a number of politically conservative positions and been put to uses that quite a few anthropologists would question, from the disapproval of cross-racial adoptions to the need for political representation based on skin color. It has also revived, with much less criticism from anthropologists, versions of the white man's burden. The "cultural argument" defense now has precedents in U.S. jurisprudence. The "culture of welfare" is a favorite phrase of pundits everywhere. Since Edward Banfield (1974) made a number of working and lower-class social attributes a matter of cultural choice in the 1970s, culture has become a preferred explanation of socioeconomic inequality within and across countries. All along this public trajectory, the conservative and racialist connotations of "culture" have increased.[40]

Both the politically conservative use of culture and the late liberal versions of the white man's burden have theoretical roots in anthropology itself: first, in the unchecked explanatory power many anthropologists endowed in culture; second, in the use of culture to delineate ever smaller units of analysis. These delineations ("the culture of science," "the culture of academe," "political culture," etc.) make the concept of society and the entire field of social relations less relevant both analytically and politically to any topic under study. The social order need not be analyzed, let alone acted upon; we need only to change morally dubious or politically ineffective subcultures. On a different scale but in similar manner, the burden of the North Atlantic today can be formulated as a duty to bring the enlightenment of Protestant Liberalism to the rest of the world (Harrison and Huttington 2000).[41]

Many cultural anthropologists are appalled by these uses, which they tend to discover too late anyway.[42] Indeed, few non-anthropologists now bother to ask us what we mean by culture, since it is often assumed that our expertise is limited to cultures of the Savage slot anyway. Since the early 1980s, a vibrant discussion has centered in economics around the relation between culture and development (e.g., Buchanan 1995; Mayhew 1987) with little participation from anthropologists. In policy circles we are often left out of debates about multiculturalism, which are accepted as "really" about race. When solicited we reject the engagement, preferring the isolation of our place of enlightenment. Even within academe we are losing ground to Cultural Studies in the debate over the appropriation of the word culture, a loss that seems to irritate some of us even more than the political capture of the word in the world outside. We keep telling all sides: You've got it wrong. But a lot of it they got from us—not only through our epiphany of culture but also through our clinging to a space where we feel conceptually safe. If some Afrocentrists today believe that an inner-city Chicago kid is culturally closer to a Kalahari bushman than to her white counterpart on the North Side of town, and if the inequalities between the two are ascribed to culture, however misdefined, anthropology has to take part of the blame.

Adieu Culture

Blame is not enough, nor is it the most effective attitude. Solutions are necessary. They will not come from a single individual or group but from the discipline's collective engagement with the context within which we operate. I do not mean by this a political engagement, which remains a matter of individual choice. Anthropology's primary response as a discipline cannot be a political statement, however tempting or necessary that solution is in critical circumstances. While the primary context of our practice as professionals remains the academic world, the ultimate context of its relevance is the world outside, usually starting with the country within which we publish rather than with those that we write about.[43] While I am not suggesting that anthropologists abandon theory for political discourse, I am arguing for a theory aware of its conditions of possibility, including the politics of its surroundings.

The nineteenth century generated a particular model of the relations between academe and politics premised on an alleged difference of nature between scientific and social practices. Challenged as it was at times, this model continues to dominate North Atlantic academic life. The most visible alternative emerged perhaps in the 1960s and remains alive under various guises, including some trends of identity politics. That alternative model negates the autonomy and specificity of academic life and research. It solves the problem of the relation between academe and politics by collapsing the two: Science is politics and theory is insurgency. One does one's politics in the classroom or in academic journals. There is no need to problematize a relation between academe and its context because the two entities are the same, except that the first is a disguised version of the second.

Neither model is convincing. While the first assumes a liberal space of enlightenment where concepts can be cleansed by academics, the second belittles academe's specific rules of engagement and the relative power of different institutional locations. It perniciously allows academics to claim the social capital of political relevance while comforting them in their privileged space. Yet concepts honed in academe become most problematic in their non-academic deployment, regardless of their political bent in that initial setting, and most anthropologists today would be uncomfortable with the role that "culture" has come to play in politics and how little influence they actually have over its use. A major hope behind this book is that anthropologists can explore together the possibility of a third model of engagement that reflects our awareness of the true power and limits of our position as academics.

No single individual can or should define that model, yet I venture to say that its collective elaboration requires a responsible reflexivity. We are indeed speaking from a privileged space, but that privilege is fundamentally institutional, rooted less in our individual or collective wisdom than in the economic and administrative shields that surround academe. Within North Atlantic democracies, imperfect as they may be, we are paid to speak our minds with relatively few personal risks, and we should use this privilege responsibly yet fully, lest someone takes it away from us. For cultural anthropologists in particular a responsible reflexivity includes the awareness that we constitute a major source of "expert" knowledge on non-European populations everywhere and that the knowledge we produce matters much more outside than within the discipline.

Until a collective engagement that makes use of this reflexivity manifests itself forcefully, what do we do about culture? If the story told here is somewhat accurate, the word is lost to anthropology for the foreseeable future. To acknowledge this is not to admit defeat.[44] Rather it is to face the reality that there is no privileged space within which anthropologists alone can refashion the word. Culture is now in an orbit where chasing it can only be a conservative enterprise, a rearguard romance with an invented past when culture truly meant culture—as if culture ever meant culture only. If concepts are not words, then Brightman (1995) is correct that strategies of "relexification" are not useful either.[45] There is a conceptual kernel to defend, but that defense need not be tied to a word that the general public now essentializes on the basis of our own fetishization.[46] We need to abandon the word while firmly defending the conceptual kernel it once encapsulated. We need to use the power of ethnographic language to spell out the components of what we used to call culture.

Quite often the word culture blurs rather than elucidates the facts to be explained. It adds little to our description of the global flows that characterize our times or to our understanding of their impact on localized populations—especially since globalization itself has become thing-like much faster than culture. Expressions that just ride the wave—such as "global culture" or "world culture"—have little methodological purchase. Their methodological or even descriptive effectiveness has yet to be demonstrated. Words such as style, taste, cosmology, ethos, sensibility, desire, ideology, aspirations, or predispositions often better describe the facts that need to be studied because they tend to better limit the range of traits and patterns covered and are—at least in their current usage—more grounded in the details that describe living, historically situated, localized people.[47] These words actually allow for a better deployment of the conceptual kernel to which I hold.

Do we gain or lose by describing clashes between *beur* and white youth in France as a clash between Arab (or Muslim) and French (or Western) culture? How close do we want to approach Huttington's clash of civilizations? Is the spread of McDonald's in France or China proof of the globalization of American culture—whatever that may be? We may be more precise in exploring how successfully North American capitalists export middle-class American consumer tastes. We may want to investigate how U.S. corporations—often dominated by white males—are selling speech forms, dress codes, and performance styles developed in Northern American cities under conditions of segregation as "black culture." The "black culture" being promoted worldwide is a recent product of the entertainment and sports industries, based on a careful repackaging of these styles for commercial purposes. What are the mechanisms through which these forms and styles are accepted, rejected, or integrated into the South of the United States, into the rest of the Anglophone world, into Africa, Brazil, or the Caribbean, or into European neighborhoods that have substantial numbers of African immigrants? We may want to look at how the expansion and consolidation of the world market for consumer goods, rather than creating a "global culture," actually fuels a "global production of desire." What forces and factors now reproduce the same image of the good life all over the world and push individuals in very different societies to aspire to the same goods? We may want to ask how the current wave of collective apologies for historical sins is propelled by the production of new sensibilities and subjectivities and the virtual presence of a Greek chorus now naïvely called "the international community" (Trouillot 2000). The production of these new subjects, the rise of new forces and new sites, makes it increasingly perilous to hang our theoretical fate on a single word over whose trajectory we have absolutely no control.

Abandoning the word "culture" would free practitioners from within all the subfields of the discipline, and enhance dialogue between sociocultural anthropologists, archaeologists, and especially biological anthropologists. Biological anthropologists would not have to find "culture" in the behavior of humans or other primates. Rather, they would have to specify the role of biology in patterning particular instances of cognition, volition, and activity among the groups—human or otherwise—that they study, and detail the degree to which symbolic constructions inform these patterns. Debates would turn on specifics, not on generalities. Anthropologists will undoubtedly find that those specifics can open new discussions by providing links across disciplinary boundaries.

Urging fellow physical anthropologists to abandon the word "race," Ashley Montagu (1964 [1962]:27) once wrote: "the meaning of a word is the action it produces," suggesting that the only reasons to deploy racial terms were political. Sociocultural anthropologists need to demonstrate a similar courage. The intellectual and strategic value of "culture" depends now, as it did then, on use and historical context (Knauft 1996:43–5). There is no reason today to enclose any segment of the world population within a single bounded and integrated culture, except for political quarantine. The less culture is allowed to be a shortcut for too many things, the more sociocultural anthropology can thrive within its chosen domain of excellence: documenting how human thought and behavior is patterned and how those patterns are produced, rejected, or acquired. Without culture, we will continue to need ethnography. Without culture, we may even revitalize the Boasian conceptual kernel, because we will have to come to the ground to describe and analyze the changing heads of the hydra that we once singularized.

Chapter 6

Making Sense: The Fields in which We Work

Anthropology could not have simply landed where it did had the deployment of the culture concept not influenced its disciplinary path. To ask where anthropology is—or should be—going today is to ask where anthropology is coming from and to assess critically the heritage that it must claim. But it is also to ask about changes in the world around us, inside and outside of academe, and how these changes should affect our use of that heritage, and what is best left behind as obsolete, redundant, or simply misleading in this new context of global transformations.

When Charles Darwin wrote *The Descent of Man* (1871), the humanity he purported to connect with its animal cousins counted about a billion individuals. *Homo sapiens* had grown at first haphazardly over more than 200,000 years to reach close to 200 million during the lifetime of Jesus of Nazareth.[1] As humanity strengthened its mastery over a growing number of species, it took only 1,500 years for that number to double. As the global transformations emphasized in this book started, the pace of demographic growth accelerated further. World population jumped to 750 million by 1750; a century later it was over one billion; a century later it had more than doubled. In 2003 world population reached the 6.3 billion mark. By the end of the twentieth century humanity added more members in any single year than it had in any of the *centuries* before Columbus reached the Americas. By 2025 we will have surpassed the ten billion mark, barring no major catastrophe.

Many observers see in these numbers the harbinger of further massive changes, especially when juxtaposed with the rate of technological growth, including increases in communications technology. Others have insisted on the effects of speed rather than mass. As the speed of change increases, so does the speed of immediate response, as we have seen earlier; but so too does the gap between the devastation caused by new problems and the application of long-term strategies. Humanity faces an increasing inability to envision and implement durable solutions to the transformations it generates (Bodley 1976).

Does sociocultural anthropology—a painstaking enterprise that requires slow years of preparation and relishes in the long-term observation of small groups—have a role in that speeding and massive world? The answer to that question depends largely on what kind of anthropology one has in mind and who takes part in the conversation that shapes it. As of yet the situation is equivocal. Most anthropologists aspire to fundamental change in the discipline: indeed, they see it as inevitable. Yet there is little open debate about the heritage to claim or the directions to pursue.

Anthropologists may agree more easily than other academics that the world has changed and that our discipline must face those changes, first because—for better and often for worse, and for reasons yet unclear—the discipline has valued newness over accumulation as far as theory is concerned (Barrett 1984). Second, the traditional populations of anthropological study are among those most visibly affected by recent global flows. With refugees at the gates, diasporas in the midst, and peasant kids dreaming of Nike shoes, most anthropologists cannot deny that the world has changed and that therefore the discipline that claims to cover the whole of humankind must also change.

Anthropological practice itself, however, tends to vacillate between an overly loud rejection of previous thinkers and a quiet reproduction of the very same research techniques and methodological assumptions. In announcing their new products to a market increasingly attuned to change, quite a few anthropologists feel the need to distance themselves from their predecessors. Claims that the wheel has just been invented are now common within academe: Newness sells everywhere, from literary criticism to the epistemology of science. Promotion and search committees in all disciplines now insist on such claims as a condition of advancement.

In anthropology, at least, it is striking that these claims are not always supported once the package is opened.[2] The loud repeal of the elders and the reproduction of their practice also weaken the guild as an intellectual force. But together they enhance individual recognition, which partly explains their resilience: The claim to newness with the guarantee of normal science combine to produce great careers. Yet as far as the future of anthropology is concerned, a third strategy may be more productive—one that explicitly embraces a disciplinary legacy as a necessary condition for present practice, but systematically identifies specific changes that would help redefine that practice.

This admittedly formulaic proposition immediately raises two sets of questions. First, since the past is always a construction, a choice that silences some antecedents to privilege others, which legacy should anthropology claim? And why? How does one establish a critical distance vis-à-vis that legacy? Second, since not all innovations can be equally beneficial, how do we measure their relative intellectual worth? How do we distinguish between the fads that appeal to our academic sensibilities and the ideologies of our times, and the methods, approaches, and themes that are likely to be relevant in a distant future at which we can only guess? What are the zones of last retreat and the risks worth taking? Finally, how do we help achieve, if not a better future, at least a better reading of possible futures? Obviously these are public questions and my answers to them can only be contributions to a public debate.

My initial response about the legacies for anthropology to claim is that we need to arc back to those disciplinary traditions that best help us understand the world today. If our age is indeed marked by changes in the size, velocity, and directions of global flows—and the fragmentation and confusion those changes create—anthropology should claim anew the traditions that paid special attention to such flows. If our age is also marked by the death of utopia, and if the geography of imagination of the West links utopia, order, and savagery, then anthropology should also claim the legacies most likely to challenge the Savage slot from within and from without. The deep-rooted connection between history and anthropology takes new relevance in that light.

History and Power: The Shaping of the Modern World

Throughout most of its career as a distinct intellectual practice, anthropology has overlapped with history. F. W. Maitland's famous line that anthropology will be history or it will be nothing—altogether plagiarized and misunderstood (Cohn 1987:53)—still resonates in the discipline because it reflected not only a wish but also a perception of a state of affairs. When anthropology began to emerge as a separate profession in the 1870s and 1880s, the few anthropologists practicing in the United States were historians of a kind, collecting either material history—mostly non-European artifacts for museums or oral histories of Native Americans for government agencies. The academic figures who towered intellectually over the newly emerging field in Europe as in the United States saw history, cultural or legal, as their prime material. Henry Maine (1861), Lewis Henry Morgan (1877), Edward B. Tylor (1881)—to cite only three names now recognized as founding figures—wrote treatises about "ancient societies" or "the early history of mankind."

Early on anthropology's history differed from that of most guild historians, who were then increasingly obsessed with the nationalized past of their states of origins. Instead, the first historical anthropologists stressed world history. That "world," however, was a residual category, a variation of the Savage slot that encompassed potentially anything that was deemed safely outside the newly nationalized memories of North Atlantic populations. The relevance of anthropology's universal history was its very vagueness, its capacity to speak *to* "mankind" without speaking to anyone in particular. Yet it did speak *of* mankind in the context of the times, and universal history continued to influence anthropological works well into the twentieth century (White 1949; Wolf 1982).

At the end of the nineteenth century anthropology took a second and much more precise historical turn. New trends—such as diffusionism in Germany and the historically oriented anthropology that emerged with Boas in the United States—prompted a growing number of practitioners to investigate, in varied ways and often for quite different purposes, how particular groups of people came to possess the cultural attributes and artifacts that were said to characterize them.[3] It is fair to say that by the beginning of the last century most anthropologists knew that local "traditions are invented" long before that phrase became fashionable in the late 1980s.

Yet it is fair also to concede that this acknowledgment, however widespread in theory, became less relevant to anthropological practice with the institutionalization of the discipline in degree-granting departments. In North America where Boasian practitioners focused almost exclusively on American Indians, anthropology's history became the story of a pre-conquest past, the remoteness of which guaranteed that the people under study would be severed "from the modern industrial society in which they lived, from which they could hardly escape, and to which they were clearly subject" (Mintz 1984:15).

In the United States as in Europe, institutionalization also meant a very limited geographical specialization. One became an expert on a sub-continent, on a culture-area, or even on a single tribe. The further narrowing of geographical specialization reinforced historical blindness. As we noted in the previous chapter, the more doctoral students produced monographs devoted to supposedly discrete groups and cultures, the more the ethnographic trilogy emphasized culture or structure at the expense of history.

It took the political tremors of the late 1960s for history to return vigorously to the center of anthropological practice. The political and ideological clashes of the times raised vital questions to which many anthropologists felt their disciplinary tradition had no answers (Gough 1968a,b; Hymes 1972). How did the world turn out the way it is, so varied yet so unified? What should be the terms of the relations between the North Atlantic and the rest of that world? Should anthropology's contribution to shaping these relations be ethical and practical, or safely academic? Did anthropologists have a duty to be on the side of the people they study? These questions, which resonated throughout the North Atlantic, were exacerbated in the United States when news of the clandestine use of anthropologists for intelligence purposes in Latin America and Southeast Asia shook the American Anthropological Association.

Looking for answers while striving to "reinvent anthropology," a growing minority of practitioners returned to history, including the history of anthropology itself. But that third historical turn in the evolution of the discipline differed from its predecessors in two related ways. First, it was a history meant to put the past in direct relation with the present, rather than a bifurcation meant to discount or even to hide the immediacy of that relation. In sharp contrast to the earlier Boasians, history served to bridge distances between cultures rather than to isolate them.[4]

Second, power—until then a theoretical oxymoron outside of the reserved area of political anthropology—became the key mediator of the new relation between past and present. Since power launched on a global scale was what tied world populations, power became the theoretical axis connecting anthropology and history, the central concept—sometimes implicit, often explicit—in accounting for the many ways in which the past helped to shape the present.

The repeated appearances of words hitherto absent from anthropology's standard vocabulary—such as colonialism, racism, imperialism, domination, or resistance—is only a superficial sign of that turn to a history of power that started in the late 1960s. More fundamental was the now widespread acknowledgment that the world in which we live is a product of a capitalist expansion, of which the domination of non-European peoples is an inherent chapter. For a growing number of anthropologists, non-European peoples stopped being "primitive" and became oppressed, marginalized, colonized, or racial minorities somewhere in the 1970s (Hymes 1972; Whitten and Swzed 1970). At about the same time the

relation between anthropology and forms of domination—notably colonialism—
was repeatedly exposed (Asad 1973; Leclerc 1972), generating no small amount of
soul searching—and guilt—among some North Atlantic practitioners.

But neither guilt nor political stance alone could generate a fecund research
program. As the excitement of the 1960s withered, the sober exploration of the
links between colonialism, capitalism, and European expansion soon became the
most tangible development within the new historically oriented anthropology.
Since the mid 1970s that exploration has generated a substantial share of anthropological production within the North Atlantic.

In that context, Marx, who had been largely absent from anthropology—and
kept at bay in the United States by the era of McCarthyism—became both a key
interlocutor and a claimed predecessor (Godelier 1973; Meillassoux 1975; Mintz,
Godelier, and Trigger 1984; O'Laughlin 1975).[5] Anthropologists engaged various
blends of Marxism with world historical pretensions, such as dependency theory
(Frank 1969) and world-system theory (Wallerstein 1976). The least controversial
yet most fundamental propositions of these schemes, notably the historical unity
of the modern world, have now been integrated into the discipline. Current
anthropology assumes constitutive links between the past and the present, the
Here and the Elsewhere, the colonizers and the colonized, the North Atlantic and
the postcolony (Alexander and Alexander 1991; Blanchetti-Revelli 1997; Carter
1997; Chatterjee 1989; Comaroff and Comaroff 1991; Feierman 1990; Heath 1992;
Nash 1992; Ong 1988; Smith 1984; Stoler 1985; Trouillot 1988).

Yet even when they are openly sympathetic to world historical schemes,
anthropologists seldom adopt them without serious modifications. Practicing
anthropologists are rarely satisfied with affirming or even demonstrating that the
world today is a product of power, or that colonialism within a loosely defined
capitalist world system was a crucial manifestation of that power on a global scale.
Rather they tend to pay attention—at least more attention than others—to the
less obvious ways in which power is deployed and subtly impacts global interac-
tions. They favor the less obvious mechanisms of North Atlantic domination—
dress codes, religious campaigns, cuisine, literacy programs, linguistic change, and
botanical gardens—over more blunt military and political deployments of power
(Brockway 1979; Heath 1992).

Most anthropologists working in the historical mode also tend to focus their
research on local dynamics within the colony and the post-colony, paying great
attention to the particulars of what Sidney Mintz (1977) calls "local initiative and
local response."[6] Local dynamics and global power are indeed what best distinguish this historical turn from preceding ones in anthropology. Early anthropologists such as Maine and Tylor were interested in universal history. The first
Boasians focused on particular histories severed from the world. Historical
anthropologists today deal with global history in local contexts. They are anxious
to demonstrate how the global deployment of power never fully achieves, on the
ground, the results expected by those who unleashed that power. Juxtaposing
structures and events, necessity and contingency, they aim to document how local
responses vary from relative retrenchment to relative incorporation within the
world system, from relative accommodation to subtle or overt resistance

(Comaroff and Comaroff 1991; Price 1983; Trouillot 1982). At times, local response can be the integration of the colonizer's presence into symbolic structures that preceded contact and conquest—a reinforcement, albeit awkward and perhaps temporary, of the very tradition challenged by the deployment of North Atlantic power (Sahlins 1985). At other times, resistance can take the form of a newly invented tradition adopted by colonized groups, a reworking of the past in response to that deployment of power.

Such an anthropology is by definition multidisciplinary, reaching out to historians and other human scientists (Cohn 1987).[7] It has developed strong ties with other attempts to write a history from below, such as subaltern studies (Chatterjee 1989; Said 1993; Trouillot 1995), and ends up questioning the North Atlantic historicity that made it possible in the first place. Ultimately, the analysis of power problematizes the very power to write the story.

... And Then Came Fieldwork

Anthropology's long-standing interest in time and history overlaps a more ambiguous relation with space and place. A naïve conception made spaces into places—or more exactly, into locales and localities: things that existed out there, the reality of which, although central to anthropological practice, was not to be questioned or analyzed. Spurred by an empiricist epistemology that often equated the object of observation with the object of study, anthropology's overemphasis on localities preceded the rise of fieldwork as a marker of the discipline. Fieldwork reinforced both the influence of that epistemology and the centrality of localities in anthropological practice. Critiques and eulogies of fieldwork today reach their full potential only to the extent that they address both the assumptions of empiricism and the naïve construction of locales and localities.

When anthropology solidified as a discipline in the nineteenth century, the naïve treatment of space paralleled a general tendency in the human sciences to empirically set the boundaries of the object of study and to take for granted the unit of analysis. Both that object and that unit were thought to be contained within the place observed. Various disciplines defined or redefined themselves by imposing their mark on their preferred object of observation: the body, the nation-state, the surface of the earth, language, social organizations, or political institutions.

None of these could be anthropology's reserved domain to the extent that it claimed most of them. More importantly, the Savage slot restricted anthropology's claims of specialized competence to non-Western peoples. Increasingly anthropology's object of observation turned out to be defined primarily as a locality—especially after the relative decline of the universal history championed by the likes of Maine and Tylor.

The nuances between location, locale, and locality, subtle as they may be, are crucial here. We can see *location* as a place that has been situated, localized if not always located. One needs a map to get there, and that map necessarily points to other places without which localization is impossible. We can see the *locale* as a venue, a place defined primarily by what happens there: temple as the locale for a ritual, a stadium as the venue for a game. *Locality* is better perceived as a site defined by its human content, most likely a discrete population. A fishing locality is one thought to be populated by fishermen and their families, a farming locality is said to be populated by farmers, and a culture area is a locality populated by people who are said to share similar cultures. Both locale and locality, therefore, are places where something or someone can be located even if their own situatedness as locations remains vague. Anthropology's weak treatment of the field as a site for our work has to do with the fact that it always tended to conceive places at best as locales, and at worst as localities, rather than as locations.

When anthropologists write that the Tolai of New Britain and the Rukuba of Plateau State contribute to bridewealth while the Kekchi of Pueblo Viejo prefer bride service, it matters little that Pueblo Viejo is in Belize, Plateau State in Nigeria, and New Britain in Papua New Guinea. The geographical names index localities rather than locations; they are specific places, but relevant mainly because of the kinds of marriage arrangements that occur there and their classificatory effects on the populations. For the statement on bridewealth to make sense and be operative in anthropological discourse, it need not address the fact that the three places just cited are contested locations. It does not matter that their names, limits, and forms of incorporation within the larger world have been and are still open to often quite bloody debates. That in 1943 the Fifth and Thirteenth U.S. Air Force bombers shelled New Britain so much that they set a new record for bomb loads in the history of warfare is absolutely and objectively irrelevant within that discourse.[8]

Similarly, the listings of early armchair anthropologists who drew information from occasional observers can be read as various catalogues of localities and locales. In their treatment of these places, some anthropologists—notably the universalist historians and the diffusionists—did lay the groundwork for a problematization of space that could eventually question the naturalness of both locales and localities. However, as British and French anthropologists specialized along colonial lines and as culture-areas in the Americas became collections of localities and peoples, the reduction of the object of study to a place defined by its discrete human content became even more consequential. Cultures and localities were like hand and glove, perfect content for the most fitting container. By the time fieldwork became a constitutive moment of anthropological practice, it only made obvious the treatment of places as localities, isolated containers of distinct cultures, beliefs, and practices.

Fieldwork is not the theoretical villain here, only an accessory to a theoretical erasure. First, as noted above, the naïve treatment of space as locales or localities preceded the fetishization of ethnographic fieldwork. Second, the notion of the field as a source of data was shared across the human and natural sciences in the nineteenth century (Kisklick 1997; Stocking 1987). Third, the reduction of anthropological practice to fieldwork itself and the related reduction of fieldwork to ethnographic data gathering are more recent than most anthropologists recognize. Fourth, this double reduction did not proceed from a theoretical reassessment. On the contrary, fieldwork merely confirmed the crossing out of locations.

When Bronislaw Malinowski's *Argonauts of the Western Pacific*, now held or criticized as the ethnography par excellence, first came out in 1922, only a minority saw it as a methodological watershed in anthropological practice. Those who did see it as such did not insist so much on the unusual length and carefulness of the ethnographic fieldwork behind it. Rather, their immediate methodological praise was focused on Malinowski's exhortation to anthropologists to lay bare the means through which they gathered their facts and the relations they produced between facts and statements.[9] The consecration of Malinowski or Boas as archetypal fieldworkers, the reduction of ethnography to fieldwork, and the fetishization of fieldwork itself as the defining moment of sociocultural anthropology belong more to the second than to the first part of the twentieth century.[10] Only after World War II does ethnography become synonymous with fieldwork, especially in the English-speaking world, and the anthropologist become primarily a fieldworker.[11] Only then do we find the proliferation of statements as strong as that of S. F. Nadel (1951:9): "Like the practical sociologist, the anthropologist is primarily a field worker."[12] A decade later Joseph Casagrande was even more emphatic: "For the anthropologist the field is thus the fountainhead of knowledge, serving him as both laboratory and library" (1960:x).[13]

More than a theoretical reflection on the epistemological status of ethnography, changes in the world at large were behind this new euphoria. Coming on the heels of a world depression and ending with a victory against evil, World War II fundamentally transformed both the mood and the composition of North Atlantic campuses. A different world opened up to the young men who joined graduate school in those times and who shaped various fields of knowledge for the next fifty years. In anthropology, the war increased both the desire for and the feasibility of fieldwork, at least in the English-speaking world (Cohn 1987:26–31; Penniman 1974). The 1960s built upon that base. The demographic boom in North American social science—propelled by tighter relations between the federal state and academe and the expansion of the world economy—offered anthropologists, among others, what Bernard Cohn (1987:30) calls with biting humor "irresistible opportunities" for growth. With increased specialization justifying expansion, ethnographic fieldwork became the first credential of the specialist, the proof of *his* expertise on *his* locality.[14]

However, localities—just like locales—preceded fieldwork, which cannot be blamed for artificially isolating them from global flows and transformations. That isolation was first premised in the Savage slot. Recall that the geography of imagination inherent in the West requires a complementary space, but recall also that this space need not be localized. As place, it can be anywhere. Recall also that anthropology's relative disregard for the geography of management, which is also inherent in the West, severed the study of populations deemed non-Western from the deployment of North Atlantic power.

The inability to construct places as locations derives from these two fundamental choices. It also derives from an empiricist epistemology that reduced the object of study to the thing observed. It also rests on a refusal to address the epistemological status of the native voice. The specificity of anthropology is not "the field" but a certain way of doing fieldwork that is premised on the locality as a place both severed from the world and constitutive of the object of study. The emphasis on fieldwork, prompted as it was by institutional reproduction and expansion, only fused the locality as the place observed with the place within which observation occurred.

Margaret Mead understood quite well the connections criticized here—except that she approved of them. She concludes a 1933 article on field methods with these words: "The ethnologist has defined his scientific position in terms of a field of study rather than a type of problem, or a delimitation of theoretical inquiry. The cultures of primitive peoples are that field" (Mead 1933:15). The entire article is premised upon the triangular relation and equivocation between the field as object of study, the field as object of observation (the place observed), and the field as the place within which observation occurs.

Constructing "The Field"

Seen from that viewpoint, the critiques of fieldwork that sprang up in the 1980s and 1990s (e.g., Gupta and Ferguson 1997; Marcus 1997; Marcus and Fischer 1986; Ruby 1982) launched a much-needed reevaluation of anthropology's most acclaimed practice. Their relentless assault on the naïve epistemology and the naïve notion of space on which fieldwork rests leads to a reevaluation of the assumptions that made *a certain kind of fieldwork* so central to anthropology's claims and practice. The problem is not fieldwork per se, but the taking for granted of localities upon which the fetishization of a certain kind of fieldwork was built and the relationship between such supposedly isolated localities and supposedly distinct cultures.

The two illusions are intertwined and a full reevaluation of ethnography requires a critique of the culture concept (Abu-Lughod 1991; chapter 5 this volume). But whereas the illusion of self-enclosed cultures still attracts many anthropologists, the obviousness of massive global flows makes it impossible for anthropologists to maintain the illusion of detached localities. Not surprisingly, a number of new topics, emerging themes or—more rarely—explicit proposals coalesce into a new tendency to bypass the traditional localities once seen as necessary sites of anthropological research. I welcome these new trends: Complex objects of observations may indeed lead to complex studies. Yet if localities are only the byproducts of a naïve treatment of the object of study, these new turns in anthropological practice can fully succeed only to the extent that they lead to new modes of constructing *both* the object of observation and the object of study.

One example will make the point: that of multi-sited ethnography, a practice which somewhat preceded the critique of the 1980s (Steward et al. 1956) and reemerged as a more systematic proposal in the 1990s (e.g., Marcus 1997). Just like team-ethnography, a multi-sited ethnography can be a partial answer to the limitations of the ethnographic trilogy (one observer, one time, one place). That partial answer is insufficient, however, if it does not address head-on the role of localities as objects of observation. After all, nineteenth-century anthropologists collected data from more than one site. There is no theoretical ground for claiming that an ethnography of Haitian vodoun sited simultaneously in New York City, southern Cuba, and rural Haiti would inherently address the issue of locality any better than an ethnography that follows Haitian peasants from house to farm to town. To assume this is to assume that multi-sited means to cross the boundaries of national states, an assumption that sends us right back to nineteenth-century postulates. A multiple-site ethnography is quite reconcilable with an empiricist epistemology if it constructs the object of study as a mere multiplication of the places observed. The multiplication of localities does not solve the problem of their construction as given entities "out there."

Another move away from the traditional locality is the ongoing development of an anthropology that tries to capture global encounters in their very movement, an anthropology of streams and flows in the making, which takes the linkages, junctures, and borders created or transformed by global movements, when not the actual movement itself, as the object of observation (Clifford 1994; Hannerz 1992; Heyman 1995; Pi-Sunyer 1973; Rouse 1991). That anthropology takes the commodities, institutions, activities, or populations that constitute central—though not always obvious—linkages or streams in the movement of global flows as its favorite sites. Thus a commodity like seaweed, unfamiliar to most individuals yet a key additive for the food industry, links the Philippines and the United States by way of McDonald's hamburgers (Blanchetti-Revelli 1997). A McDonald's restaurant in Beijing, in turn, becomes a privileged site to access not "Chinese culture" per se but the cultural transformations brought about by what many Chinese perceive as a new and top-notch form of eating and socializing (Yan 1997).

This latter example is the sort of occurrence that common sense identifies as a major sign of globalization, and that the food, clothing, and entertainment industries clamor as proof of a new global culture. Yet a close ethnography of that linkage raises a number of issues that go beyond the obvious, including the extent to which that new presence is a cultural intrusion. How much is the sociocultural direction of McDonald's in Beijing redirected by Chinese groups and individuals of various ages and classes? In this case as in others—such as ethnographies based on the observation of NGO-run clinics, immigration offices, advertising agencies, and banks—the move from traditional ethnographic localities to sites where global flows are empirically inescapable does not by itself solve the need for localization. On the contrary, the visibility of global flows in these new sites begs the question of their situatedness: What else is there for me to know about the individuals seen in that place?

Empirical global markers make these places fascinating sites for fieldwork in our times. They provide clearer opportunities for localizing the places they so mark, but they can also blind the ethnographer to the situatedness of these sites and their local conditions of possibility. Anthropologists cannot fall for the obvious sameness of airport lounges. A Nike shop in Mumbay is not the same site as a Nike shop in Johannesburg, and it should not be treated the same. On the contrary, the ethnographic challenge is to discover the particulars hidden by this sameness. Empirical global markers alone cannot transform these newly found *localities* of new consumers of global products, into historically situated *locations*, each exhibiting global markers, yet unique nonetheless.

The move to bypass traditional localities is also inherent and most obvious in the growing number of studies that focus on human global flows such as tourists, migrants, diasporas, and refugees: people caught between the Here and the Elsewhere and carriers of multiple directions. Here again, the opportunities are numerous, but the pitfalls are plenty if only because of the sensibilities involved.[15]

Flows of population have marked the history of humankind since its beginnings, and the conquest of the Americas produced some of the most important diasporas of all time. Thus, in some ways mass migrations are not new (see chapter 2). Furthermore, current flows are not as massive as they sometimes seem. The vast majority of human beings continue to be raised and buried within the same immediate area of their birth. This is true even in the North Atlantic states and even more so in Latin America and the Caribbean, Africa or Asia.

In another way, however, demographic growth and the transformations emphasized in this book together point to qualitative differences. World population grew from a contested 300 million to over six billion in the 500 years between the start of the Castilian conquest of the Americas and our times. The very definition of what constitutes a mass migration changes in light of that growth. Flows of population take on different meanings in that changing context. Those meanings are shaped not only by the numbers involved but also by the specific history of those who move and those who see them leave or arrive. To put it this way immediately suggests that the object of observation cannot be only the individuals who compose the diasporic population in the present they live or in the space they occupy. It suggests a necessary turn to multiple places and times, all of which are relevant to our understanding of the management of a specific diaspora by local and transnational institutions, of its responses to these institutional pressures, and of the changing meanings that precede, follow, or accompany this reception and these responses. Just as the ethnography of the state cannot take the state as a given object of observation "out there" (see chapter 4), an ethnography of diasporas cannot assume the conflation of the object of study and the object of observation.

The lesson is worth spelling out because diasporas, as a topic, bypass the naïve notion of the isolated locality premised in traditional ethnographic fieldwork better than any of the other new themes, topics, or sites spurred by the empirical visibility of global flows today. One could write the ethnography of a tourist village as a mere locality through which populations flow. One could pretend to study a refugee camp as a self-enclosed temporary site for transplanted populations. In both of these cases, as in that of banks, agencies, or restaurants, the most obvious empirical facts do not necessarily force us outside of the site—seen as a locality. They push us in this direction but we could resist and refuse to see the signs of a larger world, just like previous anthropologists sometimes refused to see the links between their villages and the world around them. Compare the possibility of two ethnographies: one of a fishing village (locality defined by content) that happens to be in the Caribbean island of Dominica, and a Pakistani neighborhood (locality also defined by content) that happens to be in Leeds. Leeds here is much more operational than Dominica. It is much more difficult to pretend that a Pakistani neighborhood in Leeds is not located in Leeds and that Leeds itself is not located in England. Everything about that neighborhood keeps reminding us of its localization. Although the theoretical and methodological issues are the same in these two situations, our perception of the situations makes some shortcuts harder in the case of the Pakistani neighborhood. Because the situatedness of diasporas is obvious and indeed part of their definition, the ethnography of diasporas inherently bypasses the locality.[16] Yet at the same time this situatedness forces us to admit that the disappearance of the locality does not erase the need for localization, and that the object of study—here as elsewhere—cannot be reduced to the object of observation.

If everything about Leeds' Pakistani neighborhood evokes localization, everything there and around also reminds us that this localization is not an empirical given. In my ethnography of that neighborhood I need not, in fact cannot, say everything I know, let alone everything that is there to be known, about Leeds, England, or Pakistan. Yet everything I would want to say about that neighborhood has to do with the fact that it is located.[17] Thus it is not only that I need to be selective empirically. The impossibility of clinging to a fictitiously closed locality imposes upon me the fact that *localization is not an empirical process*. Localization is part of the process through which I construct my "field," it is part of the construction of the object of observation as it relates to the object of study.

While empirical data never speak for themselves, anthropologists cannot speak without data. Even when couched in the most interpretive terms, anthropology requires observation—indeed, often field observation—and relies on empirical data in ways and to degrees that distinguish it as an academic practice from both literary and Cultural Studies. That such data is always constituted and such observation is always selective does not mean that the information they convey should not pass any test for empirical accuracy. The much welcome awareness that our empirical base is a construction in no way erases the need for such a base. On the contrary, this awareness calls upon us to reinforce the validity of that base by taking more seriously the construction of our object of observation. Ideally this construction also informs that of the object of study in a back and forth movement that starts before fieldwork and continues long after it. But the preliminary conceptualization of the object of study remains the guiding light of empirical observation: "What is it that I need to know in order to know what I want to know?"[18]

What I want to know in this case is never merely an empirical fact, let alone what I could learn from someone else—from a book, for instance. It is the knowledge that I want to produce. It is what I want to say about this topic, this site, these people—the "burning questions" I want to share even with myself as interlocutor. In that sense, the construction of the object of study is always dialogical.[19] But if that is so, then issues of methodology and epistemology are inherently tied to issues of purpose. What is the purpose of this dialogue? Who are the interlocutors? To whom does it—and should it—make sense?

Burning Questions

To the extent that anthropologists have shared their burning questions, our dialogues have been between interlocutors within the North Atlantic. The limitation is in part practical: The vast majority of our readers reside in Europe and North America. It has also a political dimension: The distribution of writers and readers reflect the uneven distribution of economic and political power on a world scale. I would like to insist, however, on an epistemological dimension of this limitation that is directly related to the discussion of ethnography as a knowledge-producing practice—the issue of the status of the native voice in anthropological discourse. That issue opens the door to a critical appraisal of both the privileges and limitations of anthropology's position between the social sciences and the humanities.

The scholar and the text. Academic discourse never gives full epistemological status to speech produced outside of academe. Since universities—and like institutions—became the primary centers of scholarly production in the North Atlantic in the mid-nineteenth century, part of the distinction of academe is its claim to a level of competency—a relationship to truth, established through a specialized construction of the object of study—that cannot be reached outside of that institutionalized frame.[20]

We should not be surprised that anthropologists never give the people they study the right to be as knowledgeable or, more precisely, to have the same kind of knowledge about their own societies as ethnographers. North Atlantic sociologists, economists, or political scientists do not extend such a right to the people of Norway, Germany, Italy, or Canada. They only concede that the populations under observation have empirical information and phenomenological experiences. French scholars may unanimously agree that the residents of Normandy know how to produce the best raw cheese in the world. They may also agree that these villagers have strong feelings about the United States's ban on raw cheese from France. Few French chemists, however, will claim that the villagers of Normandy understand the chemical process behind cheese production the way a chemist does, and no French economist will admit that the villagers' understanding of the economic stakes behind the U.S. ban is equal to that of a graduate of the École Nationale d'Administration. On the humanities end of the continuum, part of the claim of literary criticism is a competency over the meaning of an author's voice that extends beyond any autobiography or self-analysis produced by the author in question.

Social scientists and literary critics differ in their construction of authorship and authority. The claim of the most quantitative sociologists, economists, and political scientists with a positivist bent is that they have summarized the voice of the participants in such ways that the lived experience embedded in that voice has become inconsequential. Affect has been transformed into a reference. Beliefs can be reduced to actions. At the other end of the spectrum, most literary critics are eager to convince us that if we read them we will be better able to understand or appreciate the voices of a Joyce or a Baudelaire. But few literary scholars are likely to tell us that we do not need to read Baudelaire or Joyce if we read their critiques. None would venture to suggest that the effect of reading their work is the same as reading Baudelaire or Joyce. While statisticians—the extreme summarizers—may tell us that lived experience does not matter once it has been summarized in a referential language, literary critics as interpreters are telling us that lived experience—in this case our aesthetic encounter with an author's voice—can only be consumed raw, that is, by reading the text.

For different reasons, these two constructions of authority allow some autonomy to the voice of the observed—or the voice observed, as in the case of literary criticism. Even the most epistemologically naïve economists, sociologists, and political scientists assume—often implicitly—that in summarizing the voice contained in lived experience, they somehow must create an object of study that is slightly different from that voice. Raw experience cannot encapsulate fully the object of study: It becomes data.[21] At the other end of the continuum, literary scientists concede that their own object of study is different from what the voice of the author says in and of itself or about itself. In both cases, the claim to a unique competency goes through a dual acknowledgment. The observer acknowledges a minimal difference between the object of study and the object of observation and a relative autonomy of voice to the first actor. Even when that double acknowledgment comes as a reluctant compromise, as it does for most positivists, and even when it is implicit, as it is for many literary scholars, it is necessary to the scholar's claim of competency.

The native in the text. Projected against that background, anthropology's control over the native voice seems unique. Caught between the hard social sciences and the humanities, anthropology makes claims of competency that span the entire spectrum of the human disciplines. Ethnography's distinction is that it claims to summarize the voice of the native in a manner akin to that of a pollster, yet it also claims to encapsulate the lived experience embodied in this voice in ways that would make the reading of Baudelaire or Joyce redundant. This is the deep claim behind Clifford Geertz's famous comment that the cockfight is "a Balinese reading of Balinese experience, a story they tell themselves about themselves" (1973:448) and that the ethnographer reads over the natives' shoulders.

Geertz's prose is so enticing that we may miss the fact that the same word "read" refers to two different operations or experiences. The three "texts" treated here do not have the same status. As a reading of the Balinese experience to be itself read by the ethnographer, the cockfight is not a primary text. It is a commentary on that experience. A first construal of that passage would have the ethnographer looking at a Balinese textual commentary (the cockfight) over the primary text of Balinese cultural production (Balinese daily experience). The Balinese collectivity here is both Baudelaire and Joyce writing their primary texts and commenting on their writing—as both authors and critics. But if that is so, then what is Geertz doing there? Is he merely reporting to us as readers what the Balinese commentators have written about their own texts? If so, then contrary to both pollsters and literary critics, the ethnographer is not producing new knowledge. He is reading in the most literal sense.

Naïve as it may seem today, this vision of ethnography as mere reportage would have satisfied quite a few anthropologists for nearly a century—from about the 1880s to the early 1980s.[22] Today, however, the vision of ethnography as mere realist reportage is unsatisfying to most ethnographers.[23] Most anthropologists would opt for the solution that makes the second reading or the third text—that of the ethnographer—also an interpretation. The emphasis on ethnography as realist description and the ethnographer as observer has been replaced by an emphasis on ethnography as genre and the ethnographer as author. Clearly that is the direction Geertz (1988) himself prefers. In that second construal, the ethnographer *qua* critic reads both Baudelaire and Joyce *and* what Baudelaire and Joyce have written about their own work.

But if that is the case, the status of the first two texts in relation to their author(s) is quite different than the status of the texts produced by Baudelaire and Joyce as viewed by literary critics. Both Baudelaire and Joyce were not only aware of their primary production, but they were also aware of any commentary they made about it as being commentaries. The literary critic needs to assume that double awareness in order to proceed with a third level of analysis that constructs differently the object of study.

The ethnographer is in the opposite position. Geertz writes: "The culture of a people is an ensemble of texts, themselves ensembles, which the anthropologist strains to read over the shoulders of those to whom they properly belong" (1973:452). There is some fuzziness here. Is the ethnographer actually reading the Balinese daily experience—the primary text as culture—or the cultural commentary on that primary text, or both? One could concede that the line between the primary text and a meta-text (as commentary) is blurry—that Baudelaire did comment on writing within his writing. Yet that concession still requires that we afford Baudelaire's voice a degree of autonomy and self-definition. Quite the opposite occurs in the claims of ethnography, whether mere reportage or interpretation. The Balinese need not be aware that they are producing a culture that is an ensemble of texts, nor that they are commenting upon that text, in order for the ethnographer to proceed. The Balinese may not know—and need not know—that the cockfight is a story they are telling themselves about themselves.[24] Worse still, the less the Balinese know about the cockfight as commentary, the more relevant the ethnography.

This extraordinary claim is not due to anthropologists' arrogance. Nor does it start with Geertz whose fame and brilliance at formulations make his the most obvious illustration. Geertz's interpretive stance only highlights a relation of domination that was always part of anthropology but was masked by the illusions of positivist social science. That domination over the native voice comes first from anthropology's position within the human disciplines.[25] It stems also from anthropology's constitutive relation with the Savage slot. While anthropologists draw consequences—some quite debatable—from their academic hybridity, we rarely consider the academic consequences of our insertion into the Savage slot.

Anthropologists are quite aware of the ambiguity inherent in the fact that we straddle the humanities and the social sciences. Geertz himself (1988) has written: "Anthropology is going to have to find out if it is to continue as an intellectual force in contemporary culture...if its mule condition (trumpeted scientific mother's brother, disowned literary father) is not to lead to mule sterility." But are anthropologists willing to go as far as their disowned literary fathers? Once Baudelaire's correspondence was published, literary critics had to integrate his personal statements about his work into their discourse. This incorporation required that the critics attribute to Baudelaire what some of them call a "competency effect," a limited recognition of Baudelaire's authority on Baudelaire as writer. The passages in Baudelaire's letters to his mother, his mistresses, and his friends that speak of literature do not become "scientific." They do not have the epistemological status of the critics' own prose, but they cannot be ignored. Thus, Baudelaire has become an interlocutor, although at a lower level of exchange. When Baudelaire takes upon himself the right to write about aesthetics and modernity, albeit not an academic, he becomes a full-fledged interlocutor insofar as the critic cannot escape the issue of the relation between Baudelaire's scholarly discourse and his writings.

Geertz is thus quite wrong: Anthropology's dual inheritance from the social sciences and the humanities is not an impediment. It is a blessing that need not lead to sterility. However, the luxury of that mixture has too often been used to protect the anthropologist against the native, regardless of theoretical positions within anthropology. While anthropologists with a positivist bent tended to assume the epistemological passivity of their object of observation, anthropologists with an interpretive bent construct that passivity by silencing the competency effect of the native voice in their commentary. Although Geertz insists that the treatment of the cockfight as text makes obvious the "use of emotions for cognitive ends" (1973:449), the reader does not actually know what the Balinese know, think they know, or aim to know about Balinese society. Ultimately the Balinese cockfight is a Geertzian play, more Geertzian than Balinese. It matters more in the world of the ethnographer than in the world that it supposedly describes. It is staged in that first world.

The location of this stage has little to do with Geertz as an individual scholar, or even with his extreme interpretive stance. It has to do with anthropology's relation to the Savage slot. The rhetoric of the Savage slot is what ensures that the voice of the native is completely dominated by the voice of the anthropologist. Geertz has the right positions: Anthropologists indeed stand behind the natives. But we are not so much reading over their shoulders as we are writing on their backs.

This positioning is confirmed by anthropology's flagrant contempt for the most obvious and recognized forms of metasocial commentary emanating from local voices: the discourse of local politicians, local media, and especially local scholars. The usual alibi that local scholarly voices are by definition elitist does not hold scrutiny. There is no reason to decide a priori that elitist origins make such voices theoretically irrelevant. Few of us would dare to study social reproduction in France without taking Pierre Bourdieu or Alain Touraine as serious interlocutors, especially if we disagree with their analysis of France. The argument is disingenuous inasmuch as the distance between intellectuals and the lay population is measured differently in countries where intellectuals cannot make a living protected by the ivory towers of academe, but also work as journalists, lawyers, medical doctors or politicians, as they do, for instance, in Haiti. There are other pitfalls in this positioning. Yet when a North American anthropologist tells me that she can study Haiti with a bare knowledge of French because French is the language of the elites, she is affirming her right to dismiss local knowledge that most Haitians think necessary to study their own country.[26] Worse, she is affirming her right to decide which Haitians belong to the Savage slot.

A sparkling minority of anthropological writings demonstrates vividly that while the native cannot face the anthropologist, some anthropologists have tried to face the native. The ways and means of a disciplinary encounter that takes the native voice more seriously—as knowledge, as affect, or as project—are varied. They reflect the moral, political, and aesthetic choices of individual anthropologists. Still the choices are there to explore and debate. I will mention only three cases that reflect the range of this exploration and the possibilities for such a debate.

Richard Price's work on Saramaka historical consciousness (1983, 1990) gives Saramaka historical discourse a competency effect rarely seen in anthropology. Price does remain the dominant voice in this encounter (Trouillot 1992:24) just like a critic who takes Baudelaire as a serious interlocutor retains the epistemological high ground and the power to reorganize Baudelaire's voice. But this reorganization goes beyond the mere collection of what Baudelaire wrote about his work or what the Saramaka say about history, and immediately gives a new status to the quoted voice. Because Price attempts to face his natives, his readers can read over *his* shoulders and glimpse the Saramaka as historians directly and long enough to pretend to become a third interlocutor. In a different vein and with different purposes, Jennie Smith's ethnography of rural Haiti (2001) systematically searches for a vision of Haitian development, social justice, and social change that would give equal competence to Haitian peasants. On yet a different register, Anna Lowenhaupt Tsing (1993) uses creative shifts in positioning author, native, and reader to allow the Meratus Dayaks of Indonesia to return the Western gaze. The reader can develop the impression that the gaze is returned because we can read over Tsing's shoulders.

Each of these examples demonstrates that ethnographers can do much more than most have done so far to give to the native voice a competency effect that makes it an inescapable and thus specific—even if partial—interlocutor. In restoring the specificity of Otherness—if taken seriously Haitian voices cannot be the same as those of the Dayaks or of the Saramaka—these strategies undermine the stability of the Savage slot. Each of these strategies also has its limits, since above and beyond the ethnographer's choice, the Western gaze remains the stumbling block that makes it impossible for the native to become a full interlocutor.[27]

The Rhetoric of the Savage Slot

It is a stricture of the Savage slot that the native never faces the observer. In the rhetoric of the Savage slot, the Savage is never an interlocutor, but evidence in an argument between two Western interlocutors about the possible futures of humankind. More than five hundred years after the debate at Valladolid about the humanity of the American Indians, Las Casas's brief against the arguments of Sepulveda remains a most powerful—and brilliant—example of that rhetoric.

We can summarize its three steps as follows:

1. You have suggested that there are different levels of humanity because the Savage is a cannibal, a pagan;

2. I will show you that the Savage is human because his behavior demonstrates that he is perfectible and thus open to Christ's word;
3. So that you (my Christian interlocutor) and I can envision a future in which humanity becomes one under God.

The first proposition recaps the interlocutor's argument—an argument often backed by evidence from the life of the savage or evidence deemed universal. The second proposition challenges that argument on the basis of empirical evidence supposedly collected through meticulous observation—or evidence that leads to a more accurate analysis—of the Savage. The third proposition returns to the possible future envisioned with the interlocutor, a future in which the Savage is neither an active participant nor deciding subject, since he has fulfilled his role as evidence and has no further epistemological or decisional relevance.

With slight changes and the necessary dose of humor, we can reproduce the scheme ad infinitum in North Atlantic discourses about non-Western peoples inside and outside of anthropology:

(1) You have argued that human beings can only be controlled by fear by pointing to past or contemporary states of savagery;
(2) I will show you cases in which savages organize themselves through choice;
(3) So that you and I can envision a future based on our own free will.

(1) You have suggested that human behavior proceeds from individual greed;
(2) I will show you savages whose behavior cannot be explained in either individualistic or material terms;
(3) So that you and I can envision a future where individual human behavior is driven by values other than money.

(1) You have suggested that biological descent determines behavior;
(2) I will show you that beliefs, attitudes, and actions vary within and across racial lines even among savages;
(3) So that you and I can envision a future where one race does not dominate another.

(1) You have argued that Haiti cannot attain democracy because Haitians are culturally challenged or are too ignorant to conceive of such a state of affairs;
(2) I will show you that Haitian peasants have a sophisticated sense of social justice and that Haitian predicaments are in fact due to foreign hegemony;
(3) So that you and I can envision a world where the United States government does not have to impose its will on the Americas.

(1) You have suggested that capitalism is invincible by pointing to its conversion (or domination) of non-Western people;
(2) I will show you how savages resist capitalist indents into their world;
(3) So that you and I can envision a future that is not driven by sheer accumulation.

Two points are worth making about this rhetoric. First, it is most powerful when it does not hide its grounds, that is, when the stakes become immediately public, either because the interlocutor is identified or because the rhetorical use of the Savage is explicit. The power of the Valladolid debate is that the fight was public, the positions explicit, and the opponents well known. That publicity advertises the fact that the ultimate stake was not the range of reasons behind the Indians' alleged cannibalism, nor even their humanity, but Latin Christendom's own conception of humankind and whether that conception allowed for a Catholic (i.e., universal) Church compatible with colonial control. On a different model, the power of Rousseau's Savage in *A Discourse on Inequality* is that the philosopher is very aware, and indeed makes clear—although some readers miss the point—that the transition from savagery to civilization is a necessary construction. What Rousseau builds on the back of the Savage is a platform from which to envision a social contract based on free will that does not proceed either from Locke's individualist drives or from Hobbes's Leviathan.

Rousseau's uneasy position illustrates the second point about this rhetoric: It often stems from—and appeals to—a moral optimism about humankind. That optimism is sharpened, in this case, by Rousseau's social and political skepticism. Rousseau does not share in the certainty of progress or the necessary improvement of humanity along teleological lines. Contrary to many thinkers of his time, he does not see the inevitability of the great march forward. Yet Rousseau leaps anyway, but backward—as it were—into savagery: If I cannot bet on the Savage, how can I bet on us? He must assume, for no reason, that humanity is essentially good, its history notwithstanding.

This moral optimism permeates anthropology to different degrees. It lurks behind the mock list of arguments I listed above. It sustained anthropology's defense of cultural relativism from Boas to Mead to Geertz's magisterial lecture on "Anti Anti-relativism" (1984)—one of his best pieces precisely because he does not hide the stakes for anthropologists and for non-anthropologists. Yet anthropologists rarely make that optimism explicit. First, a false construction of objectivity—one that denies the observer the right to sensibilities, as if these sensibilities could disappear by fiat—pushes anthropologists into deep denial about that moral leap, in spite of the fact that this leap—and the generosity it implies toward humanity as a whole—may be the discipline's greatest appeal for entering graduate students. Second, as these graduate students mature, they learn—incorrectly—to associate that moral optimism with social optimism, with teleology, or worse, with political naïveté. Moral optimism need not produce political naïveté. The two become close only when that optimism is shameful, when it refuses to present itself as a primal act of faith in humankind, however qualified by history and politics.

Facing the Native, Facing the West

This moral optimism is anthropology's best bet in these times of fragmented globality that are marked by the death of utopia and where futures are so uncertain (see chapter 3). But this optimism comes with duties, responsibilities, and some personal discomfort. We cannot bury it under weak social analysis flavored by political optimism, the way we sometimes do in studies of resistance that any semi-illiterate dictator in the Caribbean or in Africa can easily dismiss as exemplars of liberal political naïveté. When we do that, we add insult to injury for we merely aestheticize the natives' pain to alleviate our own personal uneasiness. Instead, optimism requires that we abandon some of the comforts of the Savage slot and take some risks. I see four worth taking:

(1) an explicit effort to reassess the epistemological status of the native voice in ethnography, to recognize its competency so as to make the native a potential—if not a full—interlocutor;

(2) an explicit effort to publicly identify anthropology's hidden interlocutors in the West who are the ultimate targets of our discourse;

(3) an explicit effort to publicize the stakes of this exchange about humankind within the West;

(4) an explicit claim to the moral optimism that may be this discipline's greatest appeal and yet its most guarded secret.

I have already mentioned examples of strategies that pay more attention to the status of the native voice and aim at restoring the specificity of Otherness in ethnography. In addition to the always limited promotion of such native interlocutors, anthropology also needs to abandon its contempt for local scholarly discourse. All societies produce a formalized discourse about themselves within which there is a scholarly component. Touraine sees this metacommentary as indispensable to a society's historicity. If he is correct in that regard, it means that anthropology has produced not only peoples without history, but also people without historicity. If we acknowledge local scholarly discourse as part of that commentary—as we do for North Atlantic societies—we necessarily construct that commentary as changing, contested, and multiple. We thus recognize the society's historicity and thus pluralize the native. Once we pluralize the native, the category itself becomes untenable and the Savage slot becomes open to deconstruction.

Anthropology also needs to clearly identify its inescapable interlocutors within the West itself. If in the rhetoric of the Savage slot the Savage is evidence in a debate between two Western interlocutors, if indeed that rhetoric is most powerful when couched as a response to a clearly identified addressee, then anthropology should abandon the fiction that it is not primarily a discourse to the West, for the West, and ultimately, about the West as project. On the contrary, we should follow the steps of Las Casas in addressing the Sepulvedas of our times directly, in identifying clearly the ultimate listeners. Some prominent anthropologists have done this in different ways. Margaret Mead and Claude Lévi-Strauss are two strikingly different examples. I have argued that Franz Boas saw his work on race and culture as counter-punctual and saw the need to make this counter-punctual stance more explicit toward the end of his life. Yet the more anthropology solidified as a degree-granting discipline, the more the mechanics of institutionalization made anthropologists act as if their primary interlocutor was not the West and as if the primary goal of the discipline was not a counter-punctual argument—even if inherently diverse and always renewed, enriched, and recapped—to some primary Western narrative. We need to return as confidently as Boas had wished—too late—to the identification of these primary interlocutors without whom the detour into the Savage slot remains a self-congratulatory exercise.

The better we identify such interlocutors—inside and outside of anthropology, and indeed outside of academe, from rational choice theorists, historians, and cultural critics to World Bank officials and well-intentioned NGOs—the more chance there is for savages to jump into the discussion, establish themselves as interlocutors, and further challenge the slot by directly claiming their own specificity.[28] The identification of the interlocutors and their premises facilitates the identification of the stakes. Las Casas and especially Rousseau are spectacular precursors who showed great political and intellectual courage in spelling out what they saw as the stakes behind their counterpunctual arguments. Institutionalized anthropology has tended to choose comfort over risk, masking the relevance of its debates and positions and avoiding a public role.[29]

The time is gone when anthropologists could find solace in the claim that our main civic duty—and the justification for our public support—was the constant reaffirmation that the Bongobongo are "humans just like us." Every single term of that phrase is now publicly contested terrain, caught between the politics of identity and the turbulence of global flows. Too many of the Bongobongo are now living next door, and a few of them may even be anthropologists presenting their own vision of their home societies, or studying their North Atlantic neighbors. The North Atlantic natives who reject them do so with a passion. Those who do accept them do not need anthropologists in the welcoming committee. The political field within which the discipline operates is fundamentally different from that of colonial eras and the world of the 1950s. Not enough dust has yet settled to point to a safe haven of unequivocal neutrality. Anthropology's substantive contributions in this modified context should be a matter of debate among anthropologists inside and outside of academe, but relevance will likely depend on the extent to which the discipline rids itself of some of its shyness and spells out its stakes for a wider audience.

That will not be easy. The last two decades of the twentieth century saw an opening of anthropological discourse to other disciplines, with anthropologists such as Geertz influencing practitioners in all the human sciences. Yet the same period also saw a closing academic discourse to the problems felt by the majority of the world population. Media claims notwithstanding, the influence of academic research that could be labeled politically "progressive" has decreased—if only because these works are increasingly inaccessible to lay readers. Beyond the absolute need for a technical vocabulary to which research contributes and without which it cannot be sustained, beyond the specific need for syntactic structures that express the complexity of thought and the gracefulness of language, academics—especially in the humanities—have basked in what I call "the aestheticization of theory." By that I mean a process through which theory not only acquires a birth right of its own—a legitimate claim, indeed—but spends its life spinning in a proselytical circle, the main purpose of which is to verify its own beauty.

This retrenchment, more critically felt in the United States and Britain, may be a delayed consequence of the Reagan-Thatcher era as academe slowly adapts to larger economic and institutional changes. More widely, it may also be linked to the perception that capitalist laissez-faire has eliminated all possible alternatives to its own rules of survival. The market economy now reigns supreme in the worldwide distribution of consumer goods. The temptation to read into that domination the omen of a global *market society* is understandable, wrong-headed though it is (see chapter 3). Torn between suspicion and seduction, and dazed by the speed and multiple directions of global flows, the retreat of alarmed academics into an aesthetics of theory is also understandable.

That solution, however, is not the only one at reach. It is not even the safest one inasmuch as the life expectancy of irrelevance tends to be short. More courageous and healthier is the acknowledgment of the many dead ends within the human disciplines brought about or brought to light by current global transformations, including the death of utopia. We might as well admit that all the human sciences may need more than a mere facelift; most will be deeply modified and others, in their current institutional shape, might disappear. As the world changes, so do disciplines.

Anthropologists are well placed to face these changes, first by documenting them in ways that are consistent with our disciplinary history. The populations we traditionally study are often those most visibly affected by the ongoing polarization brought about by the new spatiality of the world economy. They descend directly from those who paid most heavily for the transformations of earlier times. We are well placed to detail the ongoing effects of the power unleashed over five centuries by the West's twin geographies. We are particularly well placed to document these effects on the lived experience of real people everywhere, but especially among those who happen to be the ones most disposable from the viewpoint of capital. The need to renew our topical interests is real, but it should not lead into the temptation to aestheticize the native or to study only natives that suddenly look like us. We cannot abandon the four-fifths of humanity that the Gorbachev Club sees as increasingly useless to the world economy, not only because we built a discipline on the backs of their ancestors but also because the tradition of that discipline has long claimed that the fate of no human group can be irrelevant to humankind.

The claim is somewhat philosophical, but values are among the highest stakes in and behind all arguments about our fragmented globality. Anthropologists are well placed to make those stakes public because they coalesce into topics over which we have some claim of competency: conceptions of humankind, religious differences, cultural relativism, and the ideals, ideologies, and social models specific to particular groups, to name a few among such stakes. While prominent social scientists are urging cultural homogenization as the sole path to global happiness (Harrison and Huttington 2000), anthropologists are well placed to show what conceptions of humankind are behind this call, what vision of the future it promotes, and what imaginary it evokes. When powerful financiers, politicians, and economists tell billions of humans that they should adopt the market as sole social regulator, anthropologists are well placed to show that what is presented as a logical necessity is actually a choice. We can demonstrate that this choice serves the material interests of certain groups, and may not be beneficial even in material terms to the majority of humankind. We can expose the historical and cultural specificity of this new faith: Why and how is this secular religion emerging here and now, and who are its priests? What is its language of conversion, what are its ritual practices? We can remind our readers inside and outside of academe that one cultural specificity of this new faith is the ability to predict social futures, one that North Atlantic leaders have claimed since the sixteenth century—and especially since the nineteenth—with a resounding rate of failure. We can compare these new omens to older ones and see how they overlap or differ. We can study their charisma without falling for the attraction (Ohnuki-Tierney 2001; Tsing 2000).

A thick description of this new religion also requires that we expose its foundation in a vision of humanity that constructs economic growth as the ultimate human value. We owe it to ourselves and to our interlocutors to say loudly that we have seen alternative visions of humankind—indeed more than any academic discipline—and that we know that this one may not be the most respectful of the planet we share, nor indeed the most accurate nor the most practical. We also owe it to ourselves to say that it is not the most beautiful nor the most optimistic.

At the end of the day, in this age where futures are murky and utopias mere reminders of a lost innocence, we need to fall back on the moral optimism that has been anthropology's greatest—yet underscored—appeal. But we need to separate that optimism from the naïveté that has been liberalism's most convenient shield. We need to assume it as a choice—whether we call it moral, philosophical, or aesthetic in the best sense. We need to hang on to it not because we are historically, socially, or politically naïve—indeed, as social scientists we cannot afford such naïveté—but because this is the side of humanity that we choose to prefer, and because this choice is what moved us to anthropology in the first place. We need to assume that optimism because the alternatives are lousy, and because anthropology as a discipline is the best venue through which the West can show an undying faith in the richness and variability of humankind.

Notes

Introduction

1. In this book, unless otherwise indicated, the word anthropology will be used as a short-cut to designate sociocultural anthropology.

Chapter 1

1. Pre-publication drafts of the 1991 article that sections of this chapter are based upon capitalized "Savage" when this term referred to the abstract category, rather than to a specific and historical subject or group of individuals. That distinction was obvious in Trouillot 1991; in this volume capitalization of the term will be used for clarity.
2. For reasons of space, I cannot retrace here all the connections between recent debates in philosophy and literary theory and recent critiques of anthropology. Our readings are too parochial anyway—to the point that any major thinker needs to be translated into the discipline by an insider. Anthropology has much more to learn from other disciplines, notably history, literary criticism, and philosophy, than the reflexivist interpreters assume. There are blanks to be filled by the reader with proper use of the bibliographical references.
3. Other reasons aside, long-term fieldwork in the so-called Third World, after the initial dissertation, is becoming more difficult and less rewarding for a majority of anthropologists. Unfortunately, issues such as the increased competition for funds to do fieldwork abroad or the growing proportion of two-career families within and outside of academe only make good conversation. Practitioners tend to dismiss them in written (and therefore "serious") assessments of trends in the discipline. The sociology of our practice is perceived as taboo, but see Wolf (1969), whose early appeal for such a sociology fell on deaf ears, and Rabinow (1991).
4. In that sense, I take exception to Renato Rosaldo's formulation that the conservative domination "has distorted a once-healthy debate" (Rosaldo 1989:223). What a certain kind of anthropology can demonstrate is exactly that the debate was never as healthy as we were led to believe.
5. See Graff (1977), Jameson (1984), Arac (1986a,b), Lyotard (1986), Ross (1988b), and Harvey (1989) on conflicting definitions of postmodernism. I am not qualified to settle this debate. But if postmodernism only means a style, a bundle of expository devices, characterized (or not) by "double coding" (Jencks 1986), then it does not much matter to anthropologists—as long as they note that double coding has been part of the cultural arsenal of many non-Western populations for centuries. On the connection between postmodernism and metanarratives, see Lyotard (1979, 1986), Eagleton (1987), and Harvey (1989).
6. Carlos Castañeda's ethnographic research was conducted while he was still a graduate student in anthropology at University of California at Los Angeles with Yaqui informant Don Juan Matus in Mexico. This collaboration resulted in numerous books about Don Juan's shamanism and ancient wisdom offered freely (through the anthropologist)

to those of the North Atlantic (1968, 1973). While enormously popular among New Age spiritualists and others seeking such ancient wisdom, anthropologists questioned his knowledge of Yaqui history and environment and asked whether even his informant existed. There are numerous critiques of Castañeda's work; see De Mille 1976; De Mille and Clifton 1980.

7. The book *Shabono*, by Florinda Donner (1982), was an account of her fieldwork experiences among the Yanomamo in Venezuela. She was later accused of plagiarizing the narrative of a Brazilian woman who was kidnapped as a child by the Yanomamo and lived with them until adulthood. For a detailed description and discussion, see Pratt 1986.

8. The Tasaday of the Philippines were "discovered" in 1971 and declared by journalists, anthropologists, and others to be a "primitive" or even "paleolithic" forest people with only stone tools and no knowledge of weapons, war, agriculture, or the world outside their forest. By 1986 some were declaring the group a hoax. Given the politics within anthropology discussed here, and Filipino land developers and loggers angered that profitable lands are protected for Tasaday use, there are no neutral observers of this case. The controversy continues today.

9. The first consists of two chapters in *Les Bijoux indiscrets*. The second is the fantastic *Supplément au voyage du Bougainville*, a primitivist utopic where Tahiti is the Other in more than one way, being both savage and female (Trousson 1975:140; Brewer 1985).

10. On Morgan's anti-black racism, see Mintz 1990.

11. I owe my ideas on the black or plantation pastoral to conversations with Professor Maximilien Laroche and access to his unpublished paper on the subject. In Bernadin Saint Pierre's successful *Paul et Virginie* (1787), whose setting is a plantation island, a group of Maroon slaves surprises two lovers. But to the heroes' amazement, the chief of the runaway slaves says, "Good little whites, don't be afraid; we saw you pass this morning with a negro woman from Rivière-Noire; you went to ask her grace to her bad master; in gratitude, we will carry you back home on our shoulders."

12. Some writers have made this point. Others have assembled the necessary information to make it without always drawing the same conclusion from their juxtapositions. I have read over the shoulders of so many of them, and imposed my readings on so many others, that credits for this section and the next were sometimes difficult to attribute in the main text, but see Atkinson (1920, 1922, 1924), Baudet (1965 [1959]), Chinard (1934), De Certeau (1975), Droixhe and Gossiaux (1985), Duchet (1971), Gonnard (1946), Rupp-Eisenreich (1984), Todorov (1982), and Trousson (1975).

13. For example, consider the success of popular North American television shows predicated on the Savage slot, the international sales of Saddam Hussein punching balls during the 1991 Persian Gulf War, and the sales of Osama bin Laden T-shirts in 2001 as indications of a future.

14. My phrasing of this issue in terms of order owes much to conversations with Ashraf Ghani. I remain responsible for its use here and its possible shortcomings. Empirical elements to an analysis of the role of order within the symbolic horizons of the Renaissance are plentiful in Hale's *Renaissance Europe: Individual and Society, 1480–1520* (Hale 1977 [1971]).

15. Utopian fiction also emphasized human control. Alexandre Cioranescu (1971:108) remarks that the perfection of More's *Utopia* was due to human choice, whereas Plato's *Atlantis* was a work of gods, doomed to failure once left in human hands.

16. Genealogies that trace the beginnings of anthropology to Herodotus (why not Ibn Battuta?) partake of that naïve history. They serve the guild interests of the "discipline," its construction of tradition, authorship, and authority and the reproduction of the

Savage slot upon which it builds its legitimacy. Note, however, that it was only in the eighteenth and nineteenth centuries that Romantics and racists abandoned the ancient Greeks's own version of their cultural origins, denying the contributions of Africans and Semites to "civilization." Classical studies then invented a new past for Greece with an Aryan model (Bernal 1987).

17. Even Pliny the Elder—often the most blatant example of ethnocentrism of Roman antiquity—did not operate with a spatial dichotomy opposing the Here and the Elsewhere. Pliny's fanciful accounts of "strangeness" sometimes mention people "among ourselves," and in one case at least "not far from the city of Rome" (Pliny VII:517). For Pliny also, there is no question that even his monsters are somewhat part of humankind. Similarly, Marco Polo's organization of space is not premised on a Western/non-Western dichotomy, in spite of the invented tradition that makes him the first "Western" traveler. For Polo (1958 [c.1298–1299]), the Elsewhere could be anywhere within or around the fragmented world of Christendom. Furthermore the Polo family did not have a Christian mandate, let alone a Western one. Half a century later, the Islamic world was still the only constructed space with practical claims to universal standards and clearly defined boundaries (Ibn Battuta 1983 [c. 1354]); its "West" was not Europe, but the Maghreb—even though Islam still dominated parts of what later became Europe.

18. From then on, descriptions of savagery would grammatically inscribe the absence in a way now all too familiar (and unquestioned) by anthropologists. The savage is what the West is not: "no manner of traffic, no knowledge of letters, no science of numbers... no contracts, no successions, no dividends, no properties..." (Montaigne 1952:94). This language is quite different from that of Polo (1958 [c. 1298–1299]) or even from that of Pliny. But its immediate antecedents are in the very first descriptions of the Americas: Columbus, for instance, thought the "Indians" had "no religion"—by which he probably meant "none of the three religions of Abraham."

19. One cannot suggest that Francis I consciously foresaw a French nation-state in the modern sense, but the absolutist order he envisioned revealed itself as historically untenable without the invented tradition necessary for the symbolic construction of the nation. It is only by one of these ironies of which history is full that this tradition became fully alive at the time of the Revolution and was solidified by a Corsican mercenary with no claim to Frank nobility, namely, Napoleon Bonaparte.

20. The attraction to a hierarchized universality was first confined to intellectuals, politicians and religious leaders, for it took quite a long time for "the West" to convince itself. In the midst of the Renaissance the awareness of foreignness did not automatically "bring about any clear sense of personal involvement with an individual's own country, let alone with Christendom as a whole" (Hale 1977 [1971]:119). Yet at the same time, one was already far away from the organization implicit, say, in Marco Polo's introduction: "In the year of Our Lord 1260, when Baldwin was Emperor of Constantinople..." Since then, "Our lord" has become THE lord and Constantinople a non-place.

21. One suspects that the Savage as wise is more often than not Asiatic, that the Savage as noble is often Native American, the Savage as barbarian often Arab or black. But neither roles nor positions are always neat, and the structural dichotomies do not always obtain historically. Jews and Gypsies, for instance, are savages "within" the West—an awkward position not accounted for by the Here/Elsewhere dichotomy, but resolved in practice by persecution.

22. Anthropological insistence on, say, rebellion and resistance in Latin America, economic *qua* material survival in Africa, ritual expression in Southeast Asia, and the thematic emphases that Appadurai (1991) captures as "gate-keeping concepts" all partake of a

symbolic distribution that predates chronologically and precedes epistemologically the division of labor within the discipline. A major lacuna of the work of Edward Said (1978) is the failure to read "Orientalism" as only one set of permutations within the Savage slot.

23. My greater familiarity with Caribbean anthropology may explain why I find most of my positive examples in this corner of the world, but it is obvious to Caribbeanists that anthropology helped challenge the vision of the Antilles as islands in the sun peopled by indolent natives—a view popularized since the nineteenth century by racist yet celebrated writers such as Anthony Trollope (1859). How successful the challenge was is another issue, but 40 years before "voodoo economics" became a pejorative slogan in North American political parlance, some North American and European anthropologists took Haitian popular religion quite seriously (e.g., Herskovits 1975 [1937]).

24. To be sure, the alleged discovery of the text provokes transient hyperboles. We all knew that ethnography was also text if only because of the ABDs relegated to driving cabs when their lines could not see the light of day, or because of the careers destroyed when dissertations failed to sprout "publishable" books (the text/test par excellence?). That Marcus and Cushman (1982:27), "for simplicity...do not consider the very interesting relationship between the production of a published ethnographic text and its intermediate written versions" is not novel. Tenure committees have been doing the same for years, also "for simplicity," while we all continued to ignore politely the electoral politics that condition academic success.

25. Eric Wolf (1969) tried to generate some interest in a sociology of anthropological knowledge, but his appeal fell on deaf ears. This sociology is still much needed, though it will become even more relevant if articulated with the symbolic organization sketched here.

26. See Clifford's (1986a:21) indulgent neglect of feminism on purely textual grounds: "It has not produced either unconventional forms of writing or a developed reflection on ethnographic textuality as such." Never mind that some brands of feminism now sustain the most potent discourse on the specificity of the historical subject and, by extension, on the problem of "voice." To be sure, some white middle-class women, especially in the United States, want to make that newfound "voice" universal, and their feminist enterprise threatens to become a new metanarrative, akin to Fanon's Third-World-ism or Black Power à la 1960. But it is at the very least awkward for Clifford to dismiss feminist and "non-Western writings" for having made their impact on issues of content alone.

27. In fact, I doubt that there is a crisis *in* anthropology as such. Rather, there is a crisis in the world that anthropology assumes.

28. The limited exercises of the postmodernists would take on new dimensions if used to look at the enlarged reproduction of anthropology. For example, were we to rekindle the notion of genre to read ethnography (Marcus 1980), we would need to speculate either a metatext (the retrospective classification of a critic), or the sanction of a receiving audience of nonspecialists, or a thematic and ideological framework in the form of an archi-textual field (Genette, Jauss, and Schaffer 1986). To speak of any of these in relation to ethnography as genre would illustrate enlarged reproduction and reexamine anthropology's own grounds.

29. I thank Eric Wolf for forcing me to make this important distinction.

30. The matter of the status of "halfies" (approached by Abu-Lugod 1991) can be further analyzed in these terms. We need not fall into nativism in order to raise epistemological questions about the effect of historically accumulated experience, the "historical surplus value" that specific groups of subjects-as-practitioners bring to a discipline premised on the existence of the Savage slot and the commensurability of otherness. At the same time, for philosophical and political reasons I am profoundly opposed to

the formulas of the type "add native, stir, and proceed as usual" that are so successful in electoral politics inside and outside of academe. Anthropology needs something more fundamental than reconstitutive surgery, and halfies, women, people of color, etc., deserve something better than a new slot (see chapters 3 and 6).

31. The symbolic re-appropriation that Christianity imposed on Judaism, or that liberation theology is imposing on Christianity in some areas of the world, the reorientation that the ecology movement has injected into notions of "survival," the redirection that feminism has imposed on issues of gender, and Marx's perturbation of classical political economy from within, are all unequal examples of "reentry" and recapture.

32. The song "We are the World" was written by artists Michael Jackson and Lionel Ritchie to raise famine relief funds for "U.S.A. for Africa." The song was recorded at the American Music Awards on January 28, 1985, to ensure that over 35 of the most popular musicians of the day could participate. The song and the album of the same name won that year's Grammys for Song of the Year and Record of the Year.

Chapter 2

1. That relationship provides the thread of Haitian novelist Fabienne Pasquet's *l'Ombre de Baudelaire* (1996), whose title I replicate here.

2. According to Higman (1984:170–172), the head sugar boiler added lime, controlled evaporation, and decided when to strike the sugar at the point of crystallization. He "was depended on by the planters to make correct decisions in what required 'practical chemical knowledge' but remained more an art than a science" (1984:172). Mintz (1985:49–50), who discusses striking at length, notes: "boiling and 'striking' ... required great skill, and sugar boilers were artisans who worked under difficult conditions" (1985:49).

3. Sometimes the data is there and only the perspective is missing. Reversing the dominant perspective, Sidney W. Mintz asks: "Who is more modern, more western, more developed: a barefoot and illiterate Yoruba market woman who daily risks her security and her capital in vigorous individual competition with others like herself; or a Smith College graduate who spends her days ferrying her husband to the Westport railroad station and her children to ballet classes? If the answer is that at least the Smith girl is literate and wears shoes, one may wonder whether one brand of anthropology has not been hoisted by its own petard" (1971c:267–68).

Chapter 3

1. Both "globalization" and "global village" date to at least the 1960s, with Zbigniew Brzezinski and Marshall McLuhan respectively emphasizing the universal status of the North American model of modernity and the technological convergence of the world (Mattelart 2000).

2. Economists do not fully agree on the list of changes that make up globalization. I have tended to rely on the more critical observers. François Chesnais (1994), Serge Cordellier (2000) and René Passet (2000) provide accessible summaries. Passet (2000) and Linda Weiss (1998) provide fundamental critiques, while journalists Martin and Schuman (1997) excel at fleshing out characters and plots. See also Adda 1996a,b; Beaud 2001; Reich 1991; Rosanvallon 1999; Sassen 1998; Wade 1996. World statistics are difficult to reconcile. When not attributed directly, the figures describing recent world patterns tend to follow the series *L'Etat du monde* (updated as Cordellier and Didot 2000) and Pearson's (1998) *Atlas of the Future*.

3. In 1970, 64 of the world's top 100 corporations were based in the United States. The United Kingdom was a far second with nine, followed by Germany, Japan, and France. By 1997, 29 corporations on *Fortune*'s top list were based in Japan, 24 in the United States, 13 in Germany, and 10 in France.

4. Outside of the North Atlantic, only China's share (US$37.7 billion) was significant. All of Latin America received about as much as Sweden alone. China is Japan's second-largest trading partner. Japan's is China's largest trading partner.

5. During the presidency of Ronald Reagan, the banking industry, including Savings and Loan associations, were deregulated. In 1989, the Lincoln Savings and Loan Association in California collapsed, followed by 800 other S&Ls, causing near-depressions in Florida, Massachusetts, California, and Texas, where nine of the state's largest 10 banks failed. The cost to U.S. taxpayers was a quarter of a trillion dollars. It was later discovered that the chairman of Lincoln's parent company, Charles Keating, had given over a million dollars in campaign contributions to five U.S. senators who pressured to end investigations into Keating and the Lincoln S&L. In 2002, some looked back to this fiasco to understand the 2001 Enron scandal, since both the S&Ls and Enron lobbied for deregulation of their respective industries.

6. St.-Onge's first chapter (2000:19–38) insists on the planning and the organization behind the campaign to promote what he calls "the neoliberal imposture," notably the role of some academics, fundraising millionaires, and political think tanks.

7. That illusion also assumes that the prevalence of a market economy entails a market-oriented society in all its ramifications. Yet the history of Northern Europe and recent political debates in France and Germany not only suggest that the correlation is not a logical or historical necessity even in a single polity, but also demonstrate that the reach of the market in all spheres of social life is a political decision.

8. *bon gré mal gré:* willingly or unwillingly.

9. Elections are a good case in point. They now occur more often and in more places than ever before. Yet they seem to encapsulate less than ever the political will of the people, itself an increasingly quite elusive notion, especially in the North Atlantic.

10. The *future sans avenir* (my coinage based on Targuieff) does not translate well in English since both the French *future* and *avenir* are usually rendered by the same word, "future."

11. If I say *cet homme est sans avenir* (this man has no future), I do not necessarily have knowledge about his temporal chances—i.e., that he will die tomorrow—but rather that this future is empty of positive markers, i.e., that he has few prospects.

12. We can choose to mourn that project and silence the damage that came with the promises. We can pretend that the project is still alive as a package but has become increasingly irrelevant. Or we can decide to analyze the package, its history, its appeal, and its demise in order to reenvision the future under different terms. That is not the central project of this book.

13. When I read the classics of Western social science with my graduate students, Condorcet almost always stands apart not as the least understood or the less liked, but the most peculiar to them—a writer from a different planet.

Chapter 4

1. Anthropological attempts to look at institutions of the national state ethnographically since the publication of that review include Gupta 1995, Heyman 1998, 1999, and Nugent 1994.

2. Since the state is an ideological projection, the purpose of state studies is to decipher this exercise in legitimacy, the processes behind the idea of the state, and its cultural acceptance.

3. Gramsci's enlarged view of the state is inseparable from concepts such as hegemony, civil society, and historical bloc, and offers the fundamental point of departure that within the context of capitalism, theories of the state must cover the entire social formation because state and civil society are intertwined. The intellectual and political implications of that starting point cannot be over estimated. See Buci-Glucksman 1975, Macchiocci 1974, Thomas 1994, and Trouillot 1990, 1996a.

   Miliband launched the Marxist critique of Leninism's implication that seizing control of government meant seizing control of state power. That critique, implicit in Gramsci, arose timidly in the 1960s and grew in the 1970s, especially in England and France. For Miliband the state is not reducible to government although government is invested with state power. The leadership of the state elite includes individuals who are not in government proper but often belong to privileged classes. Miliband barely cites Lenin but the critique is evident. Miliband (1969:49) also suggests that the study of the state must begin with the preliminary problem of its existence. "This is the fact that 'the state' is not a thing, that is does not, as such, exist. What 'the state' stands for is a number of particular institutions which, together, constitute its reality, and which interact as part of what may be called the state system." On Poulantzas's contribution, see Thomas 1994 and Jessop 1985. On Althusser, see Resch 1992.

4. For a critical assessment of the state-nation homology, see Trouillot 1990:23–6.

5. "Né à Paris, d'un père uzétien et d'une mère normande, où voulez vous Monsieur Barrès que je m'enracine?"

6. As part of their bold move to link economy, society and the ideological-cultural tenets of neoliberalism in our times, Comaroff and Comaroff (2000:318–30) provide a more ambitious summary of the debate about state and globalization than I can do here.

7. Ironically, the two big losers of World War II formalized this new trend better and faster than their competitors. Japan and West Germany reaped the benefits of having to renounce, both by choice and by force, the threat of war. But this argument does not invalidate the benefits of a war machine in revamping a national economy, as the tenure of both Reagan and Clinton demonstrate.

8. There are areas of great controversy, as the ongoing banana wars between the United States and the European Community suggest. Also, trans-state government interventions to remove trade barriers tend to pressure the South to remove its tariffs and protections much more than the North.

9. The recent history of France makes the point. From Francis I to Louis XIV to Napoleon, De Gaulle and Mitterand, French governments have always taken seriously the role of the state as cultural container. Against that background, the speed at which expectations in that regard have declined in recent years is telling.

10. The overall erosion of ideological state apparatuses in the former colonies is obvious. An overview of either the Catholic Church in France or the educational system in the United States from the 1950s to the present could illustrate the point for the North Atlantic.

11. The first wave of decolonization occurred in the Americas in the nineteenth century with the successive declarations of independence of the United States, Haiti, the former Spanish colonies, and Brazil.

12. Emily's List or the Sierra Club in the United States, as well as the fate of the German Greens, suggest that the capacity of social movements—feminist, ecological, or otherwise—to bypass national state-like institutionalization is not as evident as once thought.

13. Thus, almost all separatist movements have branches outside the geopolitical borders of the state they contest.

14. At least some street children in Mexico seem to be aware of the social overlaps and flows between the personnel of state agencies and that of NGOs, an overlap that is not

unique to Mexico. I read Magazine (1999) as saying that the governmental/-nongovernmental divide is not significant for the street children. On the power and limits of NGOs as transnational forces see also the work of Beatrice Pouligny.

15. A repeat of the Iranian revolution is not likely today, not only because of changes in the balance of forces within the periphery, but also because of the ways in which changes in the North Atlantic have affected the periphery's perception of itself. Yet the incapacity to replicate the model does not mean that the model is dead or that it has lost its inspirational power. Quite the contrary: It resonates ever more loudly among the very few to whom it still makes sense. The fanaticism of these few does not guarantee that they will convince or control a majority of citizens long enough to harness state power for a considerable period of time.

16. These three stories also suggest that the state's gate-keeping is not always efficient—or at least that its performance is marred by increased ambiguity. After all, Mr. Sen did go to Davos. He received a public apology from the Swiss government. Since 1999, Germany recognizes *jus solis* (citizenship right by birth) as well as *jus sanguinis* (right by descent). Other difficulties facing ethnic Turks are now being addressed by German courts, offering one more sign of the global expansion of judicial rhetoric and reach.

Chapter 5

1. The first person in this paper registers strategic location(s) rather than identity: anthropologist(s) emphasizing sociocultural processes, writing primarily from—or against the background of—North American institutional hegemony.

2. The exaggerated focus on Cultural Studies that turns fellow academics into prime political targets, as well as early reactions to previous versions of this paper, though obviously different in scope and relevance, include some dominant themes: we do not have a *public* problem, only an academic one that can be solved within academe; we have a public problem but it can be solved with conceptual adjustment; we have only a North American problem: culture—and Cultural Studies—are quite healthy everywhere else.

3. An avid newsreader, I do not see the need to document the extent to which "culture" now operates in the sites of power where it is recycled for mass consumption. Bits of evidence are scattered all over the world and anthropologists need only to tune their eyes to recognize the urgency. Some of my favorite items include: the 1994–1995 campaign for legislation against unemployed workers in Virginia as a mechanism to end "the culture of welfare," a slogan soon echoed in Massachusetts, Chile, Canada, and England where it became a favorite of British Prime Minister Tony Blair; the promotion of Lynne V. Cheney's book (1995) as a strategy to recapture "American culture" from the exaggerated demands of postmodernists and minorities; the reception of *Culture Matters* (Harrison and Huttington 2000). In early 2001 a new president in the United States explained his first executive order denying federal funding to agencies that recognize a woman's right to abortion elsewhere in the world as a step toward "a culture of life."

4. Africa and the Caribbean are prime targets in these politics of blame. *Culture Matters* echoes arguments that Harrison makes elsewhere (e.g., Harrison 2000) about Nicaragua and notably Haiti—where he was a USAID official—and the woes of which he blames on "Vodoo politics" and "the imprint of African culture." (Note the singular. See Trouillot 1994 for a refutation). The focus on Africa and the Caribbean recalls the rhetoric of the eugenics movement when prominent figures such as Charles Davenport and Lothrop Stoddard used their allegedly "scientific" readings of Jamaica and Haiti to document a political agenda on the home front. "Science" functions semiotically in

most of the essays in *Culture Matters* as it did in the eugenics texts—a strategy Boas recognized perhaps too late.

5. Not accidentally, Richard Shweder is the only real contrario voice in *Culture Matters*.

6. White acknowledges the symbolic coding but makes it epiphenomenal to the point of irrelevance.

7. After insisting that symbolic representations are part of human behavior, Nadel (1951:29) writes: "The subject matter of our enquiry is *standardized behaviour patterns;* their integrated totality is *culture*" (emphases in original).

8. In Boas's early writings, the word culture is first used interchangeably with civilization, and there is a marked preference for the adjectival form "cultural" (as in "cultural traits") over the noun itself in actual descriptions. I should emphasize, though it should be clear, that I do not equate definitions and conceptualizations. At their most successful, the former are conceptual short cuts. In no way can they encapsulate a conceptualization. Nor are they necessary to a conceptualization.

9. The first Alexandre Dumas, a French general, was born in what is now Haiti to a petty French nobleman and his Congo slave, Cessette Dumas. His son, better known as Alexandre Dumas the first, wrote *Les Trois Mousquetaires* and other epic novels. Plays by his grandson, Alexandre Dumas fils, include *La Dame aux Camélias*.

10. The deployment of the same conceptual kernel, the indispensable core of "culture," in Europe both before and after Boas does not generate the same excitement or the same quibbles, the racist practices of many white Europeans notwithstanding.

    An important aspect of the issue is the relationship between racial consciousness and racist practices, including institutional practices. I am not arguing that white North Americans are more (or less) racist than whites elsewhere. Nor am I arguing that racist practices can be found only in the behavior of whites against blacks. In a not too distant past, not all whites were equally white (Jacobson 1998). My contention is that the centrality of the black/white divide in the construction of North American racial consciousness uniquely informs the joint deployment of both "race" and "culture" in the United States and that even variations of whiteness—or other oppositions to it—are best understood within that context.

11. Eric Wolf similarly links the academic division of labor and the solidification of geo-historical entities. He writes:

    The habit of treating named entities such as Iroquois, Greece, Persia, or the United States as fixed entities opposed to one another by stable internal architecture and external boundaries interferes with our ability to understand their mutual encounter and confrontation.... We seem to have taken a wrong turn in understanding at some critical point in the past, a false choice that bedevils our thinking in the present.

    That critical turning point is identifiable. It occurred in the middle of the [nineteenth] century, when inquiry into the nature and varieties of humankind split into separate (and unequal) specialties and disciplines. This split was fateful (1982:7).

    See also Trouillot 1991.

12. Too often such acknowledgments were made as mere arguments between theoretical adversaries. When Franz Boas (1940:286) praised Elsie Clew Parsons for a study that demonstrated early European influences on the Zuni, it was primarily to prove the impossibility of establishing general laws of cultural evolution.

13. One wonders to what extent the extreme formulations of Boasian anthropology were linked to its incapacity to control its own rhetoric as it grasped for institutional power in a racist and conservative context.

14. Studies of culture contact or acculturation increased both in England and in the United States in the 1940s and 1950s. Their nevertheless limited impact is best seen in the conclusions of an influential Wenner-Gren conference on American Indian affairs. "[Most] of the presently identifiable Indian groups residing on reservations (areas long known to them as homelands) will continue indefinitely as distinct social units, preserving their basic values, personality and Indian way of life, while making continual adjustment, often superficial in nature, to the economic and political demands of the larger society" (Provinse 1954:389).

15. Whether or not this emphasis on wholeness was inherent in Boas's own views remains debatable. I do not, however, see evidence of a fundamental theoretical break between Boas and his students—a rupture that would beg the question as to why so many prominent Boasians read Boas wrong in a scenario that would evoke the muddled relations between Marx and Marxism. In that case, as in this one, I think that at least some of the seeds of the many "misreadings" were in the fruit itself, and that the misinterpretations—if that is what we want to call them—were *possible outcomes among many*. It is a characteristic of great thinkers that their work leads to many roads, but that very richness makes it unjust to place all the burden of future developments on misguided followers. Boas, like Marx, can survive the criticism. Furthermore—and the parallel with Marx is still valid—I am not arguing that essentialism was a necessary *theoretical* outcome of Boas's work, but a product of the historical context of its theoretical deployment.

16. The relatively recent proliferation and official recognition of subfields such as economic anthropology, medical anthropology, kinship, and gender under the larger umbrella of social cultural anthropology has alleviated the need to claim cultural exhaustiveness within a single monograph.

17. Lieberman's survey on race among professors at Ph.D.-granting institutions in the United States found that 31 percent of cultural anthropologists and 50 percent of biological anthropologists agreed with the statement "there are biological races in the species Homo Sapiens." Of course, the biological anthropologists disagreed widely on what counts as a biological race.

18. Debates tend to focus on the degree of integration of the patterns involved, the degree of consciousness about such patterns within the populations who share them, and the extent of the patterning itself. As such, they tend to orient the conceptual core in one or another direction; but in so doing, they also reinforce it.

19. The *Anthropology Newsletter* entries and Shanklin's data lead us to question whether there is a fundamental agreement even among anthropologists about the domain within which and for which such a conceptual core for culture obtains.

20. Let me repeat that the central point here is not a critique of political silences. At the same time, if my critique is legitimate, it is also more politically relevant than a mere critique of political positions. The theoretical refuge of culture makes it very difficult for the discipline as a whole to deal with racism.

21. Note that this coining only postpones the issue of the biological and phenotypical markers of human populations. See Memmi 2000 [1982] for a critique of definitions of racism—including his own earlier views—that avoid these phenotypical-biological dimensions.

22. The relationship between anthropology and black Americans has deteriorated greatly since the first generation of black students that Boas attracted to the field. Today the number of Ph.D.s in anthropology climbs much faster than in other fields, with a majority of the diplomas going to women. Yet while we attract increasing numbers of Asians, American Indians, and Latinos (except Puerto Ricans, whose numbers are shamefully small), blacks received a mere 3.5 percent of our doctoral degrees in 1999. The national average for that year for blacks in all fields is 5.9 percent, excluding

professional schools. In comparison to peer disciplines, anthropology is clearly becoming less attractive to blacks (Sanderon et al. 1999, 2000).

23. Attempts to conform to the hyphen rule (e.g., African American) or to avoid it (e.g., Latino) through the mere manipulation of labels are ineffective at displacing the need for an equivalence to whiteness that the labeling process verifies (see Williams 1989 for one of the most complex treatments of classificatory labels and identity). What matters here is how the changing construction of whiteness intersects with the maintenance of a white/black divide that structures *all* race relations in the United States. Whether significant numbers of the people now called Latinos or Asian Americans—or the significant numbers of their known "mixed" offspring with whites—will become probationary whites and thus reinforce the structure is an important indicator of the future of race relations in the United States.

24. The inability to connect theory and practice explains a number of inconsistencies in the AAA official position. The AAA does have a grouping of black anthropologists. And we have yet to systematically petition administrators at U.S. universities to eliminate race or color from student admissions forms or from discussions about faculty hires.

25. Williams (1989:402) writes: "Like race and class, however, ethnicity along with the systems of classification associated with them in different places, has been, and continues to be, the product of combined scientific, lay, and political classification. As a result, contemporary efforts to understand what these concepts label and what places these labels mark in the identity-formation process, must identify *the assumptions underlying the linkages* among their lay, political, and scientific meanings" (emphasis added).

26. Darnell (1998:274) quotes a 1947 letter from Kroeber to White in which Kroeber contrasts his casual interest in racial issues with that of Boas who "put so much energy and strength behind his convictions that one got the impression there must be something important about the beliefs."

27. Benedict not only contributed to the reconsolidation of whiteness, but she also reaffirmed the divide between science and context that Boas had started to question.

28. Wissler taught anthropology at Columbia under Boas's recommendation, and also at Yale. He became Chief Curator of the Anthropological Division at the American Museum of Natural History.

29. The 1921 Congress helped to launch the American Eugenics Society of which the journal *Eugenics* was published by Galton Publishing. The Galton Society itself—of which Wissler was a member—was founded in 1918 at the house of Wissler's future Museum supervisor, Henry Fairfield Osborn, by the avowed racist and anticommunist Madison Grant, author of *The Passing of the Great Race*. Although not all eugenicists were avowed racists, and the movement garnered much academic prestige for a short time, both societies were dominated by figures such as Grant, Stoddard, and Davenport, whose racism cannot be questioned notwithstanding the academic references of some (Allen 1995; Kamin 1995).

30. Gender is an inherent part of that story. Davenport's obsession about the potency of Negro blood and Stoddard's nightmares about Haitian slaves raping white women demonstrate that much. Herskovits's rebuttal falls for the "science" trap. One cannot answer with certitude whether mixture discredits the qualities of the "superior" races since the knowledge of biology is in its infancy and contemporary world populations are already products of race mixtures. Therefore, there is no reason to be "unduly alarmed" (Herskovits in Davenport et al. 1930:59). Compare to Frank H. Hankins's answer in the same. A few years later, Herskovits and Wissler both contributed to the reader *Making Mankind*, edited by Baker Brownell (Wissler et al. 1929).

31. Wissler's degree was in psychology (Wissler 1901). Some of his statements contradict those of Boas on biological inheritance. Yet at least many cultural anthropologists did know his positions and his affiliations were public. Stocking, who notes Wissler's ties

to the eugenics movement, reluctantly concedes to him an appearance of neutrality in the institutional fight that opposed Boasians and anti-Boasians in the first two decades of the twentieth century (Stocking 1982 [1964]:217, chapter 3 passim). I agree with Stocking's reading but I would add that it is exactly the restrictions in the terms of the debate that allowed Wissler to maintain the suspicious "neutrality" that turned him into an institutional power broker. See also Cole (1999:251–253).

32. The entire "scientific reaction against cultural anthropology" (Stocking 1982 [1964]) and most notably the eugenics discourse as publicized by the likes of Davenport (1930) can be seen as the political use—at times, successful—of an alleged scientific neutrality to defeat the culture concept in the public sphere. See most of the articles and the readers' letters in *Eugenics* from 1929 to 1931.

33. I thank Richard G. Fox for calling my attention to the role of exceptionalism in the early decades of the twentieth century.

34. In his remarkable book *Whiteness of a Different Color*, Jacobson (1998) provides a trenchant critique of Benedict—among others—exactly on those grounds. (For a more sympathetic reading, see di Leonardo 1998:183–190, 194–196). Boas himself wavers on American exceptionalism until the end of his life, when he is willing to affirm loudly that racism is constitutive of North American democracy (e.g., Boas 1945).

35. Memmi (2000 [1982]:95) writes of those who hold racist views: "One can denounce their information as false, or reveal it to be pseudo-knowledge...It makes no difference." Likewise, Haroun Jamous warns us that it is a grave mistake to see racism as the collective delusion of a group of subjects or of a group-subject.

36. Political relexification—the mere replacement of old words by new ones—is also central to the strategies of "political correctness." Claims to a public debate aside, these strategies also rely on an enlightened private space where political and intellectual elites can decide which words the rest of us can use.

37. Eric Wolf (1999:19) phrases a similar proposition: "Cleaving to a notion of 'culture' as a self-generating and self-propelling mental apparatus of norms and rules for behavior, the discipline has tended to disregard the role of power in how culture is built up, maintained, dismantled, or destroyed. We face a situation of complementary naïveté, whereby anthropology has emphasized culture and discounted power, while 'culture' was long discounted among the other social sciences, until it came to be a slogan in movements to achieve ethnic recognition."

38. Lest one thinks I am singling out biological anthropology as the fall guy, let me remind us that most biological anthropologists—including a majority of those who believe in the existence of biological races—were trained in four-field departments dominated by culturalists. The real issue is how anthropology connects culture and racism, not the biological boundaries of race.

39. I will note only some markers. The Moynihan report was an explicit appropriation of cultural determinism with a racialist bent in American public space (but the trail goes back to Myrdal). By the 1980s, politician David Duke was launching a racist campaign in defense of "Western culture." By spring 2000, a *New York Times* series "How Race is Lived in America" inadvertently yet fully documented the equation of race and culture in all spheres of American life.

40. The paper trail is enormous. For examples, see:

- "Courts: Saying Cultural Values Caused Woman to Try to Kill Her Children, Lawyers Will Recall 1985 Episode." *Los Angeles Times*, February 17, 2000.
- "Brothers Under the Skin; Why Is Trans-Racial Adoption Seen as a Bad Idea?" *The Independent* (London) Features; pg. 4, Jan 9, 2000.

- "Bureaucratic Maze Breeds Frustration Culture of Violence, Poverty Must Turn to Hope, Opportunity." *Denver Rocky Mountain News*, July 31, 1995.
- "A Broken Welfare System Threatens to Break American Society." *The San Diego Union-Tribune*, September 24, 1995.
- "Bell Tolls for Welfare Legislature to Face Tough Decisions as Colorado Moves Poor into the Job Market." *Denver Rocky Mountain News*, December 29, 1996.
- "Evidence Is Scant That Workfare Leads to Full-Time Jobs." Series: Does Workfare Work? *The New York Times*, April 12, 1998.
- "The Work Has Just Begun on Welfare Reform." *The San Francisco Chronicle*, January 10, 1999.
- "Longtime Welfare Recipients Face Many Challenges in New Jobs." *The Buffalo News*, June 6, 1999.
- "Giuliani Proclaims Success on Pledge to Curb Welfare." *The New York Times*, December 29, 1999.

41. Many thanks to Brackette Williams, whose early critique of "multiculturalism" (Williams 1993) and more recent comments on this paper helped me spell out this point.
42. Shanklin (2000) seems surprised at the negative views of anthropology she discovered in her study of public opinion. Yet the whiteness of the discipline (extreme among the human sciences and made more blatant by anthropology's favorite objects of study), the conservative and essentialist deployments of culture, and the near-total disconnect between anthropology as a theoretical practice and the public deployments of concepts and images together beg for a public relations disaster. The wonder is that the image is not worse.
43. Given the power of the United States, the relative responsibility of those of us privileged to write in the United States is obvious.
44. My solution is not passive, but it is adamantly anti-voluntarist: We do not change the world by pretending that it is different. In correctly assessing the balance of forces, I fall back on Gandhi's notion of a protracted struggle and on Gramsci's war of position.
45. Inventing a new word is futile if the central problem is in the terms of engagement; it is like renaming a currency without attention to production and the terms of exchange. Although I find Brightman's (1995) critique of relexification and disciplinary amnesia useful, I wonder how much his collapsing most of the critics of culture under "relexification" conceals important conceptual advances. Relexification does not always obtain alone. It can also be an index of conceptual debate.
46. Powerful arguments for the defense of that kernel—rather than for the defense of culture as a unit of analysis—are outlined in Wolf 1999. I disagree, however, with Wolf's implicit equation of word and concept; it is an equation belied by his own work, including the cases treated in that book.
47. A central issue is exactly how much, how, and why patterns that may be ideationally sustained—what we (used to?) call "cultural traits"—develop among specific groups uniquely located in time and in space. Fieldwork matters to help us deal with "how much" these patterns obtain, but we also need to demonstrate how they obtain. We cannot ignore the "why" questions about origins, causes, or possible alternatives to the explanation of these patterns (Wolf 1999:47–49).

Chapter 6

1. World population figures are always contested, but especially before the seventeenth century because of debates about the population of the Americas before the conquest.

2. I used to ask graduate students in theory classes not to read the prefaces and introductions of books based on dissertations, but to try to guess a posteriori from the readings of the ethnographic sections how innovative the authors were. This was by no means a scientific study, but it did confirm my own prejudice that empiricist strategies were being deployed with the same naïveté that was their hallmark since at least the eighteenth century, in spite of self-congratulatory nods to deconstruction and many references to the likes of Foucault or Derrida.

3. Boas (1940 [1920]:284) writes, "The whole problem of cultural history appears to us [American anthropologists] as a historical problem. In order to understand history it is necessary to understand not only how things are, but how they have come to be."

4. Contrary also to the history of Maine or Tylor, the chronological interest turned to post-Renaissance, rather than to ancient history.

5. Citations of Marx are extremely rare in anthropology in the first half of the twentieth century. In the United States, where the human disciplines were stifled by the anti-communist witch hunt, passing and timid mentions of Marx start a few years after the official end of the hunt and Senator McCarthy's censure (e.g., Wolf 1959:252).

6. The loudest controversies have been about the nature of that response and the ways in which it matters (Obyesekere 1992; Price and Price 1999; Sahlins 1995).

7. See in particular the first two chapters of Cohn (1987) for a penetrating and lively discussion of the relationship between history and anthropology and the state of historical anthropology up until the mid-1980s.

8. The devastation of Cape Gloucester (New Britain) was so total that "Gloucesterizing" came to mean the complete destruction of a target in Fifth Air Force parlance.

9. Malinowski (1922:3) wrote: "In Ethnography, the distance is often enormous between the brute material of information...and the final authoritative presentation of the results." "Wholesale generalisations are laid down before us, and we are not informed at all by what actual experiences the writers have reached their conclusion...."

Inasmuch as anthropologists—like all professional researchers, from art historians to physicists—draw principled conclusions from privileged information, Malinowski's admonition remains relevant in spite of three related issues to which it cannot be reduced: (1) whether Malinowski himself heeded his own call; (2) whether art historians, anthropologists, and physicists construct information in the same way; (3) whether they build— or should build—the same kind of connections between information and conclusion.

10. T. K. Penniman (1974:9–17) of Oxford, writing originally in 1935, defines ethnography as "the study of a particular race, people or area *by any of the methods of anthropology....* It furnishes the data required by anthropology, and employs the methods based on such data" (emphasis added).

11. In a 1955 addendum to the same book (1974:366), Penniman singles out Malinowski's long fieldwork as having given him a unique opportunity to analyze social structures in light of Durkheimian principles.

12. Nadel's own life work strongly qualifies that statement.

13. Both Nadel and Casagrande see anthropology through the nineteenth-century model of a natural science, and Casagrande skirts over the fact that both the library and the laboratory are scholarly constructions.

14. The "field" is gendered, with the dominance of male figures within the discipline and the preeminence of Margaret Mead in the public sphere, at least in the United States. The tension between public sphere and guild practices permeates other aspects of fieldwork. Public claims not withstanding, fieldwork alone, while often a necessary condition of access to the guild, is rarely a sufficient condition of preeminence. Few anthropologists have gained notoriety *within* the discipline with a monograph based

on traditional fieldwork in exotic lands—especially after the 1950s, that is, during the very era when fieldwork is heralded as the distinctive practice of the discipline.

15. Refugees, diasporas, and indeed tourism have become suddenly visible to academics in part because of their growing role in shaping the social and geographical consciousness of North Atlantic populations. Diasporas in particular are poised to stand as archetypes of the current state of cultural transformations on a world scale in part because of their impact on receiving countries, including their academic institutions. An anthropology of diasporas thus requires not only an awareness of change and continuity, but also the awareness of its own conditions of possibility, including the sensibilities that drive the research. Yet how much of the scholarly research on diasporas—as research on other obvious global flows—merely reflects North Atlantic common sense?

16. One could consciously restore the locality, for instance by looking at a specific diasporic neighborhood on the anachronistic model of the closed corporate community. Few anthropologists are tempted to do this today, if only because of the ridicule they would attract.

17. The sensibilities that drive and shape our work may be at play in ways yet to be determined. Why it is possible to write about a fishing village in the Caribbean or to describe a ritual in Indonesia as if they were not localized, while it is obvious that we cannot describe a Pakistani neighborhood in Leeds as if it was not in England, may have less to do with the facts on the ground—the empirical markers—than with our reaction to certain kinds of markers.

18. I owe this phrasing to Niloofar Haeri.

19. Both the content and the phrasing of this paragraph reflect years of sharing "burning questions" with Brackette F. Williams.

20. In the natural sciences, private laboratories, the eminence of which goes back only to the twentieth century, play by the same rules. The only two differences with government-sponsored research centers is the financing and the explicit possibility of profit. By the second decade of the twentieth century, even intellectuals whose individual fame did not generate directly from an institutional location became full interlocutors of academics through their institutional recognition. Furthermore, such recognition—always posthumous—is actually quite rare. In the human disciplines, Antonio Gramsci is a spectacular exception for the twentieth century, as he had no institutional location within academe.

21. We see this most clearly on post-election nights when pollsters and journalists pose at being social scientists. They must say something more than the results themselves, lest the results "speak" for themselves. Yet these analysts must also concede—at least in democratic contexts—that, whatever their second reading, the people have indeed spoken.

22. First, reportage in and of itself was satisfying because for a long time anthropologists, along with Orientalists, were the only North Atlantic scholars to pay serious empirical attention to non-Europeans. Second, the possibility of mere reportage was premised on a naïve realism: the facts were there to be observed and collected by the ethnographer. To be sure, such "facts" included ideas, motifs, cosmologies, marriage practices, myths, or stories, all the items that collectively constitute "the cultures of primitive peoples" (Mead 1933) and interpretation or analysis could follow. But they were not always necessary.

23. This dissatisfaction did not originate from a theoretical debate about the status of the native. Rather, the second moment of globality, including the spread in communications, made realist ethnography as a reportage on the culture of primitive peoples a redundant exercise. The critique of representation followed (see chapter 1).

24. Geertz concludes the list of rules for the Balinese cockfight with this unusually awkward statement: "Finally, the Balinese peasants themselves are quite aware of all this and can and, at least to an ethnographer, do state most of it in approximately the same terms as I have" (1973:440).

25. Not accidentally, the discipline in which we are most likely to encounter similar claims is history, especially in its treatment of events.

26. In contradistinction, just imagine academe's contempt for a researcher who does not speak or read the dominant language in any diglossic situation within the North Atlantic.

27. None of these authors address satisfactorily the issue of local scholarly discourse or explain its irrelevance, although in his later work Price deals with Martinican intellectuals as serious interlocutors, even though he disagrees with them.

28. Only they can gain this status for themselves. No anthropologist—not even anthropologists born and raised outside of the North Atlantic, who risk becoming anthropology's new comfort zone as indeed they have quickly become in literary criticism and Cultural Studies—can confer this right upon them. We can only facilitate their entry.

29. The number of anthropologists practicing in and out of academe has increased tremendously in the last decades of the twentieth century. Anthropologists have brought their specialized knowledge to governments, international agencies, grassroots organizations, and high-class advertisers. Yet those individualized engagements do not coalesce into trends in part because academic anthropology, the institutional core of the discipline, has not meditated much on its public role. Just as anthropology protected its "primitives" and their pristine "cultures," it also protected itself from the public eye, or at least avoided as much as possible entering the public sphere by the front door (di Leonardo 1998).

Bibliography

Abrahams, Roger D. 1992. Singing the Master: The Emergence of African American Culture in the Plantation South. New York: Pantheon Books.

Abrams, Philip. 1988. Notes on the Difficulty of Studying the State. *Journal of Historical Sociology* 1(1): 58–89.

Abu-Lughod, Janet. 1991. Writing Against Culture. *In* Recapturing Anthropology: Working in the Present. Richard G. Fox, ed. Santa Fe: School of American Research Press. 137–62.

Adda, Jacques. 1996a. La Mondialisation de L'economie T1: La Genese. Paris: La Decouverte.

———. 1996b. La Mondialisation de L'economie T2: Les Problemes. Paris: La Decouverte.

Ainsa, Fernando. 1988. L'invention de l'Amérique. Signes imaginaires de la découverte et construction de l'utopie. *Diogènes* 145: 104–17.

Alavi, Hamza, Doug McEachern, P. B. Mayer, G. R. Knight, and P. L. Burns. 1982. Capitalism and Colonial Production. London: Croom Helm.

Alexander, Jennifer and Paul Alexander. 1991. Protecting Peasants from Capitalism: The Subordination of Javanese Traders by the Colonial State. *Comparative Studies in Society and History* 33: 370–94.

Ali, Kamran Asdar. 1996. The Politics of Family Planning in Egypt. *Anthropology Today* 12(5): 14–19.

———. 2000. Making "Responsible" Men: Planning the Family in Egypt. *In* Fertility and the Male Life-Cycle in the Era of Fertility Decline. Caroline Bledsoe, Susana Lerner, and Jane Guyer, eds. Oxford: Oxford University Press. 119–43.

Allais, Denis Vairasse d'. 1677–1679. The history of the Sevarites or Sevarambi, a nation inhabiting part of the third continent commonly called Terræ australes incognitæ, with an account of their admirable government, religion, customs, and language / written by one Captain Siden, a worthy person, who, together with many others, was cast upon those coasts, and lived many years in that country. London: Henry Brome.

Allen, Garland E. 1995. Eugenics Comes to America. *In* The Bell Curve Debate: History, Documents, Opinions. Russell Jacoby and Naomi Glauberman, eds. New York and Toronto: Random House. 441–75.

Althusser, Louis. 1971 [1969]. Lenin and Philosophy, and Other Essays. Ben Brewster, trans. New York: Monthly Review Press.

Anderson, Benedict. 1983. Imagined Communities: Reflections on the Origin and Spread of Nationalism. London: Verso.

André-Vincent, Philippe. 1980. Bartholomé de Las Casas, prophète du nouveau-monde. Paris: Librarie Jules Tallandier.

Andrews, Charles M. 1937 [1935]. Introduction. *In* Famous Utopias: Being the Complete Text of Rousseau's Social Contract, More's Utopia, Bacon's New Atlantis, Campanella's City of the Sun. Charles M. Andrews, ed. New York: Tudor Publishing.

Angell, Norman. 1910. The Great Illusion: A Study of the Relation of Military Power in Nations to their Economic and Social Advantage. New York and London: G. Putnam's Sons.

Anghiera, Pietro Martire d'. 1516. De Orbe Nouo Décades. Alcalá de Henares, Spain: Impressae in contubernio Arnaldi Guillelmi.

American Anthropology Association. 1997–1998. Anthropology Newsletter.

Appadurai, Arjun. 1991. Global Ethnoscapes: Notes and Queries for a Transnational Anthropology. In Recapturing Anthropology, Richard G. Fox, ed. Santa Fe: School of American Research. 191–210.

———. 1996. Modernity at Large: Cultural Dimensions of Globalization. Minneapolis and London: University of Minnesota Press.

Arac, Jonathan. 1986a. Introduction. In Post-Modernism and Politics. J. Arac, ed. Minneapolis and London: University of Minnesota Press. ix–xliii.

———, ed. 1986b. Post-Modernism and Politics. Minneapolis and London: University of Minnesota Press.

Aronowitz, Stanley. 1988. Post-Modernism and Politics. In Universal Abandon? The Politics of Post-Modernism. Andrew Ross, ed. Minneapolis and London: University of Minnesota Press. 46–62.

Asad, Talal, ed. 1973. Anthropology and the Colonial Encounter. London: Ithaca Press; Atlantic Highlands, N.J.: Humanities Press.

Atkinson, Geoffroy. 1920. The Extraordinary Voyage in French Literature before 1700. New York: Columbia University Press.

———. 1922. The Extraordinary Voyage in French Literature from 1700 to 1720. Paris: Librairie Ancienne E. Champion.

———. 1924. Les relations de voyage du XVIIe siècle et l'évolution des idées; contribution à l'étude de la formation de l'esprit du XVIIIe siècle. Paris: Librairie Ancienne Edouard Champion.

Bacon, Francis. 1660. New Atlantis. London: John Crooke.

Baker, Lee D. 1998. From Savage to Negro: Anthropology and the Construction of Race. Berkeley: University of California Press.

Balibar, Étienne. 1991 [1988]. Racism and Nationalism. In Race, Nation, Class: Ambiguous Identities. Étienne Balibar and Immanuel Wallerstein, eds. Chris Turner, trans. London and New York: Verso. 37–68.

———. 1997. La crainte des masses: politique et philosophie avant et après Marx. Paris: Galilée.

Banfield, Edward C. 1974. The Unheavenly City Revisited. Boston: Little, Brown.

Barrett, Stanley R. 1984. The Rebirth of Anthropological Theory. Toronto, Buffalo and London: University of Toronto Press.

Barrès, Maurice. 1897. Les Déracinés. Paris: Bibliothèque-Charpentier.

Baudelaire, Charles. 1999 [1857]. Les Fleurs du Mal. Paris: Hazan.

Baudet, Henri. 1965 [1959]. Some Thoughts on European Images of Non-European Man. New Haven: Yale University Press.

Beaud, Michel. 2001. Le basculement du monde. Paris: La Découverte.

Benedict, Ruth. 1959 [1934]. Patterns of Culture. Boston, New York: Houghton Mifflin.

Benedict, Ruth and Gene Weltfish. 1943. The Races of Mankind. New York: Public Affairs Committee, Inc.

Bernal, Martin. 1987. Black Athena: The Afroasiatic Roots of Classical Civilization. The Fabrication of Ancient Greece 1785–1985, Vol. 1. New Brunswick: Rutgers University Press.

Bessis, Sophie. 2001. L'Occident et les autres: Histoire d'une suprématie. Paris: La Découverte.

Blanchetti-Revelli, Lanfranco. 1997. Keeping Meat and Diary Consumers Slim: Philippine Seaweed, American Carrageenan and the USFDA. *Anthropology Today* 13(5): 6–13.

Boas, Franz. 1932. Anthropology and Modern Life. New York: W. W. Norton & Company, Inc.

——. 1940. Race, Language and Culture. New York: Macmillan.

——. 1945. Race and Democratic Society. New York: J. J. Augustin.

Bodley, John H. 1976. Anthropology and Contemporary Human Problems. Menlo Park, California: Cummings Publishing Company.

Boucher, Pierre, sieur de Boucherville. 1964 [1664]. Histoire véritable et natvrelle des moeurs & productions du pays de la Nouvelle France, vulgairement dite le Canada. Boucherille, Canada: Société historique de Boucherville.

Braudel, Fernand. 1967. Civilisation matérielle et capitalisme, XVe–XVIIIe siècle. Paris: A. Colin.

——. 1992. The Wheels of Commerce. Civilization and Capitalism, 15th–18th Century, Vol. 2. Berkeley: University of California Press.

Brewer, David. 1985. Diderot et l'autre feminin. In L'Homme des Lumières et la découverte de l'autre. Daniel Droixhe and Pol-P Gossiaux, eds. Bruxelles: Editions de l'Université de Bruxelles. 81–91.

Brightman, Robert. 1995. Forget Culture: Replacement, Transcendence, Relexification. Cultural Anthropology 10(4): 509–46.

Brockway, Lucille H. 1979. Science and Colonial Expansion: The Role of British Royal Botanic Gardens. American Ethnologist 6(3): 449–65.

Buchanan, James. 1995. Economic Science and Cultural Diversity. Kyklos 48(2): 193–200.

Buci-Glucksman, Christine. 1975. Gramsci et l'état: Pour une théorie matérialiste de la philosophie. Paris: Fayard.

Budé, Guillaume. 1967 [1518–1519]. De l'institution du prince. Farnborough (Hants.), Gregg P.

Calvet, Louis-Jean. 1974. Linguistique et colonialisme. Paris: Bibliothèque scientifique Payot.

Campanella, Tommaso. 1998 [1602]. La Città del Sole. Tonino Tornitore, trans. and ed. Milano: UNICOPLI.

Carter, Donald Martin. 1997. Media Politics and the Migrant. In States of Grace: Senegalese in Italy and the New European Immigration. Minneapolis and London: University of Minnesota Press. 133–44.

Casagrande, Joseph B., ed. 1960. In the Company of Man: Twenty Portraits of Anthropological Informants. New York, Evanston, and London: Harper Torchbooks.

Castañeda, Carlos. 1968. The Teachings of Don Juan: A Yaqui Way of Knowledge. Berkeley: University of California Press.

——. 1973. Sorcery: A Description of the World. Ph.D. thesis. Department of Anthropology, University of California at Los Angeles.

Chartier, Roger, ed. 1989. A History of Private Life, Vol. 3: Passions of the Renaissance. Arthur Goldhammer, trans. Cambridge: Belknap Press.

Chatterjee, Partha. 1989. Colonialism, Nationalism, and Colonized Women: The Context in India. American Ethnologist 16(4): 622–33.

Chaudhuri, K. N. 1990. Asia Before Europe: Economy and Civilisation of the Indian Ocean from the Rise of Islam to 1750. Cambridge: Cambridge University Press.

Cheney, Lynne V. 1995. Telling the Truth: Why Our Culture and Our Country Have Stopped Making Sense and What We Can Do About It. New York: Simon & Schuster.

Chesnais, François. 1994. La mondialisation du capital. Paris: Syros – Alternatives Économiques.

Chinard, Gilbert. 1934. L'Amérique et le rêve exotique dans la littérature française aux XVIIe et XVIII siecles. Paris: Librairie de Medicis.

Cioranescu, Alexandre. 1971. Utopia, Land of Cocaigne and Golden Age. *Diogènes* 75: 85–121.

Clairmont, Frederic. 2001. The Global Corporation: Road to Serfdom. *Economic and Political Weekly* January 8–14, 2000. Available 2001 from http://www.epw.org; INTERNET.

Clifford, James. 1983. On Ethnographic Authority. *Representations* 1(2): 118–46.

———. 1986a. Introduction: Partial Truths. *In* Writing Culture: The Poetics and Politics of Ethnography. James Clifford and George E. Marcus, eds. Berkeley, Los Angeles, and London: University of California Press. 1–26.

———. 1986b. On Ethnographic Allegory. *In* Writing Culture: The Poetics and Politics of Ethnography. James Clifford and George E. Marcus, eds. Berkeley, Los Angeles, and London: University of California Press. 98–121.

———. 1994. Diasporas. *Cultural Anthropology* 9(3): 302–38.

Clifford, James and George E. Marcus, eds. 1986. Writing Culture: The Poetics and Politics of Ethnography. Berkeley, Los Angeles, and London: University of California Press.

Cohn, Bernard S. 1987. An Anthropologist among the Historians and Other Essays. Delhi, Oxford, and New York: Oxford University Press.

Cole, Douglas. 1999. Franz Boas: The Early Years, 1858–1906. Vancouver and Toronto: Douglas & McIntyre; Seattle and London: University of Washington Press.

Comaroff, John L. 1997. Reflections on the Colonial State, in South Africa and Elsewhere: Factions, Fragments, Facts, and Fictions. *Bulletin, Institute of Ethnology, Academia Sinica* 83: 1–50.

Comaroff, Jean and John Comaroff. 1991. Of Revelation and Revolution: Christianity, Colonialism, and Consciousness in South Africa, Vol. 1. Chicago: University of Chicago Press.

———. 2000. Millennial Capitalism: First Thoughts on the Second Coming. *Public Culture* 12(2): 291–343.

Comte, Augusté. 1974 [1830–1842]. The Essential Comte. Stanislav Andreski, ed. and intro. Margaret Clarke, trans. London: Croom Helm Ltd.; New York: Barnes & Noble Books.

Condorcet, Jean-Antoine-Nicolas de Caritat, Marquis de. 1955 [1793]. Sketch for a Historical Picture of the Progress of the Human Mind. June Barraclough, trans.; Stuart Hampshire, intro. London: Weidenfeld and Nicolson.

Cordellier, Serge, ed. 2000. La mondialisation au-delà des mythes. Paris: La Découverte.

Cordellier, Serge and Béatrice Didot, eds. 2000. L'état du monde: Annuaire économique géopolitique mondial. Paris: La Découverte & Syros.

Coronil, Fernando. 1997. The Magical State: Nature, Money, and Modernity in Venezuela. Chicago: University of Chicago Press.

Darnell, Regna. 1997. The Anthropological Concept of Culture at the End the Boasian Century. *Social Analysis* 41(3): 42–54.

———. 1998. And Along Came Boas: Continuity and Revolution in Americanist Anthropology. Amsterdam and Philadelphia: John Benjamins.

Darwin, Charles. 1871 [1885–1886]. The Descent of Man. New York: Humboldt Publishing Company.

Davenport, Charles B., Louis I. Newman, C. M. Goethe, Melville J. Herskovits, Frank H. Hankins, and Ales Hrdlicka. 1930. Intermarriage Between Races, A Eugenic or Dysgenic Force?: Eugenics and Racial Intermarriage, a Symposium. *Eugenics, a Journal of Race Betterment* 3(2): 58–62.

Davies, Hunter. 1991. In Search of Columbus. London: Sinclair-Stevenson.

De Certeau, Michel. 1975. L'Ecriture de l'histoire. Paris: Gallimard.

———. 1986. Heterologies: Discourse on the Other. Minneapolis and London: University of Minnesota Press.

Debien, Gabriel. 1974. Les esclaves aux Antilles françaises (XVIIème-XVIIIème siècle). Fort de France: Sociétés d'histoire de la Guadeloupe et de la Martinique.

Defoe, Daniel. 1719–1720. The life and strange surprising adventures of Robinson Crusoe, of York, mariner: who lived eight and twenty years, all alone in an un-inhabited island on the coast of America, near the mouth of the great river Oroonoque; having been cast on shore by shipwreck, wherein all the men perished but himself. With an account how he was at last as strangely deliver'd by pyrates. Written by himself. London: W. Taylor.

De Mille, Richard. 1976. Castaneda's Journey: The Power and the Allegory. Santa Barbara: Capra Press.

De Mille, Richard and James A. Clifton, eds. 1980. The Don Juan Papers: Further Castaneda Controversies. Santa Barbara: Ross Erickson Publishers.

Diderot, D. 1965 [1748]. Les Bijoux Indiscrets. In Oeuvres Romanesques. H. Benac, ed. Paris: Garnier.

———. 1955 [1784]. Supplément au Voyage du Bougainville. H. Dieckmann, ed. Geneve: Droz. Lille, Giard.

Di Leonardo, Micaela. 1998. Exotics at Home: Anthropologies, Others, American Modernity. Chicago: University of Chicago Press.

Donner, Florinda. 1982. Shabono. New York: Delacorte Press.

Droixhe, Daniel, and Pol-P Gossiaux, eds. 1985. L'Homme des Lumières et la découverte de l'autre. Bruxelles: Editions de l'Université de Bruxelles.

Du Tertre, Jean-Baptiste. 1973 [1667]. Histoire générale des Antilles habitées par les François. Fort de France: Editions des Horizons Caraïbes.

Duby, Georges, ed. 1988. Revelations of the Medieval World. A History of Private Life, Vol. 2. Cambridge: Belknap Press of Harvard University Press.

Duchet, Michèle. 1971. Anthropologie et histoire au siècle des Lumières. Paris: Maspero.

Dumas, Alexandre. 1846. Les Trois Mousquetaires. New York: P. Gaillardet.

Dumas, Alexandre, son. 1880. La Dame aux Camelias. New York: F. Rullman.

Dussel, Enrique. 1993. Eurocentricism and Modernity (Introduction to the Frankfurt Lectures). Boundary 2 20(3): 65–76.

Eagleton, Terry. 1987. Awakening from Modernity. Times Literary Supplement, 20 February.

Eliav-Feldon, Miriam. 1982. Realistic Utopias: The Ideal Imaginary Societies of the Renaissance, 1516–1630. Oxford: Clarendon Press.

Erasmus, Desiderius. 1997 [1516]. Education of a Christian Prince. Neil M. Cheshire, Michael J. Heath, and Lisa Jardine, trans.; Lisa Jardine, ed. Cambridge and New York: Cambridge University Press.

Feierman, Steven. 1990. Peasant Intellectuals: Anthropology and History in Tanzania. Madison: University of Wisconsin Press.

Fénelon, François de Salignac de La Mothe. 1987 [1699]. Les Aventures de Télémaque. Jeanne-Lydie Goré, trans. and ed. Paris: Garnier.

Fouchard, Jean. 1981 [1972]. The Haitian Maroons: Liberty or Death. A. Faulkner Watts, trans. New York: Edward W. Blyden Press.

Fox, Richard G., ed. 1991. Recapturing Anthropology: Working in the Present. Santa Fe: School of American Research.

Frank, Andre Gunder. 1969. Latin America: Underdevelopment or Revolution; Essays on the Development of Underdevelopment and the Immediate Enemy. New York: Monthly Review Press.

Froidevaux, Gérald. 1989. Baudelaire: représentation et modernité. Paris: J. Corti.

Gage, Thomas. 1958 [1648]. Travels in the New World. J. Eric S. Thompson, ed. and introduction. Norman: University of Oklahoma Press.

Gaonkar, Dilip Parameshwar. 1999. On Alternative Modernities. Public Culture (Special Issue Alter/Native Modernities) 11(1): 1–18.

Geertz, Clifford. 1973. The Interpretation of Cultures. New York: Basic Books.

——. 1984. Distinguished Lecture: Anti Anti-Relativism. *American Anthropologist* 86(2): 263–78.

——. 1988. Works and Lives: The Anthropologist as Author. Stanford: Stanford University Press.

Genette, Gérard, Hans Robert Jauss, Jean-Marie Schaffer, Robert Scholes, Wolf Dieter Stemple, and Karl Vietor. 1986. Théorie des Genres. Paris: Editions du Seuil.

Gide, André. 1929. Si le grain ne meurt. Paris: Gallimard, Éditions de la Nouvelle revue française.

Gilder, George. 1993. Wealth and Poverty. Oakland, CA: Institute for Contemporary Studies.

Gill, Lesley. 2000. Teetering on the Rim: Global Restructuring, Daily Life, and the Armed Retreat of the Bolivian State. New York: Columbia University Press.

Glissant, Edouard. 1989. Caribbean Discourse: Selected Essays. J. Michael Dash, trans. Charlottesville: University of Virginia Press.

Godelier, Maurice. 1973. Horizon, trajets marxistes en anthropologie. Paris: F. Maspero.

Godzich, Vlad. 1986. Foreword. *In* Heterologies: Discourse on the Other, by Michel De Certeau. Minneapolis and London: University of Minnesota Press. vii–xxi.

Gonnard, René. 1946. La légende du bon sauvage: Contribution a l'étude des origines du socialisme. Paris: Librairie de Medicis.

Gough, Kathleen. 1968a. New Proposals for Anthropologists. *Current Anthropology* 9(5): 403–07.

——. 1968b. Anthropology: Child of Imperialism. *Monthly Review* 19(11): 12–27.

Graff, Gerald. 1977. The Myth of the Post-Modernist Breakthrough. *In* The Novel Today: Contemporary Writers on Modern Fiction. M. Bradbury, ed. Manchester: Manchester University Press, Rowan and Littlefield. 217–49.

Grant, Madison. 1916. The Passing of the Great Race; or, The Racial Basis of European History. New York: C. Scribner.

Gregory, Steven. 1998. Black Corona: Race and the Politics of Place in an Urban Community. Princeton: Princeton University Press.

Gregory, Steven and Roger Sanjek, eds. 1994. Race. New Brunswick: Rutgers University Press.

Gupta, Akhil. 1995. Blurred Boundaries: the Discourse of Corruption, the Culture of Politics, and the Imagined State. *American Ethnologist* 22(2): 375–402

Gupta, Akhil and James Ferguson, eds. 1997. Anthropological Locations: Boundaries and Grounds of a Field Science. Berkeley: University of California Press.

Hale, J. R. 1977 [1971]. Renaissance Europe. Individual and Society, 1480–1520. Berkeley and Los Angeles: University of California Press.

Hannerz, Ulf. 1992. The Global Ecumene as a Network of Networks. *In* Conceptualizing Society. Adam Kuper, ed. New York: Routledge. 34–56.

Harris, Marvin. 1964. Patterns of Race in the Americas. New York: Walker.

Harrison, Lawrence E. 2000. Underdevelopment is a State of Mind. Lanham, MD: Madison Books.

Harrison, Lawrence E. and Samuel P. Huttington, eds. 2000. Culture Matters: How Values Shape Human Progress. New York: Basic Books.

Hartog, François. 1988 [1980]. The Mirror of Herodotus: The Representation of the Other in the Writing of History. Janet Lloyd, trans. Berkeley and Los Angeles: University of California Press.

Harvey, David. 1982. The Limits to Capital. Chicago: University of Chicago Press.

——. 1989. The Condition of Postmodernity: An Enquiry Into the Origins of Cultural Change. New York and Oxford: Blackwell.

Heath, Deborah. 1992. Fashion, Anti-Fashion, and Heteroglossia in Urban Senegal. *American Ethnologist* 19(1): 19–33.

Herskovits, Melville J. 1975 [1937]. Life in a Haitian Valley. New York: Octagon Books.

——. 1958. The Myth of the Negro Past. Boston: Beacon Press.

Heyman, Josiah McC. 1995. Putting Power in the Anthropology of Bureaucracy: The Immigration and Naturalization Service at the Mexico-United States Border. *Current Anthropology* 36(2): 261–77.

——. 1998. State Effects on Labor Exploitation: the INS and Undocumented Immigrants at the Mexico-United States Border. *Critique of Anthropology* 18(2):157–80.

——. 1999. United States Surveillance over Mexican Lives at the Border: Snapshots of an Emerging Regime. *Human Organization* 58(2): 430–38.

Hibou, Béatrice, ed. 1999. La privatisation des états. Paris: Karthala.

Higman, B. W. 1984. Slave Populations of the British Caribbean 1807–1834. Baltimore and London: The Johns Hopkins University Press.

Hobbes, Thomas. 1670 [1651]. Leviathan. Amsterdam: Joannem Blaeu.

Hobsbawm, Eric J. 1962. The Age of Revolution, 1789–1848. Cleveland: World Publishing Company.

Howells, William Dean. 1894. A Traveler from Altruria. New York: Harper & Brothers.

Hyatt, Marshall. 1990. Franz Boas, Social Activist: The Dynamics of Ethnicity. New York: Greenwood Press.

Hymes, Dell H., ed. 1972. Reinventing Anthropology. New York: Pantheon Books.

Ibn Battuta. 1983 [c. 1354]. Travels in Asia and Africa, 1325–1354. London: Routledge and Kegan Paul.

Jacobson, Matthew Frye. 1998. Whiteness of a Different Color: European Immigrants and the Alchemy of Race. Cambridge: Harvard University Press.

Jameson, Fredric. 1984. Postmodernism, or The Cultural Logic of Late Capitalism. *New Left Review I* 146 (July/August): 53–92.

Jamous, Haroun. 1982. Israël et ses juifs: essai sur les limites du volontarisme. Paris: F. Maspero.

Jencks, Charles. 1986. What is Post-Modernism? London and New York: Academy Editions, St. Martin's Press.

Jessop, Bob. 1985. Nicos Poulantzas: Marxist Theory and Political Strategy. New York: St. Martin's Press.

Kamenka, Eugene, ed. 1987. Utopias: Papers from the Annual Symposium of the Australian Academy of the Humanities. Melbourne and New York: Oxford University Press.

Kamin, Leon J. 1995. Lies, Damned Lies, and Statistics. *In* The Bell Curve Debate: History, Documents, Opinions. Russell Jacoby and Naomi Glauberman, eds. New York and Toronto: Random House. 81–105.

Kisklick, Henrika. 1997. After Ishmael: The Fieldwork Tradition and Its Future. *In* Anthropological Locations: Boundaries and Grounds of a Field Science. Akhil Gupta and James Ferguson, eds. Berkeley: University of California Press. 47–65.

Knauft, Bruce M. 1996. Genealogies for the Present in Cultural Anthropology: A Critical Humanist Perspective. New York: Routledge.

——. 2002a. Critically Modern: An Introduction. *In* Critically Modern: Alternatives, Alterities, Anthropologies. Bruce Knauft, ed. Bloomington: Indiana University Press. 1–54.

——, ed. 2002b Critically Modern: Alternatives, Alterities, Anthropologies. Bloomington: Indiana University Press.

Koselleck, Reinhart. 1985. Futures Past: On the Semantics of Historical Time. Keith Tribe, trans. Cambridge: MIT Press.

Labarde, Philippe and Bernard Maris. 1998. Ah Dieu! que la guerre économique est jolie! Paris: Albin Michel.

Labat, Jean Baptiste. 1972 [1722]. Nouveau voyage aux isles de l'Amérique. Fort de France: Editions des Horizons Caraïbes.

Laclau, Ernesto, and Chantal Mouffe. 1985. Hegemony and Socialist Strategy: Towards a Radical Democratic Politics. London: Verso.

Laïdi, Zaki. 1993. L'Ordre mondial relâché: sens et puissance après la guerre froide. Paris: Presses de la Fondation nationale des sciences politiques.

——. 2001. Un monde privé de sens. Paris: Hachette.

Las Casas, Bartolomé de. 1992 [1552]. In Defense of the Indians: The Defense of the Most Reverend Lord, Don Fray Bartolomé de las Casas, of the Order of Preachers, late Bishop of Chiapa, Against the Persecutors and Slanderers of the Peoples of the New World Discovered Across the Seas. Stafford Poole, trans. and ed. DeKalb: Northern Illinois University Press.

Latour, Bruno. 1993 [1991]. We Have Never Been Modern. Catherine Porter, trans. Cambridge: Harvard University Press.

Leclerc, Gérald. 1972. Anthropologie et colonialisme: essai sur l'historie de l'africanisme. Paris: Fayard.

LeGuat, François. 1708. Voyage et avantures de François Leguat & de ses compagnons, en deux isles desertes des Indes Orientales. London: David Mortier.

Levin, Harry. 1958. The Power of Blackness: Hawthorne, Poe, Melville. London: Faber and Faber.

Lewis, Gordon K. 1983. Main Currents in Caribbean Thought. Baltimore and London: The Johns Hopkins University Press.

Lieberman, Leonard, Blaine W. Stevenson, and Larry T. Reynolds. 1989. Race and Anthropology: A Core Concept without Consensus. Anthropology and Education Quarterly 20(2): 67–73.

Lieberman, Leonard, Raymond E. Hampton, Alice Littlefield, and Glen Hallead. 1992. Race in Biology and Anthropology: A Study of College Texts and Professors. Journal of Research of Science Teaching 29(3): 301–21.

Linton, Ralph. 1955. The Tree of Culture. New York: Knopf.

Lundahl, Mats and Benno J. Ndulu, eds. 1996. New Directions in Development Economics: Growth, Environmental Concerns and Government in the 1990s. London and New York: Routledge Studies in Development Economics, 3.

Luxemburg, Rosa. 1951 [1914]. The Accumulation of Capital. New York: Monthly Review Press.

Lyotard, Jean-Francois. 1979. La Condition post-moderne. Paris: Editions de Minuit.

——. 1986. Le Post-moderne expliqué aux enfants. Paris: Editions Galilée.

Macchiocci, Maria-Antonietta. 1974. Pour Gramsci. Paris: Editions du Seuil.

Machiavelli, Niccolò. 1985 [1513]. The Prince. Daniel Donno, trans. and ed. Toronto and New York: Bantam Books.

Magazine, Roger. 1999. Stateless Contexts: Street Children and Soccer Fans In Mexico City. Ph.D. dissertation, Department of Anthropology, Johns Hopkins University.

Mailer, Norman. 1966. Cannibals and Christians. New York: Dial Press.

Maine, Henry Sumner. 1861. Ancient Law: Its Connection with the Early History of Society, and its Relation to Modern Ideas. London: J. Murray.

Malinowski, Bronislaw. 1922. Argonauts of the Western Pacific: An Account of Native Enterprise and Adventure in the Archipelagoes of Melanesian New Guinea. London: G. Routledge & Sons, Ltd.; New York: E. P. Dutton & Co.

Manuel, Frank E. and Fritzie P. Manuel. 1979. Utopian Thought in the Western World. Cambridge: Belknap Press of Harvard University Press.

Marcus, Georges E. 1980. Rhetoric and the Ethnographic Genre in Anthropological Research. *Current Anthropology* 21(4): 507–10.

——, ed. 1997. Cultural Producers in Perilous States: Editing Events, Documenting Change. Chicago: University of Chicago Press.

Marcus, Georges E. and Dick Cushman. 1982. Ethnographies as Texts. *Annual Review of Anthropology* 11: 25–69.

Marcus, George E. and Michael M. J. Fischer, eds. 1986. Anthropology as Cultural Critique: An Experimental Moment in the Human Sciences. Chicago: University of Chicago Press.

Martin, Hans-Peter and Harald Schuman. 1997 [1996]. The Global Trap: Globalization and the Assault on Prosperity and Democracy. Patrick Camiller, trans. London and New York: Zed Books.

Masaki, Kotabe and Kristiaan Helse. 1998. Global Marketing Management. New York: John Wiley and Sons.

Mattelart, Armand. 2000. La nouvelle idéologie globalitaire. *In* La mondialisation au-delà des mythes. S. Cordellier, ed. Paris: La Découverte. 81–92.

Mayhew, Anne. 1987. Culture: Core Concept Under Attack. *Journal of Economic Issues* 21(2): 587–603.

McNeill, William Hardy. 1992. The Global Condition: Conquerors, Catastrophes, and Community. Princeton: Princeton University Press.

Mead, Margaret. 1933. More Comprehensive Field Methods. *American Anthropologist* 35(1): 1–15.

Meillassoux, Claude. 1975. Femmes, greniers et capitaux. Paris: F. Maspero.

Memmi, Albert. 2000 [1982]. Racism. Steve Martinot, trans. Minneapolis and London: University of Minnesota Press.

Milliband, Ralph. 1969. The State in Capitalist Society. New York: Harper Books.

Mintz, Sidney W. 1966. The Caribbean as Socio-cultural Area. *Cahiers d-Histoire Mondiale* IX(4): 916–41.

——. 1971a. Le rouge et le noir. *Les Temps modernes* 299–300: 2354–61.

——. 1971b. The Caribbean as a Socio-cultural Area. *In* Peoples and Cultures of the Caribbean: An Anthropological Reader. M. Horowitz, ed. Garden City: The Natural History Press. 17–46.

——. 1971c. Men, Women, and Trade. *Comparative Studies in Society and History* 13(3): 247–69.

——. 1977. The So-Called World System: Local Initiative and Local Response. *Dialectical Anthropology* 2(4): 253–70.

——. 1978. Was the Plantation Slave a Proletarian? *Review* 2(1): 81–98.

——. 1983. Reflections on Caribbean Peasantries. *Nieuwe West Indische Gids/New West Indian Guide* 57(1–2): 1–17.

——. 1984. American Anthropology in the Marxist Tradition. *In* On Marxian Perspectives in Anthropology: Essays in Honor of Harry Hoijer. Sidney W. Mintz, M. Godelier, and Bruce Trigger, eds. Malibu: Undena Publications, Department of Anthropology, University of California at Los Angeles. 11–34.

——. 1985. Sweetness and Power: The Place of Sugar in Modern History. New York: Viking.

——. 1990. Introduction. *In* Myth of the Negro Past, Melville J. Herskovits. Boston: Beacon Press. ix–xxi.

——. 1996. Tasting Food, Tasting Freedom: Excursions into Eating, Culture, and the Past. Boston: Beacon Press.

Mintz, Sidney W. 1998. The Localization of Anthropological Practice: From Area Studies to Transnationalism. *Critique of Anthropology* 18(2): 117–33.

Mintz, Sidney W., M. Godelier, and Bruce Trigger, eds. 1984. On Marxian Perspectives in Anthropology: Essays in Honor of Harry Hoijer. Malibu: Undena Publications, Department of Anthropology, University of California at Los Angeles.

Montagu, Ashley. 1946. What Every Child and Adult Should Know About "Race." *Education* January: 262–64.

——, ed. 1964 [1962]. The Concept of Race. *In* The Concept of Race. Ashley Montagu, ed. New York: Free Press of Glencoe; London: Collier-Macmillan Limited. 12–28.

——. 1974 [1942]. Man's Most Dangerous Myth: The Fallacy of Race. 5th ed. London, Oxford, and New York: Oxford University Press.

Montaigne, Michel Eyquiem de. 1952. Essays. Chicago: Encyclopedia Britannica, Great Books of the Western World.

Montesquieu, Charles de Secondat, baron de. 1929 [1721]. Lettres Persanes. Paris: Fernand Roches.

More, Thomas, Sir, Saint. 1966 [1516]. Utopia. Leeds: Scolar Press Ltd.

Morgan, Lewis Henry. 1877. Ancient Society, or, Researches in the Lines of Human Progress from Savagery through Barbarism to Civilization. New York: H. Holt.

Mudimbe, V. Y. 1994. The Idea of Africa. Bloomington and Indianapolis: Indiana University Press.

Myrdal, Gunnar. 1944. An American Dilemma: The Negro Problem and Modern Democracy. New York: Harper & Brothers.

Nadel, S. F. 1951. The Foundations of Social Anthropology. Glencoe IL: The Free Press.

Nagengast, Carol. 1994. Violence, Terror, and the Crisis of the State. *Annual Review of Anthropology* 23: 109–36.

Nash, June. 1992. Interpreting Social Movements: Bolivian Resistance to Economic Conditions Imposed by the International Monetary Fund. *American Ethnologist* 19(2): 275–93.

Nugent, David. 1994. Building the State, Making the Nation: The Bases and Limits of State Centralization in "Modern" Peru. *American Anthropologist* 96(2): 333–69.

Obeyesekere, Gananath. 1992. The Apotheosis of Captain Cook: European Mythmaking in the Pacific. Princeton: Princeton University Press; Honolulu: Bishop Museum Press.

Ohmae, Kenichi. 1985. Triad Power: The Coming Shape of Global Competition. New York: New Press.

Ohnuki-Tierney, Emiko. 2001. Historicization of the Culture Concept. *History and Anthropology* 12(3): 231–54.

O'Laughlin, Bridget M. 1975. Marxist Approaches in Anthropology. *Annual Review of Anthropology* 4: 341–70.

Ong, Aihwa. 1988. The Production of Possession: Spirits and the Multinational Corporation in Malaysia. *American Ethnologist* 15(1): 28–42.

Pagden, Anthony. 1982. The Fall of Natural Man. The American Indian and the Origins of Comparative Ethnology. Cambridge: Cambridge University Press.

Parsons, Talcott. 1951. The Social System. New York: Free Press.

Pasquet, Fabienne. 1996. L'ombre de Baudelaire. Arles: Actes Sud.

Passet, René. 2000. L'illusion néo-libérale. Paris: Librairie Arthème Fayard.

Pearson, Ian, ed. 1998. The Macmillan Atlas of the Future. New York: Macmillan.

Penniman, T. K. 1974. A Hundred Years of Anthropology. New York: William Morrow & Company, Inc.

Pfaelzer, Jean. 1984. The Utopian Novel in America, 1886–1896: The Politics of Form. Pittsburgh: University of Pittsburgh Press.

Pigafetta, Antonio. 1994 [1522]. Magellan's Voyage: A Narrative of the First Circumnavigation. R. A. Skelton, trans. and ed. New York: Dover Publications.

Pi-Sunyer, Oriol. 1973. Tourism and its Discontents: The Impact of a New Industry on a Catalan Community. *Studies in European Society* 1: 1–20.

Plato. 1905. The Atlantis Myth. *In* The Myths of Plato, J. A. Stewart, trans. and ed. London and New York: Macmillan. 457–64.

Pliny the Elder. 1942. Natural History. London: William Heinemann.

Polo, Marco. 1958 [c. 1298–99]. The Travels. Hanmondsworth: Penguin.

Poulantzas, Nicos. 1972. Pouvoir politique et classes sociales. Paris: Maspero.

Pratt, Mary Louise. 1986. Fieldwork in Common Places. *In* Writing Culture: The Poetics and Politics of Ethnography. James Clifford and Georges E. Marcus, eds. Berkeley: University of California Press. 27–50.

Price, Richard. 1983. First-Time: The Historical Vision of an Afro-American People. Baltimore and London: The Johns Hopkins University Press.

——. 1990. Alabi's World. Baltimore: The Johns Hopkins University Press.

Price, Sally and Richard Price. 1999. Maroon Arts: Cultural Vitality in the African Diaspora. Boston: Beacon Press.

Provinse, John Henry. 1954. The American Indian in Transition. *American Anthropologist* 56(3): 387–94.

Rabinow, Paul. 1991. For Hire: Resolutely Late Modern. *In* Recapturing Anthropology: Working in the Present. Richard G. Fox, ed. Santa Fe: School of American Research. 59–72.

Radcliffe-Brown, A. R. 1955 [1940]. Preface. *In* African Political Systems. M. Fortes and E. E. Evans-Pritchard, eds. London: Oxford University Press.

Reich, Robert B. 1991. The Work of Nations: Preparing Ourselves for Twenty-First Century Capitalism. London and New York: Simon & Schuster.

Resch, Robert Paul. 1992. Althusser and the Renewal of Marxist Social Theory. Berkeley: University of California Press.

Richon, Emmanuel. 1998. Jeanne Duval et Charles Baudelaire. Belle d'abandon. Paris: L'Harmattan.

Rosaldo, Renato. 1986. From the Door of His Tent: The Fieldworker and the Inquisitor. *In* Writing Culture: The Poetics and Politics of Ethnography. James Clifford and Georges E. Marcus, eds. Berkeley: University of California Press. 77–97.

——. 1989. Culture and Truth. The Remaking of Social Analysis. Boston: Beacon Press.

Rosanvallon, Pierre. 1999. Le capitalisme utopique. Histoire de l'idée de marché. Paris: Seuil.

Ross, Andrew. 1988a. Introduction. *In* Universal Abandon? The Politics of Post-Modernism. Andrew Ross, ed. Minneapolis and London: University of Minnesota Press. vii–xviii.

——, ed. 1988b. Universal Abandon? The Politics of Post-Modernism. Minneapolis and London: University of Minnesota Press.

Ross, Dorothy. 1991. The Origins of American Social Science. New York and London: Cambridge University Press.

Rouse, Roger. 1991. Mexican Migration and the Social Space of Postmodernism. *Diaspora* 1(1): 8–23.

Rousseau, Jean-Jacques. 1984 [1755]. A Discourse on Inequality. Maurice Cranston, trans. and intro. Harmondsworth and New York: Penguin Books.

——. 1792 [1762]. Contrat Social, ou, Principes du Droit Politique. Rouen: La veuve P. Dumesnil.

Ruby, Jay, ed. 1982. A Crack in the Mirror: Reflexive Perspectives in Anthropology. Philadelphia: University of Pennsylvania Press.

Rupp-Eisenreich, Britta, ed. 1984. Histoire de l'anthropologie (xvie–xix siècles). Paris: Klincksiech.

——. 1985. Christophe Meiners et Joseph-Marie de Gérando: un chapitre du comparatisme anthropologique. *In* L'Homme des Lumières et la découverte de l'autre. Droixhe, Daniel, and Pol-P Gossiaux, eds. Bruxelles: Editions de l'Université de Bruxelles. 21–47.

Sahlins, Marshall. 1985. Islands of History. Chicago: University of Chicago Press.

——. 1995. How "Natives" Think: About Captain Cook, For Example. Chicago: University of Chicago Press.

Said, Edward W. 1978. Orientalism. New York: Pantheon.

——. 1993. Culture and Imperialism. New York: Knopf.

Saint Pierre, Bernardin de. 1796 [1787]. Paul et Virginie, Histoire Indienne. Boston: Guillaume Spotswood and Joseph Nancrede.

——. 1833 [1795]. L'Arcadie; L'amazone. Raymond Trousson, ed. Paris: Ressources.

Sanderon, A., B. Dugoni, T. Hoffer, and L. Selfa. 1999. Doctorate Recipients from United States Universities: Summary Report 1998. Chicago: National Opinion Research Center.

Sanderon, A., B. Dugoni, T. Hoffer, and S. Myers. 2000. Doctorate Recipients from United States Universities: Summary Report 1999. Chicago: National Opinion Research Center.

Sanjek, Roger. 1994. The Enduring Inequalities of Race. *In* Race. S. Gregory and R. Sanjek, eds. New Brunswick: Rutgers University Press.

——. 1998. The Future of Us All: Race And Neighborhood Politics in New York City. Ithaca: Cornell University Press.

Sassen, Saskia. 1998. Globalization and its Discontents: Essays on the New Mobility of People and Money. New York: The New Press.

Scott, James C. 1998. Seeing like a State: How Certain Schemes to Improve Human Condition Have Failed. New Haven: Yale University Press.

Sen, Amartya Kumar. 1992. Inequality Reexamined. Cambridge: Harvard University Press.

——. 1999. Development as Freedom. New York: Knopf.

Shanklin, Eugenia. 2000. Representations of Race and Racism in American Anthropology. *Current Anthropology* (Forum on Anthropology in Public) 41(1): 99–103.

Shweder, Richard A. 2001. Culture: Contemporary Views. *International Encyclopedia of the Social and Behavioral Sciences*. Elsevier Science Ltd. Available 2002 from http://www.sciencedirect.com/science/article/B6WVS-46RRM4D-15/2/1e5a62daf-9300ea1c19f81dac6268e37; INTERNET.

Silverstein, Michael. n.d. Languages/Cultures are Dead! Long Live the Linguistic-Cultural! Paper presented at the AAA 2000, San Francisco.

Smith, Adam. 1776. Inquiry into the Nature and Causes of the Wealth of Nations. London: W. Strahan and T. Cadell.

Smith, Carol A. 1984. Local History in Global Context: Social and Economic Transitions in Western Guatemala. *Comparative Studies in Society and History* 26(2): 193–228.

Smith, Jennie Marcelle. 2001. When the Hands Are Many: Community Organization and Social Change in Rural Haiti. Ithaca: Cornell University Press.

Steward, J., Robert A. Manners, Eric R. Wolf, Elena Padilla Seda, Sidney W. Mintz, and Raymond L. Sheele. 1956. The People of Puerto Rico: A Study in Social Anthropology. Urbana: University of Illinois Press.

Stocking, George W., Jr., ed. 1974. A Franz Boas Reader: The Shaping of American Anthropology 1883–1911. Chicago: University of Chicago Press.

——. 1982 [1964]. Franz Boas and the Culture Concept in Historical Perspective. *In* Race, Culture and Evolution. Chicago: University of Chicago Press.

——. 1987. Victorian Anthropology. New York: Free Press.

Stoler, Ann L. 1985. Perceptions of Protest: Defining the Dangerous in Colonial Sumatra. *American Ethnologist* 12(4): 642–58.

St.-Onge, J.-Claude. 2000. L'imposture néolibérale: marché, liberté et justice sociale. Montréal: Éditions Écosociété.

Stowe, Harriet Beecher. 1852 [1851]. Uncle Tom's Cabin: A Tale of Life among the Lowly. London: J. Cassell.

Swift, Jonathan. 1976 [1702]. Gulliver's Travels: a facsimile reproduction of the first edition, 1726, containing the author's annotations. Colin McKelvie, intro. Delmar, NY: Scholars' Facsimiles & Reprints.

Taguieff, Pierre-André. 2000. L'effacement de l'avenir. Paris: Galilée.

Thomas, Paul. 1994. Alien Politics: Marxist State Theory Retrieved. New York: Routledge.

Thornton, Robert J. 1983. Narrative Ethnography in Africa, 1850–1920: The Creation and Capture of an Appropriate Domain for Anthropology. *Man* 18(3): 502–20.

Tinker, Chauncey Brewster. 1922. Nature's Simple Plan: A Phase of Radical Thought in the Mid-Eighteenth Century. Princeton: Princeton University Press.

Todorov, Tzvetan. 1982. La Conquête de l'Amérique: La question de l'autre. Paris: Editions du Seuil.

——. 2001. The Fragility of Goodness: Why Bulgaria's Jews Survived the Holocaust. Arthur Denner, trans. Princeton: Princeton University Press.

Toussaint, Eric. 1999. Your Money Or Your Life! The Tyranny of Global Finance. London: Pluto Press.

Trollope, Anthony. 1859. The West Indies and the Spanish Main. London: Chapman & Hall.

Trouillot, Michel-Rolph. 1982. Motion in the System: Coffee, Color and Slavery in Eighteenth-Century Saint-Domingue. *Review* (A Journal of the Fernand Braudel Center for the Study of Economies, Historical Systems and Civilizations) 5(3): 331–88.

——. 1988. Peasants and Capital: Dominica in the World Economy. Baltimore: The Johns Hopkins University Press.

——. 1990. Haiti. State against Nation: The Origins and Legacy of Duvalierism. New York: Monthly Review Press.

——. 1991. Anthropology and the Savage Slot: The Poetics and Politics of Otherness. *In* Recapturing Anthropology: Working in the Present. Richard G. Fox, ed. Santa Fe: School of American Research. 17–44.

——. 1992. The Caribbean Region: An Open Frontier in Anthropological Theory. *Annual Review of Anthropology* 21: 19–42.

——. 1994. Haiti's Nightmare and the Lessons of History. *NACLA Report on the Americas* 27(4): 46–51.

——. 1995. Silencing the Past: Power and the Production of History. Boston: Beacon Press.

——. 1996a. Démocratie et Société Civile. *In* Les transitions démocratiques. L. Hurbon, ed. Paris: Editions Syros. 225–31.

——. 1996b. Beyond and Below the Merivale Paradigm. Dominica: The First 100 Days of Freedom. *In* The Lesser Antilles in the Age of European Expansion. Stanley Engerman and R. Paquette, eds. Gainesville: University of Florida Press. 230–305.

——. 1997. A Social Contract for Whom? Haitian History and Haiti's Future. *In* Haiti Renewed. R. Rotberg, ed. Washington: Brookings Institution Press. 47–59.

——. 1998. Culture on the Edges: Creolization in the Plantation Context. *Plantation Society in the Americas* (Special Issue, "Who/What is Creole?" A. James Arnold, ed.) 5(1): 8–28.

——. 2000. Abortive Rituals: Historical Apologies in the Global Era. *Interventions. The International Journal of Post-Colonial Studies* 2(2): 171–86.

——. 2001a. The Anthropology of the State in the Age of Globalization: Close Encounters of the Deceptive Kind. *Current Anthropology* 42(1): 125–38.

——. 2001b. Bodies and Souls. Madison Smartt Bell's All Souls Rising and the Haitian Revolution. *In* Novel History: Historians and Novelists Confront America's Past (And Each Other). Mark C. Carnes, ed. New York: Simon & Schuster. 184–97.

Trouillot, Michel-Rolph. 2002a. Culture on the Edges: Caribbean Creolization in Historical Context. *In* From the Margins: Historical Anthropology and its Futures. Brian Keith Axel, ed. Durham and London: Duke University Press. 189–210.

——. 2002b. Adieu Culture: A New Duty Arises. *In* Anthropology Beyond Culture. Richard G. Fox and Barbara J. King, eds. Oxford and New York: Berg Press. 37–60.

——. 2002c. The Otherwise Modern: Caribbean Lessons from the Savage Slot. *In* Critically Modern: Alternatives, Alterities, Anthropologies. Bruce M. Knauft, ed. Bloomington: Indiana University Press. 220–37.

——. 2002d. The Perspective of the World: Globalization Then and Now. *In* Beyond Dichotomies: Histories, Identities, Cultures, and the Challenge of Globalization. Elisabeth Mudimbe-Boyi, ed. Albany: State University of New York Press. 3–20.

——. 2002e. North Atlantic Universals: Analytic Fictions, 1492–1945. *South Atlantic Quarterly* (Special Issue, "Enduring Enchantments." Saurabh Dube, ed.) 101(4): 839–58.

Trousson, Raymond. 1975. Voyages aux pays de nulle part. Histoire littéraire de la pensée utopique. Bruxelles: Editions de l'Université de Bruxelles.

Tsing, Anna Lowenhaupt. 1993. In the Realm of the Diamond Queen: Marginality in an Out-of-the-Way Place. Princeton: Princeton University Press.

——. 2000. The Global Situation. *Cultural Anthropology* 15(3): 327–60.

Turner, Terence. 2002. Class Projects, Social Consciousness, and the Contradictions of Globalization. *In* Globalization, the State, and Violence. Jonathan Friedman, ed. Walnut Creek, CA: Altamira Press.

Tyler, Stephen. 1986. Post-Modern Ethnography: From Document of the Occult to Occult Document. *In* Writing Culture: The Poetics and Politics of Ethnography. James Clifford and George E. Marcus, eds. Berkeley, Los Angeles, and London: University of California Press. 122–40.

Tylor, Edward B. 1881. Anthropology: An Introduction to the Study of Man and Civilization. New York: D. Appleton and Company.

Vespucci, Amerigo. 1992 [1516]. Mundus Novus. *In* Letters from a New World: Amerigo Vespucci's Discovery of America. Luciano Formisano, ed. and introduction. David Jacobson, trans. New York: Marsilio. 45–56.

Vincent, Joan. 1991. Engaging Historicism. *In* Recapturing Anthropology: Working in the Present. Richard G. Fox, ed. Santa Fe: School of American Research. 45–58.

Voltaire. 1929 [1756]. Zadig. David Garnett, intro. New York: Rimington & Hooper.

——. 1999 [1759]. Candide. Daniel Gordon, trans., ed. and intro. Boston: Bedford/St. Martin's.

Wade, Robert. 1996. Japan, the World Bank, and the Art of Paradigm Maintenance: The East Asian Miracle in Political Perspective. *New Left Review I* 217 (May/June): 3–36.

——. 2001. Global Inequality: Winners and Losers. *The Economist* 28 April: 72–4.

Walkover, Andrew. 1974. The Dialectics of Eden. Stanford: Stanford University Press.

Wallerstein, Immanuel. 1976. The Modern World-System. New York: Academic Press.

Wallerstein, Immanuel, Calestous Juma, Evelyn Fox Keller, Jurgen Kocka, Domenique Lecourt, V.Y. Mudkimbe, Kinhide Miushakoji, Ilya Prigogine, Peter J. Taylor, and Michel-Rolph Trouillot. 1996. Open the Social Sciences: A Report of the Gulbenkian Commission for the Restructuring of the Social Sciences. Stanford: Stanford University Press.

Watts, David. 1987. The West Indies: Patterns of Development, Culture and Environmental Change since 1492. Cambridge: Cambridge University Press.

Weil, Françoise. 1984. La relation de voyage: document anthropologique ou texte littéraire? *In* Histoire de l'anthropologie (xvie–xix siècles). Britta Rupp-Eisenreich, ed. Paris: Klincksiech. 55–65.

Weiss, Linda. 1997. Globalization and the Myth of the Powerless State. *New Left Review I* 225 (September/October): 3–27.

——. 1998. The Myth of the Powerless State. Cornell Studies in Political Economy. Ithaca: Cornell University Press.

White, Leslie. 1949. The Science of Culture. New York: Grove Press.

Whitten, N. E. and J. F. Swzed, eds. 1970. Afro-American Anthropology. New York: Free Press.

Williams, Raymond. 1983. Keywords: A Vocabulary of Culture and Society. New York: Oxford University Press.

Williams, Brackette F. 1989. A Class Act: Anthropology and the Race to Nation Across Ethnic Terrain. *Annual Review of Anthropology* 18: 401–44.

——. 1993. The Impact of the Precepts of Nationalism on the Concept of Culture: Making Grasshoppers of Naked Apes. *Cultural Critique* 24 (Spring): 143–92.

Wissler, Clark. 1901. The Correlation of Mental and Physical Tests. New York and Lancaster, PA: Press of the New Era Printing Company.

——. 1923. Man and Culture. New York: Thomas Y. Crowell.

Wissler, Clark, Fay Cooper Cole, William M. McGovern, and Melville J. Herskovitz. 1929. Making Mankind. Baker Brownell, ed. New York: D. Van Nostrand Company, Inc.

Wolf, Eric. 1959. Sons of the Shaking Earth. Chicago: University of Chicago Press.

——. 1969. American Anthropologists and American Society. *Southern Anthropological Society Proceedings* (Special Issue, "Concepts and Assumptions in Contemporary Anthropology." Stephen A. Tyler, ed.) 3: 3–11.

——. 1982. Europe and the People without History. Berkeley: University of California Press.

——. 1999. Envisioning Power. Ideologies of Dominance and Crisis. Berkeley: University of California Press.

Yan, Yunxiang. 1997. McDonald's in Beijing: The Localization of Americana. *In* Golden Arches East: McDonald's in East Asia. James L. Watson, ed. Stanford: Stanford University Press. 39–67.

Index

power, 2, 7–8, 12–13, 19–22, 26, 29, 32–33,
    36, 41, 45, 47, 49, 51, 53, 57–58,
    60–61, 65–66, 69–70, 72–73, 75–77,
    80–95, 98–99, 101, 103–105, 107, 111,
    113–115, 119–122, 124, 128, 133, 135,
    138, 144, 147–149, 152–153
powerlessness, 62, 66, 77, 86, 93
price, 42, 50, 65, 75, 101, 122
Price, Richard, 133
primitives, 18, 24, 101–102, 120, 125, 142,
    155–156
privatization, 91
privilege, 65–66, 97, 109, 114–115, 118
production, 2, 8, 26–27, 33, 38–39, 42–43,
    45, 48, 51, 53, 60–61, 70, 72, 74, 81,
    89–91, 93–94, 96, 102, 104, 106, 116,
    121, 129–131, 144, 153
professionalization, 103–104
profit, 2, 32, 42, 51–56, 58, 61, 142, 155
purchasing power, 58–59, 66

race, 4, 16, 30, 40–41, 71–72, 76, 87, 90, 94,
    98–99, 103, 105–113, 116, 120, 134,
    136, 149–152, 154
racism, 18, 71, 73, 76, 99, 105–113, 120,
    142–144, 149–152
  racism in America, 18, 100
Radcliffe-Brown, A. R., 81–82, 95
refugees, 79, 88, 118, 127, 155
relativism, 135, 138
Renaissance, 1–2, 4, 13, 17, 19–21, 26, 37, 39,
    43, 45, 66–67, 69, 71, 85, 142–143, 154
resources, 1, 3, 56–57, 92
revisionism, 21, 43, 71
revolution, 29, 31, 37, 63, 67, 70, 77, 84,
    143, 148
rights, 10, 37–38, 54, 73, 89, 94, 110
Ross, Dorothy, 111
Rousseau, Jean-Jacques, 16–17, 39–40, 135,
    137

savage, 1–2, 5, 7–9, 14–25, 27–28, 39,
    71–72, 75, 77, 101–102, 107, 109–110,
    113, 119, 122, 124, 131–137, 141–144
  noble savage, 16–17, 39
  savage slot, 1–2, 8–9, 19, 23, 27–28,
    71–72, 75, 77, 101–102, 107, 109,
    113, 119, 122, 124, 131–133,
    136–137, 142–144
  savage-utopia, 19, 22

schools, 7, 16–17, 48, 54, 58, 79–80, 82, 98,
    103, 110, 124, 151
  see also education
sciences, 3–5, 9–10, 19, 45, 68, 70, 83–84,
    97, 99, 101–102, 111, 113–114, 118,
    122–124, 129–132, 137–138, 143,
    145–146, 148, 151–155
Scott, James, 79, 82
segregation, 73, 88, 115
self-definition, 75, 131
separatism, 13, 75, 80, 89, 93, 147
Shanklin, Eugenia, 105–106, 108, 150, 153
short-term, 52, 69
Sierra Club, 147
silences, 1, 5, 10, 28, 34, 36, 39–40, 47–48,
    72, 99, 102–103, 105, 107, 118, 146,
    150
slavery, 19, 29–31, 40–43, 45, 53, 73, 142,
    151
Smith, Adam, 53–54, 121, 133, 145
socialism, 15, 18, 58
society, 43, 53–55, 60–61, 71, 81, 83–84, 99,
    102, 104, 109–113, 120, 132, 136, 138,
    142, 146–147, 150–151, 153
sociocultural anthropology
  see anthropology
sociology, 3, 19, 68, 71–72, 74, 76, 83,
    101–102, 109–110, 129–130, 141, 144
Soviet Union, 13, 68, 70, 87
space
  respatialization, 95
  spatialization, 40, 48, 50–51, 81, 87, 90,
    94
Spain, 17, 20, 29–30, 45, 88
states, 5, 9, 16–17, 19, 21, 31, 37, 78–92,
    94–96, 98–99, 101–102, 106, 123, 127,
    146–148, 150, 154
  state power, 19, 80, 86, 89–90, 92–95,
    147–148
  state-centrism, 96, 99, 101–102
stock market, 32, 52, 65
symbols, 3, 11, 93

Targuieff, Pierre-André, 69–70, 146
Thatcher, Margaret, 57, 60, 85, 138
Third World, 24, 26, 37, 58, 88, 93, 141
Todorov, Tzvetan, 13–14, 142
trade, 2, 30, 32, 47, 70, 147
tradition, 16–17, 22, 27, 45, 104, 118–120,
    122, 138, 142–143